– Latin American Business Cultures

Latin American Business Cultures

Edited by

Robert Crane

and

Carlos Rizowy

Selection and editorial content © Robert Crane and Carlos Rizowy 2011
Individual chapters © the contributors 2011

All rights reserved. No reproduction, copy or transmission of this publication may be made without written permission.

No portion of this publication may be reproduced, copied or transmitted save with written permission or in accordance with the provisions of the Copyright, Designs and Patents Act 1988, or under the terms of any licence permitting limited copying issued by the Copyright Licensing Agency, Saffron House, 6-10 Kirby Street, London EC1N 8TS.

Any person who does any unauthorized act in relation to this publication may be liable to criminal prosecution and civil claims for damages.

The authors have asserted their rights to be identified as the authors of this work in accordance with the Copyright, Designs and Patents Act 1988.

First published 2011 by
PALGRAVE MACMILLAN

Palgrave Macmillan in the UK is an imprint of Macmillan Publishers Limited, registered in England, company number 785998, of Houndmills, Basingstoke, Hampshire RG21 6XS.

Palgrave Macmillan in the US is a division of St Martin's Press LLC, 175 Fifth Avenue, New York, NY 10010.

Palgrave Macmillan is the global academic imprint of the above companies and has companies and representatives throughout the world.

Palgrave® and Macmillan® are registered trademarks in the United States, the United Kingdom, Europe and other countries.

ISBN: 978-0-230-58081-7 hardback

This book is printed on paper suitable for recycling and made from fully managed and sustained forest sources. Logging, pulping and manufacturing processes are expected to conform to the environmental regulations of the country of origin.

A catalogue record for this book is available from the British Library.

A catalog record for this book is available from the Library of Congress.

10 9 8 7 6 5 4 3 2 1
20 19 18 17 16 15 14 13 12 11

Printed and bound in Great Britain by
CPI Antony Rowe, Chippenham and Eastbourne

This book is dedicated:

To the loving memory of my parents, Eva and Gustavo, for instilling in me a very deep appreciation for cultural diversity, freedom, the delicate balance between singularity and pluralism, and the limits of relativity and the tenacity to understand, appreciate, relate to, and learn from all cultures. I also dedicate this book with love to my children, Brian, Yael, and Michal, and the ever-present memory of their mother, Charlotte.

Carlos Rizowy

To Emerson Almeida, whose imagination and perseverance brought the dream of a first-class executive education center in Minas Gerais, Brazil, to life and to his creation, Fundaçao Dom Cabral, and to its faculty, thanks to whom I came to know Brazil, its culture, and its people.

Robert Crane

Contents

List of Tables	ix
List of Figures	x
Acknowledgments	xi
About the Editors	xii
Notes on Contributors	xiv

1	Introduction Robert Crane and Carlos Rizowy	1
2	Regional Organizations, Trade Blocs, and Inter-State Conflicts in Latin America: History and Evolution Antonio Mitre	8
3	Argentina Roque B. Fernández and Katherina Fernández	34
4	Brazil Luiz Alberto Machado, José María Rodríguez Ramos, Otto Nogami, and Marcus V. Freitas	52
5	Chile Hernán Felipe Errázuriz Correa	75
6	Costa Rica Ricardo Monge-González and Ana Laura Torrentes-García	104
7	Dominican Republic Roberto B. Saladín	123
8	Ecuador Luis Valencia Rodríguez	134
9	Mexico Mercedes Delgado and Bobby J. Calder	163
10	Panama Nicolás Ardito Barletta	191

11 Uruguay 216
 Carlos Steneri, Sebastián Sosa, and Ignacio de Posadas

12 Spain: Influence, Inspiration, and the Roots of
 Latin America's Development Process 247
 Alvaro Eguiron Vidarte

Index 269

Tables

3.1	Foreign trade, Argentina, 1990–2006	45
4.1	Population distribution by area and landmass, Brazil	55
4.2	Most populous cities, Brazil, 2000	55
4.3	Religions practiced, Brazil	56
4.4	Consumer market profile, Brazil	58
4.5	Immigrants, Brazil, 1870–1953	59
4.6	Major economic trends, Brazil, 1990–2007	63
4.7	Principal agricultural products, Brazil, 1995–2007 (millions of metric tonnes)	64
4.8	Foreign direct investments, Brazil, 2002–2008 (US$ millions)	72
4.9	Trade balance, Brazil, 2008	73
5.1	Indicators of housing and basic infrastructure, Chile, 1970–2002 (%)	78
5.2	Health indicators, Chile, 1970–2010	79
5.3	Annual GDP growth, Chile, 1986–2008	80
5.4	GDP per capita growth, Argentina, Brazil, Chile, and Mexico, 1900–2007 (%)	80
5.5	Exports and imports, Chile, 2009	93
5.6	International agreements, Chile	96
6.1	Summary of strategies, programs, and actions involved in the SME Policy, Costa Rica	118
7.1	Indicators for hotels, bars, and restaurants, Dominican Republic, 1980–2008	130
9.1	Comparative economic indicators, Mexico and selected countries, 2008	166
10.1	Country data, Panama	192
10.2	Macrofiscal indicators, Panama, 2004–2008	202
10.3	Most dynamic export sectors, Panama, 2003–2008	203
10.4	Growth by economic sector, Panama, 1990–2008 (%)	204

Figures

3.1	Map of Argentina	35
4.1	Map of Brazil	53
4.2	Economic and political development, Brazil, 1500–	65
4.3	Evolution of industrial production, Brazil, 1930–	66
5.1	Map of Chile	76
7.1	Economic growth, Dominican Republic and region, 1980–2008 (GDP per capita in constant dollars of 2000, 1980 = 100)	125
7.2	Growth rate of GDP and inflation, Dominican Republic, 2005–2008 (%)	126
8.1	Map of Ecuador	135
9.1	GDP distribution by region and selected states, Mexico, 2007 (at constant 1993 prices)	168
9.2	Cluster export portfolio, Mexico, 1997–2007	171
9.3	Inflows of foreign direct investment by sector, Mexico, 1999 and 2008	173
9.4	Foundations of a country's productivity	177
10.1	Zoning use plan prepared for the former Canal Zone, Panama	199
10.2	Growth of exports and GDP, Panama, 2003–2008 (%)	201
10.3	Foreign direct investment, Panama, 1999–2008 (US$ millions)	201
10.4	Country risk rating, Panama, 1997–2008	202
10.5	Cluster of complementary activities around the Canal and the "transit" area, Panama	205
10.6	World maritime ports linked by the Panama Canal	206
10.7	Main world logistics centers	207
10.8	Main tourism areas, Panama	209
10.9	Poverty map, Panama	211
11.1	Selected macroeconomic indicators, Uruguay	227

Acknowledgments

We would like to thank all those who contributed to this book, particularly the chapter authors: Antonio Mitre, Roque B. Fernández, Katherina Fernández, Luiz Alberto Machado, José María Rodríguez Ramos, Otto Nagami, Marcus V. Freitas, Hernán Felipe Errázuriz Correa, Ricardo Monge-González, Ana Laura Torrentes-García, Roberto B. Saladín, Luis Valencia Rodríguez, Mercedes Delgado, Bobby J. Calder, Nicolás Ardito Barletta, Carlos Steneri, Sebastián Sosa, Ignacio de Posadas, and Alvaro Eguiron Vidarte.

We would also like to thank Mónica Cabezas, our executive assistant, for her diligent follow-up with each of the authors, the co-editors, Palgrave Macmillan, and all those involved in the production of the new edition and new manuscripts; for her extraordinary sensitivity in bridging the communication between the authors and the editors; for extending herself and helping the authors with the English revision and translation of some of the chapters; and for organizing the final manuscript.

We also thank all of those unnamed individuals who contributed to give us inspiration, courage, and energy to start and conclude the book.

Finally, we wish to thank those who gave selflessly of the time we might have devoted to them rather than the book – that is, our families and significant other.

ROBERT CRANE AND CARLOS RIZOWY

About the Editors

Robert Crane

Having worked in the field of management education for more than 25 years, Dr. Robert Crane has built a solid reputation for competence in the areas of international development, cross-cultural business applications, and institutional entrepreneurship in Eastern and Western Europe and North and South America. Throughout his career he has been involved with such management institutions as the J.L. Kellogg School of Management at Northwestern University near Chicago, EM-Lyon in France, and the International Management Center (now the Business School of the Central European University) in Budapest. He has developed and/or run customized programs for executives for Baker & McKensie (one of the world's largest law firms), McKinsey and Company, Societe Generale, Bouygues, and many other firms.

As a result of his wide travels and long-term residence in both Europe and North America, Dr. Crane possesses a privileged viewpoint on cultural issues. This perspective has allowed him to create customized cross-cultural business programs for multinational firms such as Royal Ten Cate (NL) and to publish a series of books on cross-cultural business with publishing houses in the United Kingdom and the United States. He teaches the imams of France cross-cultural understanding in a program organized jointly by the Institut Catholique de Paris and the Grande Mosquée de Paris and funded by the French Ministry of Immigration. He also organizes cross-cultural interfaith workshops for Christian, Jewish, and Muslim clergy and laypersons.

His breadth of vision has led him to create consortia of universities offering joint degrees he helped design and of researchers working on collective publications. His long experience in advising companies has allowed him to facilitate idea sharing among firms as well as internal brainstorming for individual companies. Finally, he has had the entrepreneurial vision and daring to develop or enhance the global dimension of institutions (IMC, IGS) and companies (Baker & McKensie, Royal Ten Cate).

As an entrepreneur, he created the first global executive education program, in 1992; the first globally televised MBA program (through the National Technological University); and The Peace School, the first primary school to teach peacemaking to small children through a knowledge of cultures and religions.

Dr. Crane holds degrees in French literature (BA, MA, PhD from the University of North Carolina at Chapel Hill) and translation (maitrise or MA from the University of Lyon, France). He also studied management (Young Managers' Programme or Executive MBA at Cranfield University in the UK).

Carlos Rizowy

Dr. Carlos Rizowy was born in Uruguay, South America, and was appointed by Uruguay's President as Honorary Consul of Uruguay for Chicago and the Midwest of the United States. He is in demand as a private personal coach to CEOs and upper management and to the boards of significant American corporations doing business abroad, and as a public speaker and media commentator, routinely addressing more than 60 audiences each year. Groups he has addressed include the Council on Foreign Relations, Rotary International, Stanford University Law Forum, many major universities, and the Latin American Chamber of Commerce. In addition, he has spoken with and given interviews to a large number of trade, business, civic, and professional organizations, including The Executive Committee (TEC, a national organization of chief executives), Vistage International (the largest worldwide CEO membership organization of significant privately and publicly held companies), NPR, the BBC, ABC, CBS, and NBC. His topics of discussion include foreign policy, security, political violence, terrorism, doing business in Latin America, foreign trade, and international issues.

Dr. Rizowy's law practice as counsel to the firm of Sonnenschein, Nath and Rosenthal has focused on corporations, government relations, and international transactions. His international business consulting focuses on government relations. He has counseled governmental as well as non-governmental organizations and consults as a foreign policy personal coach to CEOs of prominent American companies doing business abroad. He has authored articles in professional and popular journals on topics in law, business, and international relations.

As former chairman of the Political Science Department at Roosevelt University in Chicago, he inspired a generation of students and faculty members.

Dr. Rizowy is listed in the 11th edition of *Who's Who in America* and the 54th edition of *Who's Who in American Law*. He is also listed in *Who's Who in the Midwest* and *Who's Who of the Emerging Leaders of America*.

Contributors

Antonio Mitre is Associate Professor at the Universidade Federal de Minas Gerais, Belo Horizonte, Brazil. He obtained his PhD in History at Columbia University in New York. Among his most important publications are *Los patriarcas de la plata: estructura socio-económica de la minería boliviana en el siglo XIX* (Lima, IEP, 1981), *El monedero de los Andes: región económica y moneda boliviana en el siglo XIX* (La Paz, Hisbol, 1986), *Bajo un cielo de estaño: fulgor y ocaso del metal en Bolivia* (La Paz, Asociación de Mineros Medianos & ILDES, 1993), and more recently *Nosotros que nos queremos tanto. Estado, modernización y separatismo: una interpretación del proceso boliviano* (El País, Santa Cruz de la Sierra, 2008). He is also the author of several articles on the intellectual history of Latin America, some of which have been gathered in book form under the title *O dilema do centauro: ensaios de teoria da história e do pensamento latino-americano* (Belo Horizonte, UFMG, 2003).

Argentina

Roque B. Fernández is a former Minister of Economics and Public Works, a former Chairman of the Central Bank of Argentina, a cofounder and Member of the Board of the Universidad del Cema, and a Member of the National Academic Board of Economic Sciences. He has a PhD in Economics from the University of Chicago. He was awarded his degree of Doctor in Economic Science by the Universidad Nacional de Córdoba, Argentina. He is a consultant to the World Bank, IMF, IDB, and other international institutions and has held academic positions in the United States, Chile, and Argentina. He has written books and other publications in Spanish and in English.

Katherina Fernández holds a Baccalaureat in Managerial Economics from the Universidad Torcuato Di Tella, and a Masters degree in Economics from the Universidad del Cema. She is an Economic Consultant for the House of Representatives of the National Government of Argentina, a Research Assistant at the Universidad del Cema, an Assistant Professor in Economics and Macroeconomics at the Universidad del Cema, and a consultant in human resources and project analysis.

Contributors xv

Brazil

Luiz Alberto Machado is currently the Dean of the Fundação Armando Alvares Penteado (FAAP) School of Economics. He holds a BSc in Economics from Mackenzie University. He has taken advanced graduate courses at Boston University, the Creative Education Foundation, and the International Alliance for Learning. He was Visiting Scholar at the University of Surrey, Guildford, UK (1985) and at Groupe ESC, Clermont Ferrand, in France (2009). He is the author or co-author of several articles in the field of economics, creativity and innovation.

José María Rodríguez Ramos holds a BA in Business Administration (1980), an MSc in Economics, and a PhD in Economics, all from the University of São Paulo. He is a Professor of Economics Ethics and Economics Methodology; he is also the author or co-author of several books and articles on economics.

Otto Nogami holds a BA in Economics from the University of Sao Paulo, an MBA in Finance from Ibmec-São Paulo, and an MSc in Economics from Mackenzie University. He is a Professor of Microeconomics at Fundação Armando Alvares Penteado (FAAP) and of Managerial Economics at Ibmec-São Paulo. He has co-authored several books and articles on economics and financial markets.

Marcus V. Freitas holds an LLB degree from the University of São Paulo, an LLM from Cornell University, and an MA in Economics and International Relations from the Johns Hopkins University School of Advanced International Studies (SAIS). He was an Organization of American States (OAS) Fellow from 1996 to 1999. He is Professor of Law and International Relations at Fundação Armando Alvares Penteado (FAAP). He is the author of several articles on international relations.

Chile

Hernán Felipe Errázuriz Correa, a lawyer, is a partner in the law firm Guerrero, Olivos, Novoa & Errázuriz; an advisor to the Chilean Foreign Minister; a member of the editorial board and columnist for *El Mercurio* newspaper; a member of the board of the Instituto Libertad y Desarrollo; a former Governor of the Reserve Bank of Chile; a former Chilean Ambassador to the United States of America; and a former Minister of Foreign Affairs of Chile.

Costa Rica

Ricardo Monge-González is currently the Director of the Technical Secretariat of the Costa Rican Council on Competitiveness and Innovation (CCI) and Professor of Economics at the Instituto Tecnológico de Costa Rica. He is a specialist in international economics and economic development, as well as in finance and welfare analysis. He has worked as an international consultant for CABEI, ECLAC, IDB, IDRC, ILO, OAS, USAID, and the World Bank. He was the Executive Director of the High Technology Advisory Committee (CAATEC), Director of Strategy and Research at CINDE, and economic advisor to the President of Costa Rica from 1998 to 2002. He was also a member of the Costa Rica National Bank's Board of Directors. He has published ten books and many articles in major journals. He has received three distinctions: the Outstanding Thesis Award from the Ohio State University, Premio Ancora La Nación, and a nomination for the 2002 World Technology Award for Policy.

Ana Laura Torrentes-García is an economist who works as Project Assistant at the High Technology Advisory Committee (CAATEC). She is also Ricardo Monge-González's assistant at the Instituto Tecnológico de Costa Rica. She has a Bachelor's degree in Economics from the Universidad de Costa Rica.

Dominican Republic

Roberto B. Saladín was born in Santo Domingo, Dominican Republic, on July 23, 1936. A graduate in Law from the Universidad de Santo Domingo, he is currently the Ambassador of the Dominican Republic to the USA. He has been involved in academic programs in Germany, France, the United States, and Japan. He has occupied various positions in the public and private sectors of his country, including Alternate Executive Director, representing the Dominican Republic and Mexico, on the Board of Directors of the Inter-American Development Bank; CEO of the Banco de Reservas, the largest commercial bank in the Dominican Republic; Governor of the Central Bank; and President of the Monetary Board. In 1990 he was a candidate for the presidency of the Dominican Republic with the support of the Christian Popular Party (CPP). Prior to that, he worked as Secretary of State for Finance. He was one of the founders of the Dominican Export Promotion Center (CEDOPEX) – an autonomous institution of the Dominican Government – in 1971 and was Executive Director of the organization.

Ecuador

Luis Valencia Rodríguez, a lawyer, was born in Quito in 1926. A member of the Ecuadorean Foreign Service he has been Minister of Foreign Affairs (twice); Ambassador of Ecuador to Bolivia, Brazil, Peru (twice), Venezuela, and Argentina; and a Permanent Representative to the United Nations. A member of the Committee for the Elimination of Racial Discrimination and Chairman of this committee (three times), he has also been Chairman of the delegation of Ecuador to the III UN Conference on the Law of the Sea, a member of the delegation of Ecuador to the UN Conference on the Law of Treaties, and a Member of the Ecuadorean Commission for the settlement of the frontier with Peru. Former Professor of International Law at the Universidad Central del Ecuador and former Professor of Private International Law at the Universidad Internacional del Ecuador, he is also the author of texts on international law and on human rights.

Mexico

Mercedes Delgado is Assistant Professor in the Department of Strategic Management at the Fox School of Business. Before joining Temple University, she completed postdoctoral fellowships at the Institute for Strategy and Competitiveness and at the NBER's Innovation Policy Group. She received her PhD in Business Economics from the Universidad Complutense de Madrid, and she was a Visiting Scholar at the Kellogg School of Management at Northwestern University. Her research focuses on the relationship between industry clusters and the performance of firms and regions, entrepreneurship, and country competitiveness. She has published several articles in the *Journal of Economic Geography* and *The Global Competitiveness Report*, and has been the recipient of several fellowships research grants.

Bobby J. Calder is the Kellstadt Professor of Marketing, and currently the Chair of the Marketing Department, at the Kellogg School of Management. He is also Professor of Journalism at the Medill School of Journalism and Professor of Psychology at the Weinberg College of Arts and Sciences at Northwestern University. His work is primarily in the areas of marketing strategy, media, marketing research, and the psychology of consumer behavior. Previously, he has taught at the Wharton School, University of Pennsylvania, and the University of Illinois, and he has been a consultant for Booz Allen and Hamilton. He is a graduate of the University of North Carolina at Chapel Hill. He has been a consultant to many companies and to government and not-for-profit organizations. His most recent books are *Kellogg on Integrated Marketing* (2003) and *Kellogg on Advertising and Media* (2008). His research work has appeared in publications such as the *Journal of Marketing Research* and the *Journal of Consumer Research*.

Panama

Nicolás Ardito Barletta is President of Asesores Estrategicos, SA, Chairman of Panama Development Corporation, and Director General of the NGO Centro Nacional de Competitividad. He has been President of the Republic of Panama, Minister of Planning and Economic Policy, Administrator of the Interoceanic Region Authority, Chairman of the Panama Banking Commission, and a negotiator on economic aspects of the Panama Canal Treaties. In his international career, he has been World Bank Vice President for Latin America and the Caribbean, founder and first Chairman of the Latin American Export Bank (BLADEX), Director of the Economics Department of the OAS and the Alliance for Progress, and Chairman and General Director of the International Center for Economic Growth (ICEG). He has been a member of the Boards of Directors of US and international NGOs, banks, the Inter-American Dialogue, the Panama Stock and Exchange Commission, and several civic organizations in Panama. He has published essays in international, regional, and local books about development, economic policies, democracy, and other public issues. He holds a PhD in Economics from the University of Chicago and an honorary doctorate from the Universidad de Guadalajara.

Uruguay

Carlos Steneri was awarded the degree of BA in Economics, in 1971, by the Universidad de la República, Uruguay, and an MA in Economics, in 1976, by the University of Chicago. From 1976 to 1986 he was Professor of International Trade at the Universidad de la República, Uruguay. From 1994 to 1996 he was Alternate Executive Director for Argentina, Bolivia, Chile, Paraguay, Peru, and Uruguay in the World Bank and Affiliates. Since 1989, he has been the Financial Representative of the Ministry of Finance and Central Bank of Uruguay in the USA. Since 2005, he has been the Director of the Debt Management Unit of the Ministry of Finance, Uruguay. He has published technical papers relating to external financing and is a columnist in the magazine *Economía & Mercado* of the *El País* newspaper, Uruguay.

Sebastián Sosa has been an economist at the International Monetary Fund (IMF) since 2006. He currently works in the Western Hemisphere Department, focusing on macroeconomic issues in Latin America, and previously served in the Middle East and Central Asia Department and the Finance Department. Prior to joining the IMF, he was a Teaching Assistant (microeconomics, macroeconomics, and statistical methods of policy analysis) at the University of California, Los Angeles (UCLA), and was an Assistant Professor (macroeconomics) at the Universidad de la República, Uruguay. He also spent four years as a researcher at the Center for the Study of Economic and Social Affairs (CERES), a not-for-profit independent public policy think tank in Uruguay. His areas of expertise and research interests include international macroeconomics and finance and public finance. He received his PhD in Economics from UCLA in 2006.

Ignacio de Posadas was born in Montevideo, Uruguay, in 1944. From 1966 to 1968 he followed studies in the humanities, social sciences, philosophy, and theology in Canada and the United States. In 1973 he completed his doctorate at the Law School of the Universidad de la República, Montevideo, Uruguay. He has occupied numerous major positions, both nationally and internationally, including Senator, Vice President of the Senate, Member of the Special Committee on the Reform of the Constitution, Minister of the Economy and Finance, General Counsel for the Latin American Integration Association, Governor of the World Bank, Governor of the Inter-American Development Bank, Alternate Governor of the International Monetary Fund, and Governor of the Fondo Financiero para la Cuenca del Plata. At present he is a Partner at the law firm of Posadas, Posadas & Vecino in Montevideo, and Director at Merrill Lynch, PF & S (Uruguay).

Spain

Alvaro Eguiron Vidarte was born in Bilbao, Vizcaya, Spain, on November 22, 1974. He was awarded a BA in General Economy in 1996 by the Universidad de Navarra, Pamplona, Spain, and his Executive MBA in 2005 by the Instituto de Empresa, Madrid, Spain. Since 1998, he has held high managerial positions at Banco Bilbao Vizcaya Argentaria, SA, acquiring experience in market analysis, the evolution of the domestic and international financial systems, and the trading of investment and savings financial products. At present, he is fulfilling Technical Management Board duties, among which the most outstanding are analysis of main market trends and main trends within the bank, strategic proposals, and external and internal reporting.

1
Introduction

Robert Crane and Carlos Rizowy

To deal with what is an inherently vague and as yet ill-defined subject, the cross-cultural relations of Latin America, we use a series of filters to detect the elusive cultural factors in Latin American life. All of the following approaches are used in the chapters, with individual authors varying the dosing and order.

First, the historical background of each nation is examined. What are the tribal origins of the people and their influence today on economic culture? What were the governments over time? Is there a democratic, monarchical, or autocratic tradition? What is the faith of the people? What are its strengths? Are several faiths juxtaposed? Do they coexist peacefully? Is there a tradition of free trade and individual initiative, or is central control of economic affairs the historical bias? What are the values of the country? In Hofstede's terms, are they more masculine and aggressive or more feminine and nurturing? What are the nation's dreams?

Second, since the collapse of the Soviet Union, the tensions between globalization and regionalism have strengthened. Thus, we study national attitudes toward the regional economic organizations, such as the new Latin American Free Trade Area (LAFTA), Mercosur, the Andean Community, the Caribbean Community (CARICOM), the Central American Common Market (CACM), NAFTA, and the Summit for the Unity of Latin America and the Caribbean. While the United States remains a superpower and the European Union struggles to reassert Europe's presence, the Latin American countries are attempting to come together to develop stronger bargaining tools to deal with both the United States and NAFTA. Regionalism seems to be one of the mechanisms evolving in the relationship between the Latin American countries and the United States as a means of protecting the former from being overwhelmed militarily, economically, socially, politically, and culturally and of advancing their newly justified global (for Brazil and Mexico) or regional agendas. The same nations that are pursuing regionalism also advocate the development of strong international organizations as a means of complementing regionalism.

Third, a look is taken at the national stake in the regional trade groups just mentioned. Naturally, this stake is perceived in large part through the national attitude previously discussed. However, in this section a closer look is taken at the economic implications of trade group membership in both financial and emotional terms – including the specific exclusion of the United States and Canada from LAFTA. This section deals with both the economic reality of group membership and the present national perception of the benefits of that membership.

Fourth, Latin America is a continent of regions that do not always correspond to national borders. The ethnic strife in Mexico and Bolivia and the ongoing border war between Peru and Ecuador are proof of this fact. One possible role for LAFTA, Mercosur, and the Andean Community is to gather these regions, often drawn from the tribes and their customs of pre-Colombian times, into their supranational structures. How do these regions fit into their national contexts, or do they not fit? What is the benefit of trade agreements to these regions? How are the groups perceived by the regions' leaders? The idea of ideology and pragmatism is reviewed in light of interstate conflict and regional groupings.

Fifth, the trend of several Latin American countries toward populism (e.g., Venezuela, Brazil, and Uruguay) and reservations concerning market economies strengthen the cultural ties of the Southern countries versus the Northern countries, as reflected in LAFTA. (Since cultural affinity acts as a complement to regionalism, we have included a chapter on Spain as a bridge between European and Latin American business cultures.) In other countries of Latin America, poor indigenous people are radicalizing politics while challenging democracy in its present form by pursuing policies of inclusion in the political system and a different income distribution to lessen the distortion created by ethnic affiliation. Will the Latin American countries affected by this trend allow the democratic process to incorporate them into the political system or will they threaten democracy? This struggle is tied to the drug trade. The indigenous people support the Latin American populist movements in Venezuela and Brazil. The clash of cultures poses a challenge to the democratic institution in Brazil, Mexico, Ecuador, Colombia, Peru, and Venezuela.

Sixth, a look is taken at the business impact of LAFTA, Mercosur, the Andean Community, and NAFTA, present and future, on the nation.

How do businesspeople see the present climate inside and outside these trading blocs? What are their predictions for the future in both cases? What is the present reality of these common markets? What are the cultural implications of LAFTA?

Latin America is an important world region with societies that are extremely different and that face major challenges in democracy, poverty, and inequity. Disparities in the distribution of wealth have created deep social problems. Politically, there are no boundaries between the public and private sectors. Political parties are generally clientelistic, with low ideological content, and opportunistic in their positions, with little discipline.

Nonetheless, most Latin American countries have such characteristics of democracy as institutionalized elections, and the exercise of political freedoms of expression, opinion, association and movement, and access to the media. There are variations in the degree of state participation and control of these elements. As a consequence, the governments lack legitimacy, which translates into discontent among the population.

In addition, recessions and crises are fertile ground for populist movements – as in Brazil with the 2002 presidential victory of a left-wing party with Lula Da Silva, and in Venezuela in 1998 with the election of a leader of the 1992 military coup (Hugo Chavez). Upheaval in Uruguay led to the democratic election of the Frente Amplio and the present president, José Mujica, the former leader of the Tupamaro guerrilla movement, who spent years in prison. The majority of these populist groups attributed their economic misery to the pro-market policies promoted by the United States. Some eight years on, where do these leaders and countries stand?

Brazil's leftist president Luiz Inácio Lula Da Silva hoped to lead a South American diplomatic bloc with the support of Argentina. However, countries such as Mexico, Chile, and Colombia wanted to maintain the Rio Group.

Another ongoing problem of the state in Latin America is that there are some areas into which its legality does not extend. Instead, authoritarian subnational regimes coexist with democratic national regimes. Thus, in Colombia, revolutionary groups still control large areas of the territory.

Multiethnicity of the populations and indigenous movements

It is important to point out that, in most cases, the construction of the Latin American state was characterized by violence and cruelty. One might say that in Latin America there were states looking for a nation rather than nations looking for a state. The establishment of political regimes was aristocratic or oligarchic from the beginning. The emergent states were the result of domination arrangements, with a legacy of colonialism that excluded a large part of the population (indigenous peoples, women). Later, these sectors of the population were included through indigenous policies. Today many of the populist movements are motivated by the neglected indigenous and mestizo population's desire to participate in and obtain a share of the national wealth.

The indigenous population in Latin America is estimated at between 34 and 40 million people, or about 8–10 percent of the total population. The majority of this population is found in Bolivia, Guatemala, and Peru. Some 30–40 percent of the total population in Ecuador is indigenous. In the other countries of Latin America, the indigenous population constitutes less than 6 percent, so the process of inclusion did not reach the status of an emergency.

We should clearly identify the problems that arise from the identification of this kind of population; in certain countries, we can observe that the indigenous population is increasing, which may be a consequence of a newfound identity and of policies recognizing that identity.

The emergence of new movements and constitutional changes in Latin American countries recognizing the multiethnicity of the populations presents new challenges for the governments and societies. There is a tendency toward a Latin American regional model of multicultural constitutionalism, and toward a democratizing process of emancipation. This trend is not yet consistent with globalization, but it is consistent with cultural regionalism.

The demands of indigenous people are included in the "second-generation" reforms. Indigenous movements can be observed in two ways: there are direct or indirect associations, which differ in their degree of government recognition of the indigenous right to self-government. There are also specific lands recognized as belonging to the indigenous peoples whose occupants remain loyal to their own political and legal cultures and traditions (e.g., the Kuna in Panama, the Resguardos in Colombia, and the Oaxaca in Mexico).

Economic culture

The individual chapters deal with each country's economic culture. However, the trend at the beginning of the 1990s was that most of the countries in Latin America had as their primary goal economic growth through reform and anti-inflationary policies.

Measures were taken to open the economy to market forces and to reduce the size of the public sector through structural reforms. As a consequence, there was an inclination toward privatization and the diminution of the role of governments. The globalization process involved all countries in specific challenges to become a part of the global economy. Most of the Latin American countries assumed that regional economic integration was a necessity in order to promote internal development and regional integration. This process of regionalism was paving the way for global integration. As an outcome of this objective, free trade agreements such as LAFTA, Mercosur, the Andean Community, CARICOM, the Free Trade Area of the Americas (FTAA), and the Summit for the Unity of Latin America and the Caribbean were created. We included Chapter 2 in order to deal with these issues. Trade liberalization in agriculture and manufactured products, the liberalization of certain services, and a reduction in barriers to trade in agricultural products and manufactured goods between developing countries are among the key subjects discussed in world trade negotiations. However, this kind of negotiation implies gains for the Latin American and Caribbean countries only if at the same time the rich countries open their markets. Hoped-for favorable results of such negotiations include the improvement of investment in the region, and the creation of a stable basis on which to open the markets and of an appropriate climate to attract foreign investment. One example is Mexico.

The NAFTA agreement established a good atmosphere for both foreign direct investment and national investments in all the industries involved in exports to the United States. One illustration of the advantages is the Mercosur free trade agreement (1991) among Uruguay, Argentina, Paraguay, and Brazil, which was made to formalize and strengthen regional trade flows. Argentina and Brazil are the pact's two major markets. Import tariffs are reduced; duties on imports of most products from outside Mercosur are set under a common external tariff (0–20 percent). Within this framework, the countries can acquire considerable advantages, enlarging their markets. Moreover, some goods defined traditionally as nontradable have become tradable as a result of this regional trade.

However, despite the commitments made by these countries, there are many regional obstacles that must be dealt with successfully for the achievement of full integration, for example:

- Exchange policy coordination is a paramount challenge.
- There is no common goal linking Mercosur to other regional agreements.

- Is a limitation to bilateral trade agreements with other countries, especially the United States, a platform for the reinforcement of macroeconomic coordination?
- What degree of flexibility is there for member countries to negotiate bilateral agreements with other regional blocs and/or individual countries to facilitate the transition toward a fully integrated regional trade area?

The extreme economic hardship suffered by most of the member countries of these groups has occasionally led them to suspend, postpone, or even default on some of their commitments to strengthening free trade within their respective subregions.

Despite the serious effects of international crises, countries have persevered to uphold and, wherever possible, expand regional cooperation substantially. Thus, Mercosur is improving regulations for settling trade disputes and strengthening joint negotiations with third parties. The Andean Community is facilitating the fuller reintegration of Peru and has finally adopted a common external tariff, initially covering some 62 percent of all tariff items.

There are also Western Hemisphere trade negotiations, looking toward a free trade zone, which should be completed by 2005. Negotiations with third world countries and groups of countries and multilateral forums are very important to strengthening regional integration and leveling the playing field of globalization. Governments are realizing that through deepened and more efficient sub-regional cooperation, they gain stronger individual ability to negotiate with more powerful trading partners. This phenomenon resulted in the formation of LAFTA.

In the Latin American region, Brazil has emerged as the political and economic leader, pushing Mexico aside. As a member of Mercosur, Brazil has great impact on key hemispheric issues such as the creation of the FTAA. However, some countries have difficulty obtaining political consensus on unilateral trade liberalization because of the internal perceived and real disparities in the groups that benefit from those policies.

In the Latin American region the pursuit by the United States of policies such as the promotion of economic and political liberalization, support for free markets, and trade liberalization did not achieve a perceived long-term benefit to the countries of the region. Economic improvement was followed by recessions, economic crises, and political instability that fed a certain anti-Americanism that translated into the failure of pro-market policies.

In sum, free trade agreements are an excellent framework both for negotiating lower trade barriers and for setting the rules for reform, transparency, and respect for the rule of law. In addition, expanding free trade with the United States could enhance economic opportunity for the region.

What then is our goal in describing cross-cultural Latin America? We want to sound the depths of feeling of Latin Americans for each other and for the region. We want to reveal the half-submerged basis of the ways people think and feel in the region. We want to lay the groundwork for others to define and predict which way Latin America will develop in the future. We want to define how those outside the region perceive Latin America and speculate on how these perceptions impinge on the evolution of Latin America's relations with the world. It is an ambitious task, but one whose time has come. We hope we have advanced it.

2
Regional Organizations, Trade Blocs, and Inter-State Conflicts in Latin America: History and Evolution

Antonio Mitre

Those who have lived during the Cold War era in Latin America will naturally identify two features of the world, neither so brave nor so new, that emerged in the preface to its crisis: the debut or the return of democracy in almost all states, and the greater autonomy that the latter came to enjoy with regards to the center of the capitalist system. The social sciences soon reflected those changes, promoting certain issues to the front line of academic endeavor and relegating others to the condition of intellectual pastimes. Thus, such terms as "dependency" and "imperialism" – common language in the analysis of the continent's structural configuration until yesterday – suggest now a remote past, neighboring the realms of archeology. One should be suspicious of so much distancing in such a short time, and ask, first, whether the pace of change has affected our capacity to perceive reality to the point that we are running away from our own shadows. This means, in regards to the subject treated here – border conflicts and inter-state wars in today's Latin America – inquiring about the transformations that took place in the regional state system after the Cold War vis-à-vis the configuration of factors that have been responsible for the relative peace in the continent. In doing so, we should be able to identify potential threats that could upset such trends in the future.

The conceptual task involves a classic challenge, namely, to discriminate novelty from what is long-standing – an effort geared not so much to separating legacy from change as to overlapping both dimensions in order to understand the workings of the present. Among the topics examined here are the secular course of inter-state conflicts in the region, the Organization of American States (OAS) as a pacifying agency, and the destabilizing potential of border conflicts within the current regional framework, characterized by ideological alliances and the crises of United States' hegemony.

Since 1825, there have been, in Latin America, ten inter-state disputes that can be characterized as important wars: five took place during the nineteenth century and the other half in the twentieth, of which three were fought before the end of the Second World War, and two after it. All five armed confrontations in the nineteenth century had to do with border definition between countries: the two Cisplatine Wars, the War of the Confederation, the Triple Alliance, and the War of the Pacific. In the twentieth century, up to the end of the Second World War, there were three inter-state armed confrontations: the Chaco War between Bolivia and Paraguay, the largest of all; the conflict that involved Peru and Colombia in Leticia (1932–1933); and the dispute between Peru and Ecuador over the territory around the navigable part of the Marañón River (1941–1942) in the Amazon region.[1] The path of postwar conflicts can be divided into two phases. The first one started with the emergence of the regional system established within the framework of the OAS, in 1948, and finished with the military intervention in the Dominican Republic in 1965. During this period there were no inter-state armed struggles. In the second phase, which goes right up to the end of the Cold War, a small number of armed conflicts occurred (Grabendorff, 1982: 272). The main ones were the Football War between Honduras and El Salvador in 1969, and the Malvinas (Falklands) War between Argentina and the United Kingdom in 1982. There were three other serious military incidents that did not end in armed confrontation: one between Chile and Argentina over the Beagle Channel, another between Ecuador and Peru in 1985 in the Condor Mountain Ridge, and, finally, the dispute in 1987 between Colombia and Venezuela over a maritime area that is yet to be demarcated in the Venezuela Gulf (Pardo, 1999: 2). The period from the end of the Cold War to the present is better characterized by the successful effort to overcome definitively old historical controversies over boundaries than by the deflagration of new inter-state clashes, with the one between Peru and Ecuador in 1995 being the only event of significant scale. In sum, since 1945 there have been around 30 situations of bilateral conflicts of variable magnitude and intensity, but, as was observed above, very few ended in wars of major proportions. In virtue of this relative peaceful course, the region is clearly different from other areas of the planet.

The exegetic charade in most studies of this topic includes the following statements: in Latin America border and territory disputes, in addition to being frequent, have a tendency to last for long periods, and, on certain occasions, they result in the use of military force, but very rarely has the outcome been full-fledged war. Among the most outstanding factors that have been proposed to explain this singular phenomenon are the marginality of Latin America relative to the nerve centers of world power, the moderating power of the United States and, finally, the existence of a host of regional organizations with great experience in the arbitration of inter-state conflicts (Domínguez et al., 2003: 358). The question asked in this chapter is whether the pacifist tradition will stand in the face of United States' hegemony crises and, on the other hand, the growing entry of Latin America into the global system, in a scenario where ideological antagonisms have flared once again in the midst of competition for regional leadership and an eventual loss of legitimacy on the part of collective security organizations.

The evolution of the Inter-American System and Pax Americana

Having the OAS's itinerary as a road map, we shall analyze the nature and evolution of the conflicts in different periods, with emphasis on the role of the United States in the hemispheric system. Studies on inter-American relations tend to consider the OAS to be an institution manipulated by Washington and, at times, a mere extension of American interests. With a few finishing touches, such an image may be an adequate representation of the organization's performance during the period from its foundation (1948) up to the US intervention in Guatemala (1954), but it should not be generalized to its entire history, nor should its course be regarded as the panacea portrayed by its most fervent apologists. There is no need to go to extremes: an empirical examination will show a complex and mutable reality. To begin with, the principles that came to be part of the OAS – recognition of the countries' sovereignty, nonintervention in domestic matters, peaceful solution of disputes, consultation, and self-determination – had shaped and structured relationships among the Latin American countries well before the United States started to play a dominant role in the regional system (Shaw, 2003: 64). On the other hand, the principle of nonintervention, explicitly targeted by the Monroe Doctrine (1823) at foreign extra-continental powers, experienced a turnabout in Roosevelt's corollary (1905), through which the United States reserved to itself the "right" to interfere in any Latin American republic that did not meet its political and financial obligations – and the number of interventions perpetrated from then up to 1947 was great (Romero, 2004: 417). In Latin America, legal instruments were being developed throughout this phase to oppose the North American thesis: the Drago (1902) and Tobar (1907) Doctrines, the first against the use of the armed forces to collect public debts, the latter against the recognition of de facto governments. Later, the Estrada Doctrine (1930) asserted the principle of nonintervention in the internal affairs of other countries.

The Inter-American System that emerged after the Second World War was sustained, in the beginning, by two legal instruments: the American Treaty on Peaceful Solutions, or the Bogotá Agreement (1948), established during the IX International American Conference, and the Inter-American Treaty of Reciprocal Assistance, better known as the Rio Treaty (1947). In both cases, the member countries made a commitment not to resort to threats or to the use of force, but to arbitrate their disputes through the procedures established by the Inter-American System, before taking them to United Nations General Assembly or to the Security Council. The OAS's charter also established that the countries could use any other peaceful resources that allowed them to settle their quarrels. Although the Rio Treaty does not compel the signatory states to solve their controversies according to the OAS's rules, the inclination has been to consider them effective in such situations (Martz, 2007: 179–81). During these years, the majority of the pleas channeled to the OAS had to do with border disputes, sometimes tinted by the tensions between democratic governments and dictatorships (Costa Rica–Managua, 1948; Dominican Republic–Cuba, 1949), and all of them were peacefully overcome by consensus.

The democratic spirit present in the initial postwar moves rapidly disappeared, giving way to security concerns that, in tune with the "Cold War's demands and language," frequently encouraged the proliferation of dictatorships submissive to the will of the great power, particularly in Central America (López-Maya, 1995: 136).[2] At the time of drafting the Rio Treaty, it had already been foreseen that the system could not depend solely on the Assembly of Foreign Affairs Ministers to respond to situations that required prompt military action and that, therefore, the Council should act as a consulting organ and make decisions with the power conferred on it by the old Pan-American Statute.[3] A year later, when the OAS was established at the Bogotá Conference, the United States insisted on the idea of continental political-military unification as the best way to fight communism, while the statements of the Latin

American representatives emphasized the need to elaborate a plan for economic aid to the region – a call reaffirmed by the Pan-American Operation – a project proposed by Juscelino Kubitschek (1956–1961) that would be taken into account and partially carried out only after the Cuban Revolution, through the Alliance for Progress sponsored by the administration of John F. Kennedy (1961–1963). Meanwhile, the region entered the Cold War trench under the United States' political and military armor.

The impact of the Cuban Revolution on the hemispheric system

Starting from the Cuban Revolution (1959–1962), political conflicts in the region began to assume a markedly ideological character and, directly or in a roundabout way, involved the United States and some Latin American governments that were suspected of being under communist influence: Cuba, the Dominican Republic, and Guatemala at different times. Disagreements within the OAS gained intensity as US interventions became more frequent and guerrilla warfare, supported by Cuba's regime, proliferated throughout the region. From the first, US expectations of finding support for military action against Cuba were frustrated within the OAS, as was its attempt to promote a collective breaking-off of diplomatic relations with the revolutionary government. This proposal was not accepted by the stronger countries of the region: Brazil, Argentina, and Mexico.[4] During the military regimes of the 1960s and 1970s, the instruments of the Inter-American Defense System were often used by the United States to justify the use of force, support dictatorships, and give legitimacy to its interventionist actions (Sotomayor, 2004: 34). At the same time, guerrilla movements – some guided by an old libertarian spirit, others by instructions from the Cuban government, or by both forces – violated the premises of national sovereignty on several fronts, thus replicating the attitude of the big power.

In any case, US hegemony in the regional system diminished the chances that inter-state conflicts would turn into open wars. The fact that there were two important armed confrontations during the peak of the Cold War – Honduras and El Salvador, Argentina and the United Kingdom – does not represent a deviation from such a course.[5] The truth is that during this phase, when the Caribbean was vital to the United States' strategic interests, the disputes over inter-state borders, which intermittently agitated the region's scenario – Chile–Argentina, Chile–Bolivia, Guatemala–United Kingdom, Honduras–Nicaragua,

Peru–Ecuador, Venezuela–Guyana – were quickly stifled, and none of them prompted military confrontation (Grabendorff, 1982: 274). The willingness to accept arbitration in their disputes, under the assumption that the principle of nonintervention would be upheld, contributed to the pacification of state relationships in the region. The OAS and, particularly, the Inter-American Committee of Peace (IACP) were put into action 34 times from 1948 until the military intervention in the Dominican Republic (1965), and played a crucial role in the solution of most of the conflicts during this phase (Grabendorff, 1982: 274).

The emergence of military regimes all over Latin America during the 1960s and 1970s marks the beginning of a new phase. The failure of guerrilla actions in Venezuela, Bolivia, Colombia, Guatemala, and Brazil led the governments of the region to consider the Cuban regime no longer an imminent threat. It was exactly during this period that the OAS's statute underwent modifications in order to inhibit interventionist practices, and, for that purpose, Article 9 was drafted to define with more precision what should be understood as "aggression." It is true that the United States, a decisive player in the system, continued to act unilaterally every time it considered that its interests were being damaged. Nevertheless, US viewpoints about security threats in the region were several times successfully rebuffed within the organization. The most emblematic case was probably the decision taken by the OAS in relation to Nicaragua in 1978. On that occasion, the United States' proposal to organize a government of national unity with the support of inter-American peace forces was rejected. In the end, the resolution approved by most of the Latin American countries, fearful that the United States' initiative would prolong the Somoza regime and turn into an excuse for another intervention, was "practically" a call for the people of Nicaragua to overthrow the dictatorship and establish a democratic government, through "elections." The prediction of one analyst, that the episode "may well have marked the nadir of US influence in the OAS,"[6] would be in part corroborated by future events.

Changes in the structure of dependency were readily translated into the OAS's normative and institutional configuration, which at that time experienced greater democratization. An agreement was reached in 1975 that sanctions stipulated by the Rio Treaty could be suspended by a simple majority, instead of the traditional two-thirds. Despite US opposition, a new article on collective economic security for development was also approved, and the Special Consulting Committee, created to monitor Cuban activities in the region, was finally abolished (Muñoz, 1984: 160). In the following years, whenever the Latin American countries took a stance contrary to that of the United States, be it with relation to Nicaragua (1978), Panama (1989), or the conflict between Argentina and the United Kingdom (1982), the US position was simply defeated, or had to be modified to follow the will of the majority (Shaw, 2003: 81). The spectrum of issues channeled to the OAS Council widened during this phase, and pending questions over borders made their comeback, once again tinted with economic motivations geared to taking control of or having access to natural resources. Matters relating to fishing rights, use of resources in frontier areas, and territorial claims intertwined in a string of conflicts: Argentina–Brazil, Chile–Argentina, Chile–Bolivia, Colombia–Venezuela, Nicaragua–Colombia, Mexico–United States, Panama–United States, Peru–Chile, and Venezuela–Guyana. But in only a couple of cases were there armed confrontations: Argentina–United Kingdom (1982) and Peru–Ecuador (1995). Guerrilla warfare, with its characteristic hybrid shape of civilian and inter-state conflict, reappeared once again in several countries. The most critical situations arose in Nicaragua and Guatemala, which managed to exit from the inferno of such two-faced wars only after "three generations of peace deals" negotiated between governments and guerrillas, with the mediation of international organizations (Matul and Ramirez, 2009: 95).

The scenario at the dawn of the new millennium: democracy and regionalism

With the end of the Cold War and the consolidation of democracy in the region, conditions for finding a negotiated way out of old conflicts improved throughout the following decades. The number of direct interventions carried out by the United States also diminished Grabendorff (1982: 272),[7] at a time when the OAS's institutional incentives made it more attractive and profitable for that power to choose multilateral options for conflict resolutions.

Nowadays, there are fewer disputes over border issues. Secular and highly inflammable quarrels were totally or partially overcome during the 1990s: Peru and Ecuador solved their disputes concerning the Amazon border in 1999; Chile and Argentina negotiated their differences in the same decade, except for a glacial strip of about 50 kilometers in the south of Patagonia. A treaty mediated by the United Nations in 2007 solved the controversies over sea limits between Suriname and Guyana. Finally, Cuba, excluded from the organization in 1962, was readmitted in June 2009, despite the United States, which conditioned its approval on a commitment on the part of the island's regime to observe the premises of democracy.

In any case, territorial and frontier questions continue to sour relations between several countries. Nicaragua has still not abandoned its claim over the Fonseca Gulf and the Colombian island of San Andrés, mostly in virtue of their symbolic political value rather than for economic motives (Briscoe, 2008: 2). Also remaining latent are the Argentinean demand over the Malvinas, which can be described as a frontier issue, since that country considers the islands an extension of its continental platform, and the Bolivian claim to at least part of the territory lost in the war against Chile.

During the past 30 years, as a result of democratization and regional integration processes, other forums were institutionalized with the purpose of securing peace between countries that are part of specific blocs. Among the most important agreements in that direction are the Framework Treaty for Democratic Security, signed by the Central American states in 1995; the Caribbean Regional Security System, established in 1996; the Mercosur Declaration, by which the country members, together with Bolivia and Chile, designated the whole area a peace zone in 1999; and the Andean Charter for Peace and Security, signed by the participant countries in 2002. These regional platforms may complement and expand the OAS's actions or, at times, function as replacements, since, as we will see later, not every country adheres with equal zeal or shows the same positive attitude with regards to the inter-American organization.

Finally, the architecture of the Inter-American System contemplates alternative forums that, created in the past to mediate disputes, have become institutionalized by virtue of their being summoned on several occasions. This is the case for the Rio Protocol, established in 1942 as a mediator in the war between Ecuador and Peru, or the role of the OAS's Secretary-General, who, by request of states, has worked on the solution of pending issues such as those between Belize and Guatemala and between Honduras and Nicaragua. All this institutional background in conflict resolution, although it does not eliminate the possibility of future wars, certainly makes more fluid, speedy, and efficient the arbitration of conflicts before they result in armed struggles of large proportions.

The beginning of a new hemispheric order

With regard to the topic under consideration, three developments stand out as most significant in the past few decades: first, the quasi-simultaneous

Latin Americanization of Brazilian and Argentine foreign policies – two countries which, despite their cultural differences and specific weights in the region's balance of power, had historically searched for and imagined their national destinies beyond the South – and, second, the growing visibility of Venezuela in the hemispheric and extra-continental scenario, once again under the banner of Latin Americanism. Finally, there is the renewed importance of the Caribbean and Central American area in the face of present-day ideological polarization. Let us consider those processes and their relevance with relation to the theme under discussion.

Brazil and Argentina: the reasons for cooperation

Throughout their history, Brazil and, even more so, Argentina have never been short of intellectuals who have struggled for the inclusion of their countries in the matrix of Latin American identity. However, in the fields of government policy and diplomacy, both states – for different reasons – have lived for centuries with their backs turned on the Extremo Occidente.[8] Notwithstanding this, the perception both countries developed of one another was in no way the most suitable to encourage cooperation. In fact, a survey carried out in urban areas just before the Malvinas War showed that only a small percentage of the Argentineans and Brazilians interviewed considered it worthwhile for their respective governments to make any effort to build up a preferential relationship with the neighboring country. Even the Soviet Union was a preferred option for the establishment of cooperative links for development, although the number of Argentineans who believed Brazil would be a good partner was higher than the number of Brazilians with the same opinion about Argentina (Selcher, 1985: 74). It was against this background of mutual distrust that the Latin Americanization of both countries' foreign policies occurred, transforming the traditional antagonism into a partnership with increasing degrees of cooperation and coordination of actions within the regional scenario.

The catalyzing circumstances of this change were reverse signals. In the case of Argentina, it was the misfortune of the Malvinas (Falklands) War; in the case of Brazil, the fortunate growth and industrial modernization reached during the 1970s: crisis and decadence on one side; hopes of prosperity and rising expectations on the other; and a simultaneous movement on both parts to drift away from the United States. Changes started in the late 1970s, paradoxically while military regimes were in place in both countries, where national security doctrines ruled promoting "geopolitical competition, market-oriented practices and a realpolitik approach" in relation to foreign affairs (Resende-Santos,

2002: 91). Up to that time, the links maintained by Brazil with eight of its nine neighboring countries had been lax, with a more intense exchange with its inevitable partner, Argentina, mostly of a conflictual nature. Thus, South–South relations were established, to a great extent, on the basis of a secular absence of direct contacts, as shown by the fact that when João Batista Figueiredo (Brazilian president from 1979 to 1985) visited Buenos Aires in 1980, 45 years had elapsed since any other Brazilian president had been there, and when he visited Lima, Bogotá, and Caracas, he was the first Brazilian president to set foot in those capital cities since the establishment of the republic (Selcher, 1985: 69).[9]

The internationalization of the Brazilian economy during the 1960s and 1970s explains, in part, the course followed by its foreign policy, but there are other intervening factors that should be taken into consideration. One of these was the suspension, during the presidency of Ernesto Geisel (1974–1979), of the military assistance accord with the United States in response to the pressure exerted by the Carter administration over human rights (Selcher, 1985: 68). Coincidental with this drifting apart from the North, there was great progress in the negotiations over the Corpus-Itaipu hydroelectric dam, which was begun in 1974. Against all predictions, the intense controversies during previous years about the project of Alto Paraná were solved by the Tripartite Agreement signed in October 1979. This cooperative attitude, increasingly supported by institutional mechanisms, was enhanced during the presidency of Figueiredo, when the conviction that Brazil's development "could not be planned outside the Latin American context" took root (Selcher, 1985: 69). During his government, the Cooperation Agreement for the Development and Pacific Use of Nuclear Energy was reached in May 1980, a step forward in overcoming a rivalry that went back to colonial times.

In the transition phase, the democratic platform offered more and better conditions for strengthening the relations with neighboring states and for creating or restructuring regional blocks. Bilateral cooperation continued during the presidency of José Sarney (1985–1990). Thus, in little more than a decade, Brazil and Argentina managed to structure "one of the most successful cooperative regimes in the world," which, in addition to the nuclear agreement, created the Southern Common Market (Mercosur) in 1991, an association which included Uruguay and Paraguay (Resende-Santos, 2002: 89).[10] Mercosur continued to be a priority in the agenda of the governments of Collor de Mello (1990–1992) and Itamar Franco (1992–1995). Its consolidation, during the consecutive governments of Fernando Henrique Cardoso (1995–2003), was accompanied by two ruling principles of the foreign policy implemented at that time: the firm defense of the autonomy of the state, especially in disputes with the United States, and the promotion of democracy as a nonnegotiable value (Cardoso, 2004).[11] Within this context, described as open regionalism, the South took a privileged place in the Brazilian agenda, beyond circumstantial gains or losses. With wording that reminds us of Ortega y Gasset, Minister Celso Lafer clearly pointed out the way to be followed by his country: "for us, [Mercosur] is destiny, a part of our circumstances. ALCA is not destiny, but an option" (Vigevani, Oliveira, and Cintra, 2003).[12] As time passed, and until the creation of the South-American Nations Community (2007) and the South-American Union (2008), the scope of these "circumstances" became increasingly large. Since then, the emphasis given by Brazilian foreign policy to its southern identity has represented a change in relation to the universalism of its previous attitude. On the other hand, it makes it difficult to perceive the structural diversity of the region – a fact that may increase the risk of ideological distortions affecting the country's standing in the event of conflict.[13]

For Argentina, two facts converged to make this country choose to cooperate with its neighbors. The first was the Malvinas War. Although the controversy with the United Kingdom goes back to 1833, for more than a century it did not affect the strong economic relations between the two states. It was precisely the decline of the United Kingdom as a world power after the Second World War that encouraged Argentina's demand and the British government's willingness to reach an agreement. To this end, there were several negotiation attempts between 1960 and 1980, and when everything pointed to a pacific and definitive solution of the secular dispute, war broke out. A premonitory article, written a few months before the event, pointed out with great precision the motives that could halt the pacification process:

> The basic obstacle to agreement is, however, that both governments while anxious to settle, were imprisoned by history – that is, by past pronouncements and obligations; which restricted their freedom of maneuver, thwarting a negotiated compromise. Thus, the British government – as illustrated in 1980 by the hostile reception given to Ridley's initiative by both the islanders and parliament – was restrained by a commitment to respect the principle of national self-determination as well as by the unchanging view of the islanders. In turn, the manipulation of the dispute for both domestic and international purposes prevented Argentine acceptance of anything short of sovereignty. (Beck, 1982: 54)

And it was precisely the manipulation of the Malvinas issue for domestic purposes, by both the Argentinean military regime and the British government, that turned out to be responsible for the transformation of the peace negotiations into a sudden war.[14] In 1982, the Argentinean military government, basically diseased, made a last attempt to overcome its domestic crisis, and launched the country into the irresponsible adventure of the Malvinas War. During the conflict, the unconditional support of the United States for the United Kingdom, notwithstanding the anticommunist alliance established shortly before by the Reagan administration with the government of Leopoldo Galtieri (1981–1982), clearly showed the real boundaries between the inter-American defense system and the old Monroe Doctrine (Feldman, 1985). As a result, the war intensified Argentina's desire to cooperate, first with Brazil, despite the apathetic position adopted by this country during the conflict, and afterward with Chile, going back to the negotiation table over the Beagle Canal, despite the surreptitious aid offered by the government of Pinochet to the United Kingdom (Selcher, 1985: 30). After its defeat, Argentina, which formerly had thought of itself as essentially European and quite different from its neighbors, began to cultivate a Latin American identity, with all the ideological features implied by such a term. At the same time, the media offered ample space to portray the culture and concerns of the region, while the political class rediscovered the old discourse tying the destiny of the country to the vicissitudes of the South.

In the wake of the Malvinas War, the nuclear question, one of the most sensitive, since it involved controlling a technology that could lead to the development of nuclear weapons, was also favorably negotiated between the two Atlantic countries. The history of this issue, full of mutual preventions, was fraught. In November 1983 Argentina, more advanced in this field than Brazil, announced that it had developed, through a secret program, the necessary technology to produce enriched uranium, creating an atmosphere of suspicion in the neighboring country. Fortunately, the expectations of a "nuclear race" that would ruin the commitment assumed three years before did not materialize. On the contrary, in the 1990s, Argentina and Brazil established collective security institutions capable of promoting cooperation with pacific purposes in this area. On November 28, 1990, Presidents Carlos Saúl Menem and Fernando Collor de Mello signed, in Iguaçu, an agreement by which both countries abandoned the development of nuclear weapons, and subjected themselves to mutual supervision institutions, and inspections by the International Atomic Energy Agency. This statement was endorsed one year later by the Guadalajara Agreement, in Mexico, which laid the foundations for the creation of the Brazilian-Argentinean Agency of Accounting and Control of Nuclear Materials (BAAAC). At present, Argentina and Brazil are signatories to the Tlatelolco Treaty and the Nuclear Non-Proliferation Treaty (Sotomayor, 2004: 49). In this case, cooperation was facilitated by the efforts of the democratic regimes to submit their armed forces to the control of the civilian government. At this stage of the democratization process, both the Argentinean Ministry of Foreign Affairs and the Itamaraty Brazilian Foreign Affairs Office showed greater autonomy with regard to the pressures from the military (Sotomayor, 2004: 49). A sign of the climate of relaxation of tensions that came to prevail in both countries was the significant reduction of Brazilian troops on the southern frontier and the change in the focus of attention toward the northeast and north of the country, particularly the Amazonian region, where Brazil's borders stretch along more than 11,000 kilometers (Pion-Berlin, 2000: 52).

It is clear that neither the political gap with respect to the United States nor the rapprochement between the countries of the region should be attributed exclusively to conjunctural factors such as the support given by the United States to the United Kingdom during the Malvinas War. As a matter of fact, the relative consensus that prevailed among countries of the Americas during the Cold War began to diminish due to factors such as the strong industrial development of some economies, the emergence of subregional blocks, changes in geopolitical strategies, and the emergence of a new consciousness among the military of the technological dependency on the United States (Selcher, 1986: 86). The result was the diversification of markets in the most dynamic economies, the local production of weapons, and the end of the US monopoly as a supplier. All these factors set the basis in the authoritarian period for the development of more autonomous policies (Muñoz, 1984: 159, 160).

Starting in the 1990s, the end of the Cold War, as well as later redefinitions of US priorities – especially after the September 11, 2001, attack – removed that power further from the regional context. On the other hand, the journey to the North, begun by Mexico when it joined NAFTA, opened the window for the introduction of new political actors in Central America and Caribbean. The Chavez regime took advantage of the empty space to strengthen its presence in the area, using, as others had done before, the enormous power of Venezuela's oil. At the same time that the rise of *Chavismo* strengthened the ties of Venezuela with the countries of the Caribbean Basin and boosted the Cuban regime, the presence of the old left in several Latin American governments – among them the largest and most modern economies, such as Brazil, Chile, and Argentina – contributed to magnify the role of Venezuela as a global player.

Venezuela and Colombia: the reasons for conflict

The conflict between Venezuela and Colombia, ongoing for some time, does not fit the traditional pattern of border controversies so recurrent in the Latin American scenario and has now become an important parameter of the new hemispheric landscape. To understand its potential to polarize the region – the United States and its preferential partner (Colombia) versus Venezuela and its closest allies (Ecuador, Bolivia, and Nicaragua) – one must transcend the temporal stamp of its most recent protagonists: Bush, Uribe, and Chávez. Currently the struggle involves the alignment of governments into two camps according to political affinities and a different stance with respect to the US guidelines on free trade, the war on drugs, military bases, and collective security. It is precisely because of the complex network of national interests set in motion in each round of the disputes between Venezuela and Colombia that the degree of uncertainty as to its possible consequences runs among the highest in the region.

The recent episode caused by the crossing of the Ecuadorian frontier by Colombian armed forces in the fight against FARC illustrates how controversies of this kind can easily become internationalized, as well as the difficulties facing the OAS in arbitrating them. The episode also reveals the entry of the civilian conflicts of some countries into regional and extra-regional geopolitical dynamics. The crisis on this occasion was catalyzed by a Colombian air strike on Ecuadorian territory, with the objective of targeting one of FARC's main leaders, Raul Reyes. In consequence, the transfer of Ecuadorian and Venezuelan troops to the Colombian border rapidly transformed this episode into a confrontation between the Chávez regime and the US government.

The accusations of the Colombian authorities that Chávez was financing the guerrillas was swiftly followed by the closing of the Venezuelan embassy in Bogotá and the expulsion of the Colombian representatives in Quito and Caracas. All these reactions brought both countries closer to an armed confrontation. According to Chávez's statement, the order given to the Defense Minister to send ten battalions to the border with Colombia and to mobilize the air force was not intended to stimulate war with the neighboring country, but fundamentally to prevent the United States, which already had Colombia under its control, from continuing to split the Latin American countries. This stereotype of a nation made to submit to the will of the empire, used abundantly in the past to refer to the condition of Central American republics, and now foisted upon Colombia by some interpreters of the conflict, feeds, with predatory eagerness, on a long and troubled history. As a matter of fact the alliance between the United States and Colombia, of considerable polarizing potential in current inter-American politics, precedes the administrations of Chávez and Uribe, and the Plan Colombia. The alliance goes back to the time when the Cuban Revolution provoked considerable fear among the Colombian elite. In particular, the military worried about the possibility that Soviet expansion in the Caribbean, together with territorial claims by Nicaragua, as well as the presence of guerrilla groups backed by Havana, could put the unity of the Colombian state at risk. The strategy developed then by the Colombian government to deal with the situation crystallized in a combination of contradictory initiatives during the presidency of Julio César Turbay (1976–1982). They involved, on one hand, waging a war against internal and external forces allied with the guerrillas and, on the other, submitting to US guidelines.[15] More than the alignment of the Turbay administration with Reagan's policies, which came as a surprise at that time, it was the substitution of traditional Colombian foreign policy with relation to the Caribbean and hemispheric matters with a course of action that led the country in the direction of an increasingly prominent role, based on a deeper structural dependency on the United States in economic, technological, and military terms, exactly when other countries of the region were trying to free themselves from such a condition (Bagley and Tokatlian, 1985: 27). Despite some later attempts to correct its course, by assuming more nationalistic and pro-Latin American stances – Contadora Group, Consensus of Cartagena – the master line of Colombian foreign policy continued to be the one established at the peak of the Cold War, and reaffirmed by Uribe and the Pan Colombia.

While this was happening, Venezuelan diplomacy seems to have gone in the opposite direction: it abandoned its traditional alliance with the United States and headed toward open confrontation with the superpower. At the same time, it passed from relative isolationism to intense regional involvement nurtured by what has been called "oil diplomacy" or "diplomacy of social power." From the beginning of Chávez's regime to the present, billions of dollars have been spent on generous aid programs, subsidized oil to Cuba and to members of "Petrocaribe," donations and disaster relief aid to Bolivia, medical equipment to Nicaragua, and free heating fuel to a considerable number of American consumers (Corrales, 2008: 4).

It is quite common to attribute Venezuela's strong and increasing influence in Central America and the Caribbean to recent policies developed by the Chávez regime, using oil as a strategic basis. Nevertheless, a retrospective view of Venezuelan foreign policy shows that the intensification of its presence in the region, capitalizing on the power of oil to that end, has been a deliberate goal of past administrations since at least the 1960s. In that sense, representative features of current Venezuelan foreign policy such as the promotion of the Bolivarian ideal of Latin American unity, generous loans to governments and regional agencies, programs to subsidize oil or compensate for increases in oil prices, and active involvement in the internal affairs of Caribbean and Central American countries were also outstanding aspects of the policies implemented by Rafael Caldera (1969–1973), Carlos Andrés Pérez (1974–1978), and Luis Herrera Campins (1979–1983).[16]

Concomitant to the unfolding of Venezuelan strategy, US foreign policy toward Latin America took an erratic course in the post-Cold War era. In the hands of petty diplomats for the most part, it often lost, not so much the subtleness it seldom possessed, but the disposition to follow regional developments systematically with a reasonable knowledge of the continent's structural diversity. Policy in Washington has fluctuated between inaction and the veiled interventionism of times past, as can be surmised from its support for the failed coup in Venezuela, its destabilizing tactics against the governments of Bolivia and Ecuador, its increase in military bases, and, more recently, its disguised attitude that ultimately legitimized the coup in Honduras in an attempt to maintain some degree of control over its former "backyard." In short, the conflict between Venezuela and Colombia, beyond the aspects mentioned above, reveals the extent to which governments allied or aligned with one side or the other interpret the drama of the Colombian state and society from an ideological standpoint still anchored in Cold War principles. Under the impact of this polarization, the mediating capability of regional players is compromised, as was proven by the quarrel between the OAS Secretary-General and representatives of the US government in regards to the conflict ignited by Colombia by its crossing the Ecuadorian border as well as by the Honduran crisis.[17]

Central America and the Caribbean in the new hemispheric arrangement

Central America and the Caribbean have been a port of entry and a stage for experimentation and the branching-out of political, cultural, and ideological institutions since the colonial era. A transmission line of ideas and goods, its impact on Latin American history has always been greater than its economic importance, which has oscillated over the long term. From the start, the area took its place on the American scene as one where powers measure their strength or face off in memorable arm-wrestling duels: such was the case long ago among Spain, England, and Holland, and more recently between the United States and the Soviet Union. Here, the clash of ideologies reverberates more intensely, and tends to beckon the South, even after the Cold War.

Perhaps more than in other regions, the consolidation of the Central American States and those of the Latin American Caribbean is a relatively recent phenomenon. The same condition that was used to explain their backwardness – namely, their being located within the gravitational pull of the United States' strategic interests – has been posited as the cause of their subsequent strengthening. In effect, according to this type of interpretation, a major factor responsible for the modernization and expansion of the Central American states to a level closer to that of the South American countries was the US Department of State itself, which, in line with the goals of military defense, contributed to the implementation of a series of bureaucratic and administrative reforms throughout the Cold War (Holden, 1999: 1–2). Even so, in most countries greater state power did not mean social and political incorporation of vast sectors of the population or effective control of the national territory. And it is precisely amid the institutional void still prevalent in border areas that threats with the potential to transform internal conflicts into inter-state clashes proliferate – due, in part, to a historical-spatial condition that is unlike any other in the continent. In fact, the degree of physical proximity and the intersection of the paths of those societies that at some point pretended to be a single state contribute to the dissemination of domestic tensions across national borders. Thus, more than in any other area, in Central America and the countries with umbilical connections to the Caribbean milieu, Venezuela and Colombia included, estimates of the chances of inter-state armed conflict occurring must shift the focus of analysis from external warfare to inter-state rivalries (Thies, 2005: 451). From this standpoint, it is fitting to recall that many of the domestic conflicts that have resulted in international wars in the course of the past 50 years had the Caribbean and Central America as their main staging ground. Today, with ideological polarization reincarnated precisely in this region, the phenomenon may sprout again and spread, feeding on the intensification of social conflict, particularly in border areas.

Frontiers, organized crime, and inter-state conflicts

The increased porosity of borders, the technological advances and the economic nexuses nurtured by globalization, the practice of multilateralism in regional diplomacy, the communion of ideals, and the will to achieve collective goals ratified by the series of American summits in the past 15 years, as well as the negotiated solution of old inter-state rivalries, allow one to forecast a future of peace and democracy for the region (Resende-Santos, 2002: 89). Yet the dynamics of the processes mentioned are not irreversible and, depending on the prevailing circumstances, may refuel past contentions and stimulate confrontations, since the territorial bond, despite the imagery of globalization, "continues to be an important source of national identity and legitimacy" (Johnson, 2001: 132). Along these lines, it is worth mentioning that although the number of areas without clear boundaries is significantly fewer today than in other periods, nonetheless a dozen territorial and boundary disputes are still pending. In the past eight years, force has been used in five of those cases, and troops were mobilized in two of them, involving ten out of the 19 independent countries of Latin America (Domínguez et al., 2004: 357). Moreover, in those instances in which a country lays claim to territories lost in past wars, the threat is greater when the conflict did not end in a politically negotiated settlement (Hensel, 1994: 281).[18]

Territorial disputes in border areas usually have a high potential for risk, due not only to their deep historical roots, but also to the fact that they involve issues of national sovereignty. It is precisely in those locations where the contrast between inter-state pacifism and the intensification of civil and criminal conflicts beyond state control becomes more explicit. From Ciudad del Este (Paraguay), in the south, to the municipality of Tecate (Mexico), in the north, the border areas possess the same characteristics of violence, human displacement, criminality, and corruption of state institutions – or sheer absence of them. The drama unfolds with particular intensity at several points along the Mexican borders due to the flux of immigrants from Guatemala, Honduras, El Salvador, and Colombia who seek to enter the United States by crossing the Suchiate River as a means to reach Tapachula, the main route of illegal migration to the target country (Briscoe, 2008: 3). In this map of despair, the most probable place for conflict is the province of Petén, in Guatemala, particularly at the border with Chiapas, a territory over which drug trafficking cartels and transnational gangs seek to maintain control. In the same way, a sort of wild-west atmosphere prevails along the extensive Colombian borders with Ecuador and Venezuela, characterized by high crime rates and the occupation of territories by armed gangs and drug trafficking networks. There, the interests of contracting companies, irregular groups, and police forces cross each other continuously; what is worse, all of them are armed and "prepared to launch a military response to any incident that may occur" (Informe sobre fronteras, 2008: 4). A particularly critical case refers to the poorly controlled frontiers between Venezuela and Colombia, where criminality has raised the level of animosity among the population to the point of eclipsing other problems caused by the guerillas and the massive migration of Colombians to the neighboring country:

> Neither the maritime borders of inconclusive definition, nor the illegal Colombian immigrants, nor the use on the part of the Colombian guerillas of official Venezuelan armament, nor the terrorist actions of Colombian guerillas within Venezuela have infuriated the common Venezuelan as much as the increase in the number of cars stolen to be sold in Colombia. (Pardo, 1999: 7)

Against such a background, crises like the one that recently took place among Ecuador, Colombia, and Venezuela due to the bombardment of a FARC stronghold near the Putumayo River entail a risk comparable to lighting a match in a flammable atmosphere. These kinds of situations promote the "militarization" of diplomacy, be it through political discourse or by transporting troops to the frontier, and jeopardize the efforts to reach a compromise (Mares, quoted in Pardo, 1999). Things can get worse when, amid the ideological cleavages already present among the governments of the region, countries of the stature of Brazil or Argentina compromise their moderating capacities by taking sides on the basis of anachronistic interpretations of the hemisphere's context.

A phoenix out of the ashes of ideology

The new configuration of ideological cleavages, historically more dangerous and destabilizing than territorial disputes, could not only reduce the margin of efficacy of regional organizations called on to arbitrate them but also increase the explosiveness of border areas where there already exist controversies over the control of strategic resources or tensions resulting from the intensification of criminality and guerilla warfare – especially given that, in the past few decades, technological modernization and the diversification of weapons supply have increased the destructive potential of military and paramilitary armies in the region. Therefore, while international borders might be dissolving in the waters of economic unification, this is not necessarily the case in regards to adjoining countries since, as Guedes da Costa rightly argues, "national defense, for the majority of the Latin American countries, still means beware of your neighbor" (Pion-Berlin, 2000: 61). In this sense, it is important to remember that, notwithstanding the successful resolution of several boundary disputes at the close of the twentieth century, many others continue and, indeed, have been aggravated since then. As a matter of fact, Guyana, Venezuela, Colombia, and several countries in Central American were involved in at least one militarized conflict with other countries during the decade 2000–2010. Within this group, Nicaragua, Venezuela, and Honduras entered into confrontation with the greatest number of neighbors (Domínguez *et al.*, 2004: 359).

Notwithstanding the fact that the formation of regional blocks has promoted cooperation in matters of security, the armed forces, especially in countries with a high degree of military autonomy, such as Chile, have not been enthusiastic about projects of hemispheric range. Economic integration has not resulted thus far in a system of collective defense that could replace the one created by the Rio Treaty. Steps in this direction have failed due to a lack of consensus among the countries, which, in general, prefer to guarantee their own security individually or form defensive alliances grounded on ideological affinities (Pion-Berlin, 2000: 59). In effect, the issue of security has been as politicized as any other, stimulating the formation of different perceptions as to the scale and degree of danger that certain phenomena represent in comparison to others. Thus, for instance, the war on terrorism, which is the articulating axis of a "solid political alliance" between the United States and Colombia, is viewed with much less interest by the other republics. Likewise, while the official discourse of the governments of Venezuela and Brazil highlights poverty as the major threat to regional security, that of the United States bestows lesser importance on the issue. The perception of the risk that drug trafficking represents is high in the cases of Brazil, Colombia, and the United States and moderate in the remaining countries, "with the exception of Bolivia, where it is low" (Bonilla and Cepik, 2004: 72–74). While the possibility of US intervention is considered from medium to high by the Andean countries and Brazil, in Colombia it is considered low, which constitutes a "reversal of the imagines manipulated [by those countries] in regards to terrorism" (Bonilla and Cepik, 2004: 74).

Although the so-called democratic thesis of Kant considers that the more democracy is consolidated and generalized throughout the region, the smaller the chance of conflict among those states, empirical analyses of the existence of such a link have shown that "democracies in Latin America are unaffected in their decision to utilize force in foreign policy by whether or not the country with which they have a dispute is democratic" (Mares and Bernstein, quoted in Johnson, 2001: 129). This is even more true in societies where the transition to democracy is still an unfinished process, since, as suggested in the analogy proposed by Edward Mansfield and Jack Snyder: "governing a society that is democratizing is like driving a car while throwing away the steering wheel, stepping on the gas, and fighting over which passenger will be in the driver's seat. The result, often, is war" (quoted in Johnson, 2001: 133). Ask the countries that have suffered the misfortune of such uncertainty. After all, the number of armed confrontations among Latin American and Caribbean countries under democratic rule has been nearly a dozen in the past few years: Guatemala and Belize, Guyana and Suriname, Venezuela and Guyana, Venezuela and Trinidad and Tobago, Venezuela and Colombia, Colombia and Nicaragua, Nicaragua and Costa Rica, Nicaragua and El Salvador, Nicaragua and Honduras, Honduras and El Salvador, and Honduras and Guatemala (Domínguez, 2004: 380).

Following the same line of thought, it is worth mentioning that the correlation between democracy and civil war, within the domestic sphere, is also statistically insignificant (Elbadawi and Sambanis, 2002: 325). The very conservation of democracy by the Inter-American System does not seem to be regarded as an absolute and, hence, non-negotiable value, as stipulated in numerous documents of the regional organizations. Notwithstanding the OAS's role in the defense of democratic stability and the reestablishment of the Guatemalan and Paraguayan constitutional processes in 1993 and 1996, respectively, the recent episode in Honduras indicates not only the limitations of the organization's performance, but also the inoperative character of the Betancourt Doctrine, when the question is over breaking relations collectively with a government that has violated the constitutional pact. In this case, regardless of the legal controversy over who in fact broke the pact, the political decision of some countries not to adhere to the line determined by the organization showed not only the fragility of the collective systems in neutralizing unilateral actions, but also the considerable weight that an (almost) unilateral action still carries when it is taken by the United States. Conversely, the episode revealed the lack of coherence among countries that work zealously for the maintenance of democracy within the hemisphere while, at the same time, keeping monastic silence when it comes to criticism of leftist authoritarianism.

In Latin America, probably because of the place that the *letrados* (educated elite) have always occupied within the power structure, ideological disputes have always been the tempests of politics, with sufficient force to transcend national frontiers. If formerly they could be more easily appeased by the dominant presence of the United States in the region, today this country's relative withdrawal has already encouraged rivalries among the states that seek to occupy this vacuum to gain greater regional and international influence. Moreover, the fact that the United States has been explicitly left aside, together with Canada, from one of the largest organizations parallel to the OAS, namely, the Summit for the Unity of Latin America and the Caribbean (Cancún Summit), in February 2010, does not necessarily contribute to hemispheric peace. Nor does the monarchical approach of US foreign policy, guided by anything but justice, help.

Regional conflicts have resumed precisely through the path of ideology that many thought the Cold War had ended. For this reason, alongside the resurgence of a left still haunted by the idea of conspiracy, the United States today likewise sees, through the eyes of its specialized agencies, the hands of the Chávez regime in every regional event regarded as harmful to its own political and economic interests (Ellis, 2005: 5). Distortions also flourish among political alliances of governments that are critical of the United States' foreign policy, while trying to uphold simultaneously the social agendas of the new left and capitalist interests. Recent tensions – between Argentina and Uruguay in the case of the paper industry, Brazil and Ecuador involving the Odebrecht firm, Brazil and Bolivia over the supply of gas, and Venezuela and Brazil in consequence of Mercosur – clearly illustrate the difficulties in foreign policy of conjugating pragmatism and solidarity on the basis of shared socialist ideals, be it those from the twenty-first century or from the twentieth (Galvão, 2009: 67). Against this landscape of growing distance from the North and splits in the South, not only the OAS – which was initially built upon the idea of a community of interests – but also other regional organs tend to lose their efficacy and legitimacy when arbitrating conflicts. Therefore today, perhaps more than ever before, it is crucial to discern the frontiers that separate reality from pure ideology so as to "protect us from our own selves, for sometimes we are our worst enemy" (Pardo, 1999: 24).

Notes

I am grateful to Mónica Cabezas, Maya Mitre, and Gabriel Mitre for the translation of parts of this chapter. Any remaining mistakes are mine.

1. The terrible massacre ordered by Trujillo against the Haitian people living at the frontier is not considered here as an interstate conflict. On this tragedy, involving a complex set of historical, ethnic, and political factors, consult Accilien, Adams, and Méléance (2006).
2. The Rio Treaty was used as a model to create NATO. The main objective was to establish an inter-American army, under the command of the United States. On this subject, see López-Maya (1995: 136).
3. Replaced by the OAS in 1948. On the Pan-American Union and the OAS's origins, see Dreier (1963: 299).
4. With the beginning of the military regimes, most of the Latin American governments suspended diplomatic relations with Cuba. Mexico was one of the few countries that maintained continuous diplomatic relations with the island's regime. On the initial impact of the Cuban Revolution within the hemisphere, see Quintaneiro (1988).
5. Dominguez and others (2004: 373) used these two examples to show that the United States' hegemony is irrelevant to explaining the prospects for war and peace in Latin America, and, in doing so, they raised the exceptions to the condition of "proofs."
6. This statement was made by Walker, quoted in Shaw (2003: 79).
7. The military occupation of Haiti lasted from 1994 to 2004.
8. A term used to refer to Latin America.
9. The visit took place during the presidency of Jorge Videla.
10. In 1996, Chile and Bolivia became associate members; that is, they participate in the free commerce zone, but are not obliged to adopt the foreign tariff system.
11. See, in this respect, the position adopted by the Brazilian government during the political crises in Paraguay (1996, 1996, and 2001) and Venezuela (2002), as well as the inclusion of the Democratic Clause in Mercosur.
12. In any case, the regional integration plans existed well before Mercosur. Remember, among other structures, the Latin American Free Commerce Association (ALALC), created in 1960, which was succeeded by the Latin American Integration Association (ALADI), created in 1980, as well as other instruments, such as the Plata Bay Treaty.
13. On the construction of the idea of South America through discourse and practice, by Brazilian diplomacy, see Galvão (2009: 63–80).
14. On this occasion, the British Parliament, going against the Executive's initiatives, defended the exercise of the principle of self-determination by the islanders.
15. On Colombian diplomacy in the 1970s and 1980s, consult Tokatlian (2000: 336–37).
16. For a good analysis of Venezuelan foreign policy in regards to the Caribbean and Central America from 1960 to 1980, see Bond (1982: 100–13).
17. On the interrogatory of the OAS Secretary-General José Miguel Insulza, see US Government (2008).
18. As it happened, for example, in the case of the War of the Pacific, which has been intermittently revived in a series of disputes that still create tensions between the countries involved. The motives for the continuous reactivation of the conflict throughout the years have been of varied nature: a quarrel over the course of a river (such as the Lauca), the supply of gas to Chile,

and others. This is so because for Bolivia no controversy with relation to Chile is merely a circumstantial issue, but necessarily involves a question of sovereignty, since it implies its secular claim over a sea outlet. On the disputes relating to the Lauca River, consult Tomasek (1967).

Bibliography

Accilien, Cécile; Adams, Jessica; Méléance, Elmide (eds.) (2006). *Revolutionary Freedoms: A History of Survival, Strength and Imagination in Haiti*. Coconut Creek, Florida: Educa Vision.
Bagley, Bruce Michael; Tokatlian, Juan Gabriel (1985). "Colombian Foreign Policy in the 1980s: The Search for Leverage." *Journal of Interamerican Studies and World Affairs*, 27(3) (Autumn), pp. 27–62.
Beck, Peter J. (1982). "Cooperative Confrontation in the Falkland Islands Dispute: The Anglo-Argentine Search for a Way Forward, 1968–1981." *Journal of Interamerican Studies and World Affairs*, 24(1) (February), pp. 37–58.
Bond, Robert (1982). "Venezuela la Cuenca del Caribe y la crisis en América Central." *Revista de Estudios Latinoamericanos Mundo Nuevo*, 15/16 (January–June), pp. 27–99.
Bonilla, Adrián; Cepik, Marco (2004). "Seguridad andino-brasileña: conceptos, actores y debates," in Cepik, Marco and Ramírez, Socorro (eds.). *Agenda de Seguridad Andino-Brasileña*. Bogotá: Frederich Ebert.
Briscoe, Ivan (2008). "Trouble on the Borders: Latin America's New Conflict Zones. Peace, Security and Human Rights Programme." FRIDE, Comment, July. http://www.fride.org/download/COM_Borderlands_Americas_ENG_jul08.pdf
Cardoso, Fernando Henrique. "Desafios do Brasil no plano internacional." http://www.iea.usp.br/artigos/fhcdesafiosinternacionais.pdf
Corrales, Javier (2008). "Venezuela's Domestic Politics and Foreign Policy: Current Trends." Testimony before the House Committee on Foreign Affairs Subcommittee on the Western Hemisphere, July 17. http://foreignaffairs.house.gov/110/cor071708.pdf
Domínguez, Jorge; Mares, David; Orozco, Manuel; Palmer, David Scott; Rojas Aravena, Francisco; Serbin, Andrés (2004). "Disputas fronterizas en América Latina." *Foro Internacional*, 44(3), pp. 357–91. [Published in English as "Boundary Disputes." August 2003, Peaceworks, 50. http://www.usip.org/resources/boundary-disputes-latin-america
Dreier, John C. (1963). "The Council of the OAS: Performance and Potential." *Journal of Interamerican Studies*, 5(3) (July), pp. 297–312.
Elbadawi, Ibrahim; Sambanis, Nicholas (2002). "How Much War Will We See? Explaining the Prevalence of Civil War." *Journal of Conflict Resolution*, 46(3) (June), pp. 307–34.
Ellis, Evan (2005). *Scenarios for the Next Generation of Crisis in Latin America*. Vancouver: Mclean, 23 June.
Feldman, David Lewis (1985). "The United States Role in the Malvinas Crisis, 1982: Misguidance and Misperception in Argentina's Decision to Go to War." *Journal of Interamerican Studies and World Affairs*, 27(2) (Summer), pp. 1–22.
Galvão, Thiago Gehre (2009). "América do Sul: construção pela reinvenção (2000–2008)." *Revista Brasileira de Política Internacional*, 52(2), pp. 63–80.

Grabendorff, Wolf (1982). "Interstate Conflict Behavior and Regional Potential for Conflict in Latin America." *Journal of Interamerican Studies and World Affairs*, 24(3) (August), pp. 267–94.

Hensel, Paul R. (1994). "One Thing Leads to Another: Recurrent Militarized Disputes in Latin America, 1816–1986." *Journal of Peace Research*, 31(3) (August), pp. 281–97.

Holden, Robert H (1999). "Securing Central America against Communism: The United States and the Modernization of Surveillance in the Cold War." *Journal of Interamerican Studies and World Affairs*, 41(1) (Spring), p. v, pp. 1–30.

Informe sobre fronteras (2008). http://www.cocasoberania.org/Fronteras%20MAR2008.pdf

Johnson, Kenneth L. (2001). "Review: Regionalism Redux? The Prospects for Cooperation in the Americas." *Latin American Politics and Society*, 43(3) (Autumn), pp. 121–38.

López-Maya, Margarita (1995). "The Change in the Discourse of US-Latin American Relations from the End of the Second World War to the Beginning of the Cold War." *Review of International Political Economy*, 2(1) (Winter), pp. 135–49.

Mares, David (2001). *Violent Peace: Militarized Interstate Bargaining in Latin America*. New York: Columbia University Press.

Mares, David; Bernstein, Steven (1998). "The Use of Force in Latin American Inter-State Conflicts," in Dominguez, Jorge I. (ed.). *International Security and Democracy: Latin America and the Caribbean in the Post-Cold War Era*. Pittsburgh: University of Pittsburgh Press.

Martz, Mary Jeanne Reid (1977). "OAS Reforms and the Future of Pacific Settlement." *Latin American Research Review*, 12(2), pp. 176–86.

Matul, Daniel; Ramírez, Alonso (2009). "El proceso de paz en Centroamérica: Agendas de paz y nuevos focos de conflictividad: Los casos de Guatemala y Nicaragua." *Pensamiento Propio*, 29 (January–June), pp. 91–125. Buenos Aires: Publicación trilingue de Ciencias Sociales de América Latina y el Caribe.

Muñoz, Heraldo (1984). "Beyond the Malvinas Crisis: Perspectives on Interamerican Relations." Review. *Latin American Research Review*, 19(1), pp. 158–72.

Pardo, Rafael (1999). "Los nuevos elementos de seguridad para América Latina." Trabajo presentado al Foro sobre Seguridad en el Hemisferio organizado por la misión permanente de Chile ante la OEA. Washington DC.

Pion-Berlin, David (2000). "Will Soldiers Follow? Economic Integration and Regional Security in the Southern Cone." *Journal of Interamerican Studies and World Affairs*, 42(1) (Spring), pp. 43–69.

Quintaneiro, Tania (1988). *Cuba e Brasil: da revolução ao golpe (1959–1964)*. Belo Horizonte: Editora UFMG.

Resende-Santos, João (2002). "The Origins of Security Cooperation in the Southern Cone." *Latin American Politics and Society*, 44(4) (Winter), pp. 89–126.

Romero, Carlos A. (2004). "El tema democrático y la seguridad multilateral," in Cepik, Marco and Ramírez, Socorro (eds.). *Agenda de seguridad Andino-Brasileña*. Bogotá: Frederick Ebert.

Scheina, Robert L. (2003). *Latin America's Wars: The Age of the Professional Soldier, 1900–2001*. Vol. 2. Washington DC: Brassey's Inc.

Selcher, Wayne A. (1985). "Brazilian-Argentine Relations in the 1980s: From Wary Rivalry to Friendly Competition." *Journal of Interamerican Studies and World Affairs*, 27(2) (Summer), pp. 25–53.

Selcher, Wayne A. (1986). "Current Dynamics and Future Prospects of Brazil's Relations with Latin America: Toward Patterns of Bilateral Cooperation." *Journal of Interamerican Studies and World Affairs*, 28(2) (Summer), pp. 67–99.

Shaw, Carolyn M. (2003). "Limits to Hegemonic Influence in the Organization of American States." *Latin American Politics and Society*, 45(3) (Autumn), pp. 59–92.

Sotomayor Velázques, Arturo C. (2004). "Civil-Military Affairs and Security Institutions in the Southern Cone: The Sources of Argentine-Brazilian Nuclear Cooperation." *Latin American Politics and Society*, 46(4) (Winter), pp. 29–60.

Thies, Cameron G. (2005). "War, Rivalry, and State Building in Latin America." *American Journal of Political Science*, 49(3) (July), pp. 451–65.

Tokatlian, Juan Gabriel (2000). "Colombia at War: The Search for a Peace Diplomacy." *International Journal of Politics, Culture, and Society*, 14(2) (Winter), p. 333–62.

Tomasek Robert D. (1967). "The Chilean-Bolivian Lauca River Dispute and the O.A.S." *Journal of Interamerican Studies*, 9(3) (July), pp. 351–66.

US Government (2008). "Crisis in the Andes: The Border Dispute between Colombia and Ecuador and Implications for the Region". Briefing and hearing before the Subcommittee on the Western Hemisphere of the Committee on Foreign Affairs House of Representatives. Second session, April 10. Serial no. 110–59. Washington DC: US Government Printing Office.

Vigevani, Tullo; Oliveira, Marcelo F. de; Cintra, Rodrigo (2003). "Política externa no período de Fernando Henrique Cardoso: a busca de autonomia pela integração." *Tempo Social*, 15(2) (November), pp 31–61. São Paulo. http://www.scielo.br/scielo.php?pid=so103-2060200300020003$script=sci_arttext

3
Argentina

Roque B. Fernández and Katherina Fernández

The land and its people

Argentina has a total population of 36,260,130, a total surface area of 3,761,274 square kilometers (continental Argentina: 2,791,310 square kilometers and Antarctic Argentina: 969,464 square kilometers), and a density of 13 inhabitants per square kilometer. It is surrounded by Chile to the west; the Atlantic Ocean to the east; and Peru, Bolivia, Paraguay, Uruguay, and Brazil to the north (see Figure 3.1). Argentines' ancestors mostly came from Europe, and were mainly Spaniards and Italians. There were also, in smaller numbers, German, French, and English immigrants. In 2004–2005 a national survey revealed that a total of 600,329 people recognized themselves as being pure aboriginals or descendents of the first generation. There is freedom of religion but Argentines are for the most part Roman Catholic. However, Jews, Protestants, Muslims, and many other religions live together peacefully. Since the adoption of the 1853 National Constitution the form of government has been representative, republican, and federal. The country is divided into 23 provinces and the federal capital, which has been an autonomous city since a modification of the Constitution in 1994.

The government is divided into three branches: the Executive, formed by the President and Ministers; the Legislative, with two houses – the Senate and the House of Representatives; and the Judicial, with a Supreme Court of Justice and different jurisdictions.

Taking advantage of the good climatic conditions of the temperate pampas, the main economic activity in Argentina is agriculture and food processing industries. Other important activities are livestock raising and fishing. As in many developing countries, the nonagricultural industrial sector is of moderate size and has been influenced by periods of protective measures and periods of free trade policies.

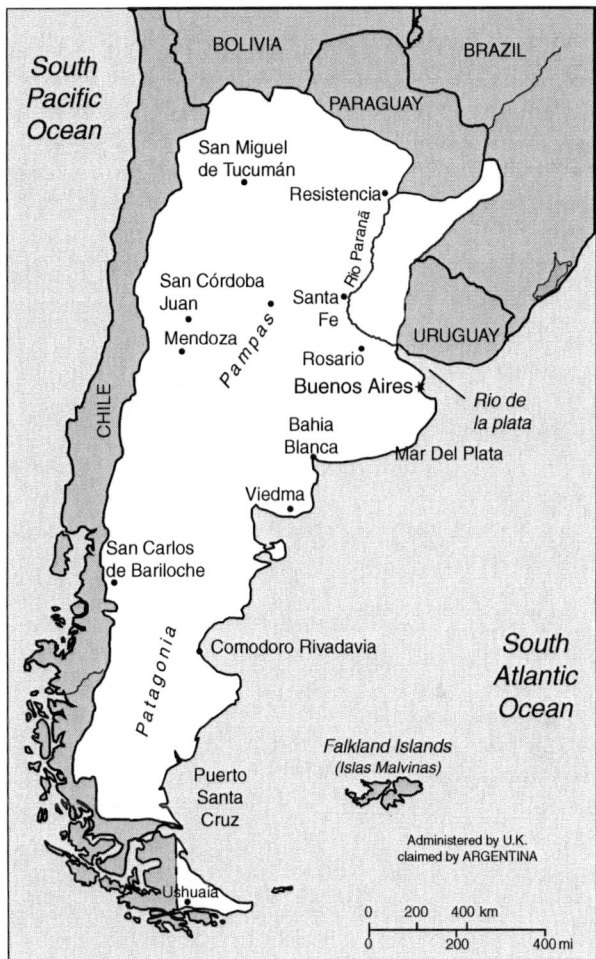

Figure 3.1 Map of Argentina

Cultural and economic history

The beginnings

The survival of many heterogeneous aboriginal groups has shaped the culture in Latin America. Argentina has incorporated many characteristics of European culture, introduced mainly by conquerors and afterward by immigrant streams mainly from European countries at the end of nineteenth and beginning of the twentieth centuries.

Many indigenous groups from different cultures occupied the Argentine territory before its colonization. The Diaguitas and Comechingones from the middle-west territory domesticated animals, wove and hunted. The Querandies, Patagones, and Onas inhabited Patagonia, the Litoral and Pampa regions. These people were nomads and lived by hunting and fishing. The Calchaquies and Matacos inhabited the north region, cultivated the land and domesticated animals.

Juan Díaz de Solís, a Spanish colonist, discovered the River Plate in 1516. Sebastian Cabot first penetrated the territory in 1526 and established the first Spanish colony in the region. In 1536, Pedro de Mendoza founded Santa María del Buen Ayre, but the rebellious natives, who refused to provide food to the Spaniards, burnt down the city.

However, Domingo Martinez de Irala is considered the first colonist, since he was able to approach the indigenous groups peacefully, achieving the unification between Spaniards and natives. Colonizing streams from Peru, Chile, and Spain he started penetrating Argentine territory in 1560, populating the region and giving birth to new cities. Jesuit missionaries also began to make their way into the area during this time.

In 1776, the viceroyalty of the Río de la Plata was created, integrating Argentina, Bolivia, Uruguay, Paraguay, and southern Brazil. Buenos Aires was its capital. In 1777, the Port of Buenos Aires began free trade with ports in Spain.

The road to independence

In 1810, the viceroy was replaced by an open city council (cabildo abierto). The development sprang from popular beliefs influenced by emancipating ideas from the French Revolution and North American independence. Liberating armies propagated the revolutionary doctrine in neighboring countries, trying to evict the Spaniards from their territories.

General José de San Martín, one of the nation's most important historical characters, contributed to freeing Chile and Peru, thus assuring the independence of the south of the continent. In 1816, independence from Spain was declared. In 1853, the National Constitution was created, establishing a republican, representative, and federal form of government.

The economic culture in Argentina was greatly influenced by figures such as the Frenchman Quesnay who favored wealth creation through work on the land, that is, developing agriculture. Influence also came from the British, through the ideas of John Locke and Adam Smith, favoring freedom and private property, as basic human rights, and free trade.

One major exponent of these economic principles during the viceroyalty period was Mariano Moreno, who defended the farmers' interests. He strongly defended free trade and counseled the viceroy against monopolies that tended to generate contraband. He confronted Spanish public officials who denied the Spanish colonies the right to trade directly with London merchants. However, Spain's attitude became more flexible due to its economic decadence (the result of debilitating wars with other European countries) at the beginning of the 1800s.

Releasing the constraint on foreign trade established the basis for free trade with Europe after the country's independence in 1816, and shaped Argentina's attitude until the First World War. Consequently, the trade derived from cattle and sheep – such as leather, wool, and frozen beef – began shaping external trade. Of course, the other side of the coin was the importing of manufactured goods, mainly from Britain. These imports enhanced competition and produced discomfort for the Argentines involved in businesses competing with them. Although some protectionist policies were set in motion to protect certain industries, free trade was the general policy thanks to the revenues stemming from customs duties. This policy favored internationally competitive sectors such as agricultural production.

At the beginning of the 1800s, agriculture played a subordinate role to cattle. Much of the country's interior, where agricultural conditions were optimal, had not been extensively populated. However, this tendency started to reverse in the 1820s with the stimulation of export policies for fruit and other agricultural products.

The country tried to develop mining activity, but with no success. The goal was to supplement the wealth generated by stock exports and to attend to the great financial needs of the revolution for independence. The people's lack of knowledge on how to exploit mines destroyed this dream and made the economy dependent first on cattle, second on agriculture, and lastly on manufactured goods. The direct consequence of the lack of mineral wealth was a shortage of coins to back up commercial transactions. Thus, paper money was printed with a set conversion rate to gold and silver, to substitute for the lack of coins.

After achieving independence from Spain with much effort, the young Argentine republic enjoyed a unique place in the world. It had vast natural resources, a huge internal market, and direct access to the sea. Again, derivatives from cattle easily found eager importers such as Brazil, North America, Europe, and Cuba. The following decades, however, were tainted by imbalances between Buenos Aires – the center of commercial activity due to its proximity to a port, as well as of financial, political, and economic activity – and the other provinces. Nevertheless Argentina began to position itself as one of the most powerful countries in Latin America.

The see-saw century: dealing with populism and coups d'etat

In 1904, the working class party gained representation in the government. H. de Yrigoyen assumed the presidency in 1916, maintaining the country's neutrality during the First World War. A succession of military coups took place from 1930 until 1946, replacing the elected democratic governments. In 1944, diplomatic relations were broken with Germany and its allies, and war was declared on them.

In 1946, General Juan Domingo Perón was elected president with massive support from the working class. His government was characterized by populist measures. Perón and his wife, Eva Perón (who died in 1952), favored policies to enhance social welfare. However, these policies produced unsustainable macroeconomic pressure and social unrest that ended with Perón's exile in 1955. A new succession of democratic governments and coups d'état characterized the period from 1955 to 1973.

In 1972, Perón was reelected with substantial popular support, but he died the following year. His widow, María Estela de Perón, the vice-president, succeeded him. But the period was characterized by waves of violence due to the lack of economic policies to support the nation's development and control the fiscal deficit and inflation. A new military coup again ended the democratic government.

The period called the Proceso Nacional de Reorganización (National Reorganization Process) was characterized by a sort of civil war with massive violation of human rights. The results of this era were thousands of missing people, a great increase in the external deficit, a deep recession, and the closure of many private firms, as well as the military occupation of the Malvinas Islands in 1982. The islands had been seized in 1833 by the United Kingdom.

The leader challenged: gaining stability

This last phase of Argentine history culminated in the lost war in the Falklands (Malvinas). Democratic elections were reestablished in 1983. New president Raúl Alfonsín, from the Radical Union Party, was elected for a six-year period. He worked hard on establishing and protecting the basic pillars of democracy and institutional stability. However, he was not successful in controlling the constant increases in prices that finally led to hyperinflation. As a result, a few months before the end of his mandate Alfonsín surrendered the presidency to Carlos S. Menem, from the Justicialist Party who had won the presidential election. Menem was reelected for the period 1995–1999. During his decade of administration, he achieved price stability by creating the Convertibility Plan, based on a fixed exchange rate (under which one Argentine peso equaled one dollar). He also privileged free trade and capital mobility. The outcome of these policies was an increase in gross national product (GNP) that made Argentina the second largest economy in Latin America after Brazil. However, a succession of balance of payment crises in the developing countries of South-East Asia in 1997, and the Russian debt default in the second half of 1998, forced Argentina into a period of recession, which was worsened by the Brazilian devaluation of the Real at the beginning of 1999. The economy started to recover in the second half of 1999. In 2000, the Alliance Party (named after the alliance of the Radical Union and Frepaso parties) won the presidential elections under Fernando de la Rúa. A combination of major tax increases, adverse terms of trade, and capital outflows aborted the recovery and a new period of recession began. These developments, together with the lack of attention to badly needed structural changes, produced social turmoil that ended with de la Rúa's resignation in December 2001, plunging the economy into an even bigger crisis. A new provisional government, under the Justicialist Party, declared, with the approval of the National Congress, defaults on the national debt, and later assigned the presidency to Eduardo Duhalde. One of Duhalde's first actions as president was to pass two other controversial laws: the abolition of the Convertibility Law, producing a devaluation of the Argentine peso; and the "pesofication" of dollar-denominated contracts in the banking sector. This meant that every dollar deposit in the banks was converted to $1.40 (Argentine pesos), whereas at the time, the price of the dollar in the exchange market had reached approximately $4 (pesos)., At the same time, the loans in dollars that banks had made to the public were converted to argentine pesos at the official conversion rate, , that is, one dollar for one argentine peso. That is why the process was referred to as asymmetric "pesofication": Banks' dollar assets and liabilities were converted to pesos at different exchange rates, producing a massive redistribution of wealth from lenders to borrowers. For example, a borrower holding a liquid position in US dollars was able to convert that position at an exchange rate of four pesos for each dollar in the unregulated open exchange market, canceling his previous debt converted at an exchange of one peso to one dollar. To be precise, this process represented a nominal debt reduction of 75 percent.

These policies immediately produced high country risk; the default was interpreted by the international community as a lack of willingness to pay. Moreover, the above policies also produced vast social discomfort, political uncertainty, and the deterioration of institutions. Consequently Duhalde called for anticipated elections, without primaries, an election that was won by Carlos Menem, but as he obtained fewer than 40 percent of the votes, the law required a second election. In the runoff election, Carlos Menem and Nestor Kirchner (second in number of votes), would be allowed to compete. As Carlos Menem decided not to compete in the second round, Nestor Kirchner was elected president with just 22 percent of the votes.

Although he started with weak support from the population, he was able to complete his four-year appointed term. At the end of his presidency, the high growth rate in GNP, the low unemployment rate, and the relative stability in the value of the Argentine peso, contributed to a certain period of peace among the citizens of Argentina. These positive indicators of the economy can be largely explained by the very favorable terms of trade and abundant international liquidity during Kirchner's term. However, certain manipulations of core macroeconomic indices, such as the inflation level and the amount of foreign reserves, and an increasing concentration of power in just a few people's hands – "crony capitalism" – started to undermine the confidence of the population in the real strength of the economy and its institutions.

After his first mandate, Kirchner appointed his wife, Cristina Fernandez, to compete for the elections in 2007, thus again avoiding the normal procedure of primary elections within the party. Cristina Fernandez won the elections and assumed the presidency in December 2007. Unfortunately, her term had a rough start: immediately after she gained power, a corruption case put the financing of her campaign under the magnifying glass. Her campaign was presumed to have been financed with illegal money from Venezuela. After that, she tried to pass a controversial resolution raising the tax on exports of agricultural products, thus fomenting a tax revolt by farmers. The farmers tried to reverse the situation through public demonstrations, which involved blocking traffic on the roads. They also sought support, which they successfully gained, from people not directly involved in agricultural activity. Cristina Fernandez decided to end this civil revolt by sending the resolution for approval by the National Congress. In a heated debate with tied votes for and against the law, the vice president, Julio Cleto Cobos, had to make the deciding vote. He voted against the tax hike. This represented a huge loss of power for the president and a steep fall in popularity from an original 60 percent to a low of 20 percent in just a few months in power.

Also, the world financial situation after the subprime crisis affected the Argentine economy by diminishing the price of food commodities which had greatly contributed to Argentina's recovery after the 2002 crisis. After the default in 2001, Argentina was not able to access the international financial markets. The combination of these adverse factors (high inflation rate, loss of access to capital markets, and worldwide decrease in growth at the end of 2008) has put pressure on the fiscal accounts. This phenomenon produced a sharp increase in country risk and consequently the pursuit of desperate measures by Argentina to attract foreign capital. To address this matter, the president passed a law in November 2008 that enabled capital from abroad to return to Argentina with very flexible prerequisites. The opposing parties accused the government of permitting the laundering of money. Another drastic measure was the nationalization of the private funds that workers used to save money to finance their retirement. After the law was passed through Congress (where Cristina Fernandez had a majority) these funds were automatically transferred to the national social security administration.

This and many other policies contributed to making the opposition complain, over the past few years, against policy actions which undermined the basic institutional framework of Argentina: the defense of property rights and the balance of power among the legislative, judiciary, and presidential branches of government. The years to come will surely be difficult. The national leadership will certainly be challenged.

World economic organizations: trade and growth

As mentioned earlier, Argentina enjoyed a comfortable position in world trade at the end of the 1800s. However, the country became progressively poorer compared to other nations from the beginning of the last century. For example, Argentina's output grew by 157 percent from 1900 to 1997, whereas Canada's output grew by 603 percent over the same period. The explanation for this very low growth rate seems to be an inward orientation and macroeconomic instability. President Juan Perón's administration particularly favored import substitution policies over export policies in order to encourage domestic industrial development. He also favored an expansionary fiscal policy. However, empirical evidence (Díaz A., 1970) shows that output grew 5.6 percent annually between 1900 and 1930, whereas from 1930 to 1965, output grew by only 3.7 percent, thus putting into question the success of import substitution measures. When barriers to growth were eliminated under Menem's administration, output experienced a higher annual growth rate of 6 percent. This tendency decreased as other developing countries' crises spread around the globe.

In 2002, an import substitution policy was pursued again, strengthened by a major devaluation of the Argentine peso, which has remained undervalued in the past few years. This type of policy, together with a strong increase in the price of commodities that Argentina exports has produced high growth rates, but many suggest this type of growth will not lead to development in the long run. Several export taxes and import restrictions in the past few years on products such as petroleum, meat, and agricultural goods, and the strong intervention by the government to control prices – applying cross subsidies between sectors and expropriating companies and retirement funds – have resulted in a lack of investment and the consumption of the capital stock accumulated during the freer decade of the 1990s, thus compromising growth in the long run. These results suggest that when Argentina follows relatively free trade policies, it tends to produce more sustainable growth than during periods of protectionism.

Trade liberalization: the birth of Mercosur

The recent attempts by Argentina to liberalize trade started at the end of the 1980s. The first attempt at free trade started in 1988, unilaterally, by abandoning the previous protectionist policies that tended toward autarky, import substitution, and exchange rate and price controls.

There were also efforts to open trade multilaterally by deepening the country's compromises with GATT (General Agreement on Tariffs and Trade) and the WTO (World Trade Organization) and by lowering tariffs and quota restrictions.

Regional openness started with Brazil in 1986 with the signing by both countries of the Programa de Cooperación y Integración Económica Argentina-Brasil (Argentina-Brazil Integration and Economics Cooperation Program). In November 1988, a new treaty – the Tratado de Integración, Cooperación y Desarrollo – (the Treaty in Integration, Cooperation and Development) was signed, whereby both countries agreed not only to a free trade union but to recognize the importance of coordinating monetary, fiscal, and exchange policies.

Later, in 1991, the Tratado de Asunción (Treaty of Asunción) was signed, which gave birth to Mercosur (Mercado Común del Sur). A 40 percent tariff decrease was agreed upon among the participating countries – Argentina, Brazil, Uruguay, and Paraguay – starting June 1991. The remaining tariffs would gradually decrease to zero tariffs in 1995, thus establishing a free trade area and a new external common tariff for other nonmember countries. However, the members of Mercosur agreed to keep certain products under a specific tariff. Such was the case for Argentine products related to the steel, textile, paper, and shoe industries. Moreover, the sugar and automobile industries were given special treatment ad hoc due to divergences in policy among the countries regarding the protection of these vulnerable sectors. Still, the main objective was to move to a customs union by 2001 by gradually eliminating these restrictions on trade.

Chile, Bolivia, Ecuador, Colombia, and Peru were included in the Mercosur treaty as "associate economies", which meant that they could negotiate bilaterally with Mercosur, whereas Venezuela requested to be fully incorporated as a new member in 2006 but has not received ratification from all member countries yet.

Mercosur has also served as an enforcing mechanism. Due to the international commitment among countries, the task of local lobbyists to press the government for protection for certain industries was made more difficult. This mechanism is particularly valuable for a country like Argentina, accustomed as it is to protectionist policies. In this area in particular, regionalism is preferable to unilateralism.

What is behind the trade agreement?

Many authors have analyzed the determining factors of regional trade (Sanguinetti and Garriga, 1995). Unilateral liberalization – together with geographic features – seems to be an important factor in determining intra-regional trade among countries. There appears to be a concept of a "natural bloc", drawn from common frontiers, similar cultural inheritance, and similar languages, that reduces the costs of transactions between these related countries compared to others. There is empirical evidence suggesting that Mercosur is such a natural bloc.

Although the first four member countries are neighbors with markets close enough to lower transaction costs, there are different national interests. Argentina, Paraguay, and Uruguay are economies that view integration as a way to increase trade. These nations look at Mercosur as a stage in opening commerce to other countries outside their current trading bloc. However, Brazil's economy is the largest of the bloc partners. As a result, membership in Mercosur seems to have an additional geopolitical interest: to generate a very large economic area so as to increase negotiating power relative to other trade areas in Europe, Asia, and the United States. Thus, Mercosur's pitfall is differing interests. In Argentina's case, the country would obtain more benefits by opening up to the rest of the world than by belonging to a bloc in which Brazil's economic leadership leads to higher tariffs for countries outside the bloc. Chile's reluctance to adhere to Mercosur might be taken as proof of the advantage for this country to function as a small world economy rather than as a member of a group of countries not offering all the advantages of trade creation and suffering from trade diversion within the region, as well. Despite the different interests among member countries, Mercosur is a useful tool for all of them since it can be used as a transitional stage to greater global integration and as leverage during negotiations. As a result, the member nations are more powerful as a bloc than individually.

Trade development

Table 3.1 gives some insight into the trade statistics of the Mercosur bloc. As can be seen from the information in the table, trade within Mercosur has grown much more quickly than trade outside the bloc. However, the balance of trade accounts moved from an initial surplus to a deficit starting in 1995. This phenomenon can be explained by the underlying macroeconomic movements that members of the bloc have experienced in opening their economies and abolishing external capital rationing.

These movements also explain why the balance of trade deficit has produced discomfort for those who favor protectionist policies. Nonetheless, the trade balance reverted to a surplus in 2001.This seemingly happy turn of events was due at first not to an increase in competitiveness but to an ongoing recession.

However, in 2002, the devaluation of the peso in Argentina helped to bring about a trade surplus. At present, inflation in Argentina has been eroding the real exchange rate, which has encouraged lobbyists from the industrial sector to push for an ever-greater depreciation of the peso.

Clearly then, in most sectors of the economy, Argentina is not gaining in competitiveness due to an increase in its productivity (that is, using new technologies that help reduce the costs of production) but due to continuous intervention by the central bank to maintain the exchange rate at an artificially high level.

Table 3.1 Foreign trade, Argentina, 1990–2006

Year	Exports within Mercosur	Exports to the rest of the world	Total exports	Imports within Mercosur	Imports from the rest of the world	Total imports	Balance with the rest of the world
(a) Trade statistics (US$ millions)							
1990	4228	42,191	46,419	3606	23,642	27,248	18,548
1991	5243	40,699	45,912	4789	27,357	32,146	13,312
1992	7369	42,872	50,241	7108	31,564	28,673	11,308
1993	10,057	44,018	54,075	9024	36,846	45,869	7172
1994	12,049	50,066	62,115	11,622	46,459	58,082	3607
1995	14,444	56,066	70,059	13,928	61,829	75,758	−5763
1996	17,034	57,965	74,999	17,112	66,169	83,281	−8204
1997	20,758	62,796	83,555	20,483	77,021	97,504	−14,225
1998	20,507	61,098	81,605	20,935	75,848	96,783	−14,750
1999	15,399	59,176	74,576	15,845	64,953	80,978	−5777
2000	17,697	66,901	84,598	17,431	69,191	86,622	−2290
2001	15,214	72,671	87,885	15,331	66,294	81,625	6377
2002	10,214	78,669	88,883	10,665	49,036	59,702	29,663
2003	12,631	93,467	106,097	13,059	53,083	66,143	40,383
2004	17,192	118,396	135,588	17,601	73,388	90,989	45,007
2005	21,105	142,700	163,805	21,323	88,020	109,343	54,680
2006	25,629	164,527	190,156	25,533	110,069	135,601	54,459
(b) Trade statistics (percentage change)							
1990							
1991	24	−3.6	−1.1	32.8	15.7	18.0	−28.2
1992	40.5	5.4	9.4	48.4	15.4	20.3	−15.1
1993	36.5	2.7	7.6	26.9	16.7	18.6	−36.6
1994	19.8	13.7	14.9	28.8	26.1	26.6	−49.7
1995	19.9	12.0	13.5	19.8	33.1	30.4	−259.8
1996	17.9	3.4	6.4	22.9	7.0	9.9	42.3
1997	21.9	8.3	11.4	19.7	16.4	17.1	73.4
1998	−1.2	−2.7	−2.3	2.2	−1.5	−0.7	3.7
1999	−24.9	−3.1	−8.6	−24.3	−14.4	−16.5	−60.8
2000	14.9	13.1	13.4	10.0	6.5	7.2	−60.4
2001	−14.0	8.6	3.9	−12.0	−4.2	−5.8	−378.5
2002	−32.9	8.3	1.1	−30.4	−26.0	−26.9	364.7
2003	23.7	18.8	19.4	22.4	8.3	10.8	36.3
2004	36.1	26.7	27.8	34.8	38.3	37.6	11.5
2005	22.8	20.5	20.8	21.1	19.9	20.2	21.5
2006	21.4	15.3	16.1	19.7	25.0	24.0	−0.4

Sources: Centro de Economia Internacional en base a Indec, Secretariat of Foreign Trade, Brazil (SECEX), Banco Central de Paragual, Banco Central del Uruguay, and International Monetary Fund (FMI).

The present and future of trade

Mercosur at present

Mercosur has remained relatively stable despite changes of government and economic crises. There is an ongoing debate as to whether Mercosur has been trade creating or trade diverting. There is empirical evidence that supports each position. In 1997, an economist at the World Bank released the first publicly available document that suggested that Mercosur was trade diverting (Yeats, 1997). This document produced justified discomfort for all bloc members and prompted many responses suggesting that overall Mercosur had been trade creating (Bohara, Kishore, and Sanguinetti, 2001).

Before Mercosur was founded, many of its members – especially Argentina – had relatively closed economies. So, it is not wide of the mark to consider that any degree of opening to commerce is trade creating, at least at the beginning of the agreement. Indeed, Mercosur produced a strong initial expansion and encouraged trade and investment. Nevertheless, policies that protect vulnerable industries still remain. There are tariffs, nontariff restrictions, export subsidies, and production subsidies that distort trade. This state of affairs has also produced decreased exports to both NAFTA and the European Union.

These protectionist policies have prevailed due to lobbying by different sectors of the economy. The power of these lobbyists has had considerable influence and has coddled the so-called "infant industries" in Argentina to the ripe old age of 50 years! These small business groups, which hold a more protectionist view, are suspicious of economic integration programs. They try to maintain a system of protection of the products they represent. Such is the case, for example, of industrial products represented by the Industrial Union. Nevertheless, these goods do not represent a large proportion of GNP.

On the whole, the business community has accepted Mercosur and supranational organizations as a good plan for growing international trade, and as growth enhancing. Yet they do not enjoy 100 percent public support; most of the Argentine people are strong supporters of nationalism and are accustomed to populist measures to protect them. There has also been some discomfort about the opening of the economy due to such external shocks as Brazil's devaluation in 1999. However, as mentioned earlier, in January 2002, Argentina abandoned the convertibility plan by devaluing its currency and moved to a floating exchange rate, which improved its terms of trade. Exporters received Argentina's devaluation of the peso with great relief. They felt that the rule one peso = one dollar had made tradable products less competitive, due to the artificially appreciated value of the local currency that was pegged to the dollar.

In the past few years there has been some complaint from the smaller countries – Uruguay and Paraguay – due to the protective restraints that still prevail in the bigger countries like Brazil. For example, Paraguay considers there has not been a significant increase in the living standards of its citizens since it joined Mercosur. As a result, the country might pursue bilateral agreements with other countries like the United States; Uruguay might follow this same path.

This type of macroeconomic conflict within Mercosur has caused intraregional relations to deteriorate and has produced a negative impact on direct investments from countries that could have taken advantage of the enlarged trade area. There is an urgent need to deepen international policy coordination in order to avoid these hurtful consequences.

Mercosur's future

Sadly, in the past few years, controversial policies that limit access to foreign markets by prohibiting exports of certain goods and imposing high tariffs and quotas on many exports products have produced discomfort among the exports' producers. Many foreign markets that were gained during the opening of trade during the 1990s are now closed to Argentine exporters mostly due to export tariff and export quota. This tendency, together with policies biased against international companies, has left Argentina in an uncomfortable state, isolated from the rest of the world.

Despite these last developments, many simulations have been run to determine the impact of eliminating barriers to agricultural goods – a field in which Argentina has a comparative advantage (Fundación Mediterránea, 2000). In particular, this exercise has been run for the United States and the European Union. The results for the latter are very favorable, suggesting that if barriers are eliminated for this type of produce, meat exports to the EU will increase by 350 percent and sugar exports by 143 percent, for example. This result is a direct consequence of the European Union's distorting measures toward agricultural goods. Argentina already exports this type of goods despite the European Union's policies.

If the United States eliminates agricultural trade barriers, the results are more modest compared to those for the European Union. For example, sugar exports would increase 60 percent and dairy products 20 percent. The explanation for these modest increases in exports is that there are fewer barriers and distortions to these goods and that the United States is more efficient in producing its own.

Although negotiations regarding tariff reductions and/or elimination have started among these countries, Argentina, like many other developing countries, faces additional costs when settling multilateral agreements. Due to poor management infrastructure, in order to comply with standards and technical norms, many countries require expensive tests and certificates for exporters. One example of this kind of cost was the outbreak of aftosa (foot-and-mouth disease) in the country. Argentina's ineffectiveness in controlling this type of virus resulted in the closure of the meat market by almost all importers for a very long time. Despite this incident, the country's agricultural and cattle industry is considered competitive relative to the United States. So, it might be better to improve trade with those countries that do not have a comparative advantage in this particular market segment.

There is a new debate on whether the country should try to separate itself from its present bloc and search for other markets unilaterally. Currently, given market conditions, there might be more trade creation if the country entered NAFTA directly, even if it meant abandoning Mercosur. One of the advantages of entering NAFTA is the possibility of using the fast track policy of the United States in order to negotiate tariffs more easily. The reduction of transaction costs is a valuable tool in trying to reach an agreement with NAFTA. At present, Brazil's reluctance to lower the Mercosur external tariff is unfavorable to the other members who wish to have greater trade gains.

Culture versus globalization

There is an ongoing debate as to whether the growth in globalization has been detrimental to culture and tradition within a given country. The different ethnic groups in Argentina have integrated perfectly well into the democratic system. As was previously mentioned, there is a very small indigenous ethnic population in the country. These peoples' claims concerning their territory and culture are always heard. Moreover, they have been protected by specific legislation. International agreements such as Mercosur, NAFTA, and the Andean Pact are recognized by the ethnic groups and are considered to be a normal process of integration among nations. The indigenous tribes do not believe that their cultural features are threatened since they are well protected by specific laws. Moreover, they have greatly benefited from the sale of their handicrafts and services (for example as ski instructors or tourist guides) to tourists, especially in the north of the country where these groups are mostly found.

Trade is definitely a factor of cultural integration in many other ways. Argentina has incorporated many modern practices, such as marketing structures and the development of economies of scale for mass production. All these practices are sooner or later translated into the educational or business culture. Buying bread at the bakery, meat at the butcher's shop, and then vegetables at the grocer's is, for many Argentineans, the culture of the small merchant. So, when large companies enter the country with big, efficient supermarkets, with better prices, higher quality, and mass production, people argue that such behavior destroys culture.

The argument is accurate from that point of view. That is, in a competitive system, the more efficient baker will compete successfully in the market, and the inefficient baker might find himself arranging bread on the supermarket's aisles. Thus, small merchants might argue that life was better before globalization. However, as consumers wish to optimize price and quality, this argument is not true for them.

Should consumers sacrifice themselves for culture's sake? In Argentina, although the small merchant culture still exists in some places, especially in the most rural regions, the more traditional political parties, such as the Radical and the Justicialist Parties, do not reject globalization. Moreover, they tend to promote economic integration with other countries.

Free markets and democracy were at the origin of the Argentine republic as established in the 1853 Constitution, but were gradually abandoned through time; however these principles have resurfaced in the past three decades. Freedom and democracy restarted in 1983, and freedom of the press restarted in the 1990s. Political competition is relatively new for most of the present generation.

There has not yet been enough time to allow the system fully to work in favor of efficient allocation of resources and strong monetary, fiscal and political institutions.

Conclusion

Argentina has been able to improve its terms of trade by becoming an important participant in the Mercosur trade agreement. Yet there is an urgent need to coordinate macroeconomic policies in order to minimize negative external shocks to the bloc. Until the major peso depreciation at the beginning of 2002, the debate in Argentina was whether the country should separate from the other bloc members that had previously depreciated their own currencies without allowing for compensatory measures to absorb short-run disequilibrium. An alternative proposal was to negotiate unilaterally with the United States or the European Union, or to enter NAFTA, by which means Argentina could benefit by penetrating these markets. This strategy could have also been useful to all the members of Mercosur affected by trade diversion. On the one hand, it could be stated that real exchange rate volatility has affected, and will continue to affect, regional economic integration in the future. On the other hand, culture and tradition have integrated well with globalization. The country's ancient and rich culture is maintained by the prevailing ethnic groups, which have accepted the challenge of an integrating world.

Bibliography

Bohara, A.; Kishore,G.; Sanguinetti, P. (2001). "Trade Diversion and Declining Tariffs: Evidence from Mercosur." Working Paper, January. Beunos Aires: Universidad Torcuato Di Tella.
CEI (2000). *Mercosur 2000, Crecimiento económico y nuevas oportunidades de inversión.*
Díaz, A. (1970). *Essays on the Economic History of the Argentine Republic.* New Haven, CT: Yale University Press.
Fernandez, Katherina; Fernandez, Roque B. (2007). "Willingness to pay and the sovereign debt contract." *Journal of Applied Economics* 10, May, pp. 43–76.
Fernández, R. (1991) What Have Populists Learned from Hyperinflation? *The Macroeconomics of Populism in Latin America,* ed. R. Dornbusch and S. Edwards. The University of Chicago Press.
Fernández, R.; Mantel, R. (1989). "Fiscal Lag and the Problem of Stabilization: Argentina's Austral Plan," in *Latin American Debt and Adjustment,* P. Brock, M. Connolly and C. Gonzalez (eds.). New York: Praeger Publishers.
Fundación Mediterránea (2000). *Las distorsiones de los mercados mundiales de alimentos y su impacto en la Argentina.* Mimeo.
Halperín Donghi, Tulio (1963). "La expansión ganadera en la campaña de Buenos Aires (1810–1852)," Desarrollo Económico, 1(1–2), April& September, pp. 57–110.
Kandel, P. (1983). *Claves de la Economía Argentina 1810–1983.* Beunos Aires: Editorial Sudamericana.
Krugman, P.; Obstfeld, M. (2001). *International Economics, Policy and Theory,* Fifth Edition. Reading, MA: Addison-Wesley Publishing.
Nogués, J.; Sanguinetti, P.; Sturzenegger, F. (2001). *Argentina y la Agenda de negociaciones comerciales internacionales: El Mercosur, el NAFTA, y la Unión Europea.* ABA, Buenos Aires, June.
Rock, David (1987)., *Argentina 1516–1987 (From Spanish Colonization to Alfonsin).* Berkeley, CA: University of California Press.

Sanguinetti, P.; Garriga, M. (1995). "The Determinants of Regional Trade in Mercosur: Geography and Commercial Liberation." Working Paper 016. Beunos Aires: Universidad Torcuato Di Tella.

Yeats, A. (1997). "Does Mercosur Trade Performance Raise Concerns about the Effect of Regional Trade Agreements?" World Bank Policy Research Working Paper.

4
Brazil

Luiz Alberto Machado, José María Rodríguez Ramos, Otto Nogami, and Marcus V. Freitas

Brazil was "discovered" by the Portuguese on April 22, 1500. Following three centuries under the rule of Portugal, Brazil became an independent nation in 1822. For the past 14 years under Portuguese rule, Brazil was the seat of the Portuguese throne, due to the invasion of the Iberian Peninsula by Napoleon. By far the largest and most populous nation in South America, Brazil has overcome more than 20 years of military intervention in the governance of the country and has pursued industrial and agricultural growth and development of the country's interior. Through exploiting vast natural resources and a large labor pool, Brazil had become Latin America's leading economic power by the 1970s. However, highly unequal income distribution remains a pressing problem.

A country of continental dimensions

Situated in eastern South America, bordering on the Atlantic Ocean, Brazil is the fifth largest country in the world. It has a total area of 8,511,965 square kilometers; 8,456,510 square kilometers are land and 55,455 square kilometers are water. This figure includes the archipelagos of Fernando de Noronha and Trinidade and Martim Vaz, the Rocas Atoll, and the Rocks of St Peter and St Paul.

The countries bordering Brazil (and the length of each border) are, from south to north, Uruguay (985 kilometers), Argentina (1,224 kilometers), Paraguay (1,290 kilometers), Bolivia (3,400 kilometers), Peru (1,560 kilometers), Colombia (1,643 kilometers), Venezuela (2,200 kilometers), Guyana (1,119 kilometers), French Guiana (673 kilometers), and Suriname (597 kilometers). The coastline runs for more than 9,170 kilometers, almost of all of it along the South Atlantic Ocean (see Figure 4.1).

Figure 4.1 Map of Brazil

The country is comprised of 27 states and the Federal District of Brasília, the capital. The states are divided into municipalities, which are further divided into districts.

Geographically, Brazil consists of five basic regions:

1. North (mainly the Amazon basin and the state of Tocantins)
2. Northeast (roughly, east from 46° west and north from 16° south)
3. Southeast (the coastal states south of the Northeast region as far as São Paulo, plus the state of Minas Gerais)
4. South (from Parana south)
5. Central-West (Mato Grosso, Mato Grosso do Sul, Goiás, and the Federal District)

More than half of Brazil lies at about 200 meters above sea level, and only a small part rises above 915 meters. The highest peaks have an altitude of about 3000 meters; only 12 of them exceed 2,130 meters, four in the far North and eight in the Southeast. The Great Escarpment runs the length of the coast south from Bahia and falls away inland at varying distances, most of the terrain being broken by fertile valleys.

Arable land is found mainly in the South, but this is changing with the need to develop land for agriculture throughout the rest of the country, particularly in the Central-West and the North. Forest still covers substantial areas. The river system is extensive. The Amazon and its tributaries, which are great rivers themselves, drain over half of Brazil's area. Other large rivers include the Sao Francisco in the Northeast and the Parana and the Paraguay in the Southwest, both of which are tributaries of the River Plate.

The equator runs north of the Amazon River, and the Tropic of Capricorn crosses the metropolitan area of the city of São Paulo. Most of Brazil is therefore in the tropical zone; only the southern part is in the temperate zone. The North is hot, humid, and rainy. Along the coast the tropical heat is tempered by sea breezes, whereas inland, especially along the Central Plateau, the altitude keeps the temperature lower. Humidity is high all along the coast, and rainfall is heavy. There is a semiarid desert area inland in the Northeast region. Nearly every type of climate can be found in Brazil except the very cold. The country is free from earthquakes, hurricanes and cyclones, but rainstorms, drought, and frost occasionally cause considerable damage. There are areas of great scenic beauty, particularly along the coastline.

The population

Characteristics

The Brazilian population was estimated at 189.82 million inhabitants, with a growth rate of 1.0 percent per annum in the period 2000–2007, below the geometric average rate of 1.63 percent recorded in the period 1991–2000, which confirms the fall in fertility in recent decades. Slightly more than 69 percent of the population is less than 18 years old and 10.5 percent are more than 60 years old. In 2007, in Brazil, life expectancy at birth was 72.57 years.

The biggest social problems in recent decades have still been related to the continuous flow of the population toward urban centers. The southern regions (17.8 percent) and the Southeast (18.6) are those with the lowest percentage of poor people. A comparison of the distribution of the population throughout the Brazilian territory is summarized in Table 4.1, and Table 4.2 lists the most populous Brazilian cities in 2000.

According to the latest census results available (2000), the highest growth rates occurred in the central regions and the Northwest. Here, there are migratory groups attracted by the expansion of the agricultural frontier. There is also the attraction created by certain cities, such as Brasilia and Goiânia, which have grown so quickly in recent decades.

In 2007, the population of Brazil was composed of 49.4 percent whites, 7.4 percent blacks, 42.3 percent mixed races and 0.8 percent

Table 4.1 Population distribution by area and landmass, Brazil

Region	Population Millions	%	Landmass (%)
North	15.403	8.1	42
Northeast	53.305	27.6	18
Southeast	80.845	42.6	11
South	27.704	14.6	7
Central-West	13.563	7.1	22

Source: PNAD 2007 – Pesquisa Nacional por Amostra de Domicilios (National Survey by Household Sample), conducted by the IBGE – the Brazilian Institute of Geography and Statistics.

Table 4.2 Most populous cities, Brazil, 2000

	Region	Population (millions)
São Paulo	Southeast	10.406
Rio de Janeiro	Southeast	5.852
Salvador	Northeast	2.441
Belo Horizonte	Southeast	2.233
Fortaleza	Northeast	2.138
Brasília	Central-West	2.043
Curitiba	South	1.587
Recife	Northeast	1.422
Manaus	North	1.404
Porto Alegre	South	1.360

Source: Instituto Brasileiro de Geografia e Estatística, Demographic Census 2000.

from other ethnic groups. People of active age (ten years old or older) totaled 159 million people, and of this total, 62 percent (rate of activity) were involved in the labor market. The remaining population totaled 8.1 million.

The average monthly income from work (people of ten years or older and employed with earned income) is R$956 (US$ 562), while the average real household income is R$1,796 (US$1,056). The urban population represents 86 percent of the total population (2008), with an infant mortality rate of approximately 22.58 deaths for every 1,000 live births.

Language

The language of Brazil is Portuguese. There are no significant local dialects or other deviations from the official language, but a number of words and phrases are at variance with those used in Portugal. English is the foreign language most used by the business community.

Religion

The predominant religion is Roman Catholicism (see Table 4.3). Many other religions are also practiced, since immigrants of different creeds have settled in Brazil. There is religious freedom, and religion is not a source of unrest.

Education

Government-subsidized (free) and private educational facilities from primary school through university offer full- and part-time curricula. The government also subsidizes national apprenticeship training programs,

Table 4.3 Religions practiced, Brazil

	%
Roman Catholic	73.6
Evangelicals	15.4
Kardecist Spiritism	1.3
Umbanda and Candomble	0.3
Other religions	1.8
Non-religious	7.6

Source: Instituto Brasileiro de Geografia e Estatística, Demographic Census 2000.

to develop the labor force for various industrial and commercial sectors, and an educational program to reduce illiteracy.

About 75 percent of the population above ten years of age is considered to be literate. The general level of education requires much improvement. Approximately 5 percent of all students go on to higher education.

Spending on education is around 4 percent of GDP – Gross Domestic Product (2004). According to data from the PNAD – National Survey by Household Sample, conducted by the IBGE – the Brazilian Institute of Geography and Statistics, indicates that there is still a proportion of 11.4 percent of its population aged 15 or older who cannot read or write.

The gross rate of school attendance for the age group 7 to 14 appears to be near universal, with 97 of children attending school.

Analysis of the Brazilian schooling of adults (25 years or older) shows that, on average, about 30 percent of adults are considered functionally illiterate; more than 40 percent have incomplete primary education; 9 percent have studied only up to completion of primary education; and 18 percent have completed high school. Only 8 percent had completed higher education.

Living standards

The standard of living of a large proportion of the population is very low, while that of the top stratum is extremely high. This gap between rich and poor has been a constant preoccupation of government after government. The gross domestic product (GDP) per capita in 2008 was the equivalent of about US$8,298 per annum. The percentage of home ownership is low. There is a chronic shortage of housing, especially for the working classes.

A study by Ernst & Young – Brazil and by the Fundação Getúlio Vargas (FGV) Project, before the crisis of 2008, indicated that the Brazilian market would be the fifth largest in the world in 2030. In 2007, Brazil was in eighth position.

This view is based on growth of consumption at a rate of 4 percent per year, leading to a consumer market of about US$2.5 trillion, thus surpassing countries like Germany, the United Kingdom, and France, and behind only the United States, China, India, and Japan. Despite the crisis, this number appears feasible, given that the Brazilian consumer market is strong, which – associated with its size, a sustainable macroeconomic policy, and the presence of agricultural commodities and minerals – gives the country great potential for growth.

This growth in consumption is associated with an increase in per capita income, which will cause the consumption profile to become more concentrated in the middle class and geared to an older population ranging from 30 to 55 years of age, as previously noticed. Table 4.4 shows some characteristics of the Brazilian market, according to studies of the Pesquisa Nacional por Amostra de Domicílios (PNAD).

The study indicated that the profile of the Brazilian consumer in 2030 will be determined by four variables: population (lower population growth and an aging population), universal education, stability of prices, and social mobility.

Cultural and social profile

With its mixed background of Portuguese, Italian, Spanish, German, Japanese, East European, and African immigrants, Brazil offers a wide diversity of cultural and social activities, depending on the region of the country concerned. Most major cities support cultural institutions. Leisure and recreational activities are mainly outdoors, taking advantage of the favorable climate.

Immigration to Brazil is summarized in Table 4.5.

Brazilian culture

Brazilian people spring from a mix of the original natives and a large list of nationalities and different races that have came over its 500 years of

Table 4.4 Consumer market profile, Brazil

Consumer good	Families with these goods (%)
Oven	98.2
Water filter	51.4
Refrigerator	91.4
Freezer	16.2
Washing machine	40.0
Radio	88.4
Television	94.8
Personal computer	27.0
Internet access	20.4

Source: PNAD 2007 – Pesquisa Nacional por Amostra de Domicilios (National Survey by Household Sample), conducted by the IBGE – the Brazilian Institute of Geography and Statistics.

Table 4.5 Immigrants, Brazil, 1870–1953

Country of origin	1870–1907	%	1908–1953	%
Germany	54,416	2.4	154,409	6.0
Italy	1,208,042	51.8	357,793	14.0
Japan	N/A	N/A	190,282	7.6
Portugal	519,033	22.3	951,654	37.4
Spain	287,822	12.4	356,647	14.0
Russia	54,593	2.4	64,031	2.5
Others	202,679	8.7	471,639	18.5
Total	2,328,585	100	2,546,455	100

Source: São Paulo (Estado), Secretaria da Agricultura, Departamento de Imigração e Colonização.

history. This original blend has produced a juxtaposition that includes the largest Japanese city outside Japan and the largest Italian city outside of Italy – all in São Paulo, one of the most populous cities in the world.

The influences of this variety of outsiders have produced different means of expression in the arts, music, social rules, and behavior that are included in the concept of culture. It is important to know that in this large country there are no dialects, but just small accent differences or different meanings for the same word. The particular way of occupying the land by foreign people from very different parts of the world produces this special thing called Brazilian culture. This culture is highly visible and can be found in music, from erudite composers like Heitor Villa Lobos to the original and most popular rhythm called samba, with Noel Rosa and others; the chorinho, with Pixinguinha; and more recently (about 40 years ago), the bossa nova rhythm, which has its roots in American jazz; and through the work of composers who have classical and erudite backgrounds like João Gilberto, Antonio Carlos Jobim, Chico Buarque de Hollanda, Caetano Veloso, Gilberto Gil, and many others.

In architecture Brazil's biggest name is Oscar Niemeyer, who planned and designed Brasília, and other significant buildings. There are others, like Lucio Costa and Lina Bo Bardi, who came from Italy and carried out important work such as the MASP (the São Paulo Museum of Art). Jaime Lerner, another name in contemporary engineering and architecture, did important work in the urban (re)planning of Curitiba.

Brazil is a tropical country with a friendly environment that offers an enormous variety of fruits and vegetables. From the arrival of the first adventurous Portuguese and the African slaves to the generally pacific arrival of other nationalities, the people developed one of the most spectacular varieties of culinary styles, which include dishes such as feijoada (black beans), vatapá (dendê oil, coconut milk, fish, and shrimp), pato no tucupi (duck cooked with a special vegetable), or the small "cheese bread". Most of the world knows Brazil from its wonderful beaches, soccer, and the friendliness of the people. But the country has more to offer than that, for example, the canyons in Chapada Diamantina; an original rain forest in Amazônia, where different nations of natives found only in the past few years still live; or the biggest river in the world, the Amazon, which features the phenomenon called pororoca, which happens when the river meets the Atlantic Ocean; or even the amazing waterfalls in Iguaçu.

To understand Brazilian culture, we have to take a look at the history, geography, and circumstances of colonization in the past, as well as at the consequences of world wars and crises in other countries. Also, we have to take a look at Brazil's position in the modern world and the success of its people in different fields such as business, fashion, and international politics.

Brazil has many important cultural institutions and cultural events in both big and small cities that take place year round. There are special folk exhibitions and civic and religious celebrations at which all the multicultural influences from over 500 years coexist peacefully.

Some scholars propose that the Brazilian term "jeitinho", which is translated as "to always take advantage", is actually a lovely way of life that means having a good relationship with others (people, culture, and business), and it is the best way to look at Brazil. This friendly attitude, this open mindedness toward other viewpoints, this permanent willingness to help everyone is the best way to explain the people and the Brazilian culture.

Political and legal system

The federal government consists of three branches: the executive, the legislative, and the judiciary. The president heads the executive branch. Under the president are a number of executive departments, the heads of which are appointed and known collectively as the Cabinet, and are responsible to the president. Unlike in many parliamentary democracies, Cabinet members are not also members of the legislature. Besides the executive departments there are a number of independent agencies, many of which are regulatory. Note – the president is both the chief of state and head of government.

The legislative branch, the bicameral National Congress, or Congresso Nacional, is made up of two chambers: the Federal Senate, or Senado Federal, and the Chamber of Deputies, or Câmara dos Deputados. There are 81 senators, three from each state or federal district elected by majority vote to serve eight-year terms; one-third are elected after a four-year period, and two-thirds elected after the next four-year period. The total membership of the Chamber of Deputies is 513, with the number of representatives from each state depending on its population, and the members are elected to serve four-year terms. Voting is compulsory from the age of 18 to 70, and people of 16 and 17 can opt to vote.

The judicial branch consists of a system of federal, state, and local courts throughout the country, headed by the Supreme Federal Tribunal. The federal courts rule on the constitutionality of laws and decisions appealed from the lower courts to which the Federal Union is a party. There is no appeal to the Supreme Court's decisions. The state (Higher Tribunal of Justice) and municipal (Regional Federal Tribunals) courts operate independently of the federal courts within the bounds of the Constitution. The judges are appointed for life. The Brazilian legal system is based on Roman codes, not on common law. The administration of justice is slow and cumbersome.

State governments follow a pattern similar to that of the federal government. Each state has a governor as chief executive, and power is divided among the state executive, legislative, and judicial branches.

There are many political parties. However, ideologies are not highly developed, as the democratic system of government in Brazil returned only in 1985. Parties normally represent specific economic groups and interests within the country.

History

Brazil was discovered in 1500 by the Portuguese navigator Pedro Alvares Cabral. Although it was invaded by the French and later by the Dutch, who occupied the coast of Pernambuco in the Northwest for some years, Brazil remained a Portuguese colony for more than 300 years. In 1822, Brazil declared its independence. A constitutional government has been maintained for most of the time since then. The country continued to be ruled by members of the Portuguese royal family until 1889, when the Republic was proclaimed.

In 1964, after considerable political, economic, and social unrest, a new government structure was installed by the armed forces. Considerable economic growth and development was achieved during the following 20 years, although not without political and social repercussions. In 1985, the country returned to a democratic regime. The present Constitution was promulgated in October 1988. It is lengthy, comprising 83 articles.

Economy

The economy is basically one of free enterprise, although there is still considerable state and semi-state participation in various strategic sectors, such as transport and utilities. The petroleum industry is a government monopoly, except for distribution. Special legislation was enacted to privatize many companies for which the presence of the state is not considered essential.

Natural resources and agriculture have been the traditional mainstays of the economy, backed by abundant human resources. Since the 1960s, however, emphasis has been placed on industrial development financed largely by international loans. As a result, exports today reflect a more balanced mix of commodities and manufactured items. Moreover, the profile of imports became more restricted during the 1970s and 1980s due to a policy of import substitution and the scarcity of foreign exchange. With the lowering of trade barriers, this profile is changing.

Following the oil crises of the 1970s and 1980s, Brazil developed its sugarcane alcohol industry, which for many years fueled a large part of the private-car fleet.

The official GNP in 2000 was US$587.5 billion. However, the underground economy is not included. It is said to vary between 30 and 40 percent of GNP depending on the sector. Table 4.6 details major economic indicators for Brazil between 1990 and 2007.

Mineral and energy resources

Brazil is rich in natural resources. It has some of the largest iron ore deposits in the world and is now one of the biggest gold producers. Many other metals, minerals, and precious stones are also mined on an ever-increasing scale. There is significant hydroelectric potential, which is slowly being harnessed as a source of energy. The Itaipu Dam in the extreme southwest is the largest hydroelectric power producer in the world. Participation by foreign investors in the mineral and energy sectors has not been encouraged.

Table 4.6 Major economic trends, Brazil, 1990-2007

	1990	1995	2000	2005	2007
Gross domestic product (US$ billion)	469.318	770.350	644.984	882.439	1,333.818
Per capita GDP (US$)	3,202	4,849	3,766	4,791	7,108.3
Real annual growth (%)	-4.35	4.42	4.31	3.16	5.7
Agriculture	-8.18	4.72	4.83	2.08	5.9
Industry	-0.76	3.16	3.58	3.68	4.7
Services	-3.72	5.74	2.72	0.30	5.4
Consumer price index, INPC (%)	2,863.90	65.96	6.22	5.76	5.16
General price index, IGP - DI (%)	2,740.23	67.46	13.77	5.97	7.89
Trade balance (US$ billions)	10,752	-3466	-753	44,758	40,028
Exports	31,414	46,506	55,086	118,309	160,649
Imports	20,661	49,972	55,839	73,551	120,621
Foreign currency reserves	9,973	51,840	33,011	53,799	180,334
Total foreign debt	96,546	129,313	189,500	150,674	161,896

Sources: FGV, *Conjuntura Econômica*, 63(8), August 2009; Banco Central do Brasil.

Agriculture, fisheries, and forestry

Vast areas of land are suitable or adaptable to agriculture. The advance in land clearing is mainly in the Central-West and North regions. Brazil is a major exporter of soybeans and orange juice in addition to the traditional coffee and cocoa. Ownership of rural land by foreigners is restricted. The fishing potential along the 9,170 kilometers of coastline is significant but has not been fully exploited. Forest areas still abound, particularly in the Amazon basin, and international protests have been raised against forest clearance and its potential damage to the world environment. The principal agricultural products are summarized in Table 4.7.

Manufacturing

Major manufacturing industries include petrochemicals, steel, automobiles, mining, cement, paper and allied products, the agroindustry and food processing. None of these industries is in decline. There is great potential for expansion in all areas, assuming the current economic difficulties can be overcome.

Table 4.7 Principal agricultural products, Brazil, 1995–2007 (millions of metric tonnes)

	1995	2000	2005	2007
Bananas (bunches)	5.801	5.663	6.703	7.098
Oranges	19.837	21.330	17.853	18.685
Staple crops				
Beans	2.800	2.464	3.022	3.169
Cocoa	0.328	0.346	0.209	0.202
Coffee	2.587	2.551	2.140	2.249
Cotton	1.885	1.139	1.211	1.357
Maize	30.557	29.967	35.113	52.112
Rice	9.962	10.193	13.193	11.061
Soybeans	1.915	22.710	51.182	57.857
Sugarcane	271,432	251,408	422,957	549,707
Tobacco	0.578	0.663	0.889	0.909
Wheat	2.796	2.201	4.659	4.114

Source: FAOSTAT, 2009.

High-tech industries

The high-tech sector comprises mainly the assembly of imported components and parts. Multinationals dominate, but there are several large Brazilian groups.

Service industries

Service-providing industries are now a significant and growing part of the economy. There is good growth potential for the tourist and information services areas. Business services are considered to be fairly sophisticated. In advertising, computer services, and management consultancy, multinationals are well represented. The wholesale, distribution and retail trades are populated by some very large national companies, a few multinationals, some large regional companies, and a large number of small family-owned businesses. Many large industrial groups have their own distribution networks.

Apart from restrictions on the banking, financial services, and telecommunications areas, foreign investors may participate in the service industries.

Transport and communications

There has been no significant development or modernization of the government controlled railroad network over the past years, although there are plans for some major extensions, particularly in the North and Central-West regions. Therefore, road transport dominates, both for long-distance and intercity traffic. Nevertheless, construction of new highways has been slow in recent years. Also, most of the major federal and state highways have not been well maintained. Nearly all road transport and haulage companies are privately owned.

Economic and political development

Brazilian economic and political development falls into two clearly different phases. The first is from the discovery to the early (around 1930) twentieth century. In this period the characteristic is a growth model based on exports. In the second phase, the growth model is turned inward. Each of the phases presents its own characteristics, such as can be observed in Figure 4.2.

During the phase of the growth model based on exports, the economic cycles of sugar, coffee, and rubber (as described later in this chapter) occurred. In this period Brazil became independent from Portugal. However, the Brazilian economy was not affected.

In relation to inward-turned development, a clear evolution can be observed with emphasis on different types of production over time. The strategy was based on import substitution and was related to the development of know-how and technology, as can be observed in Figure 4.3.

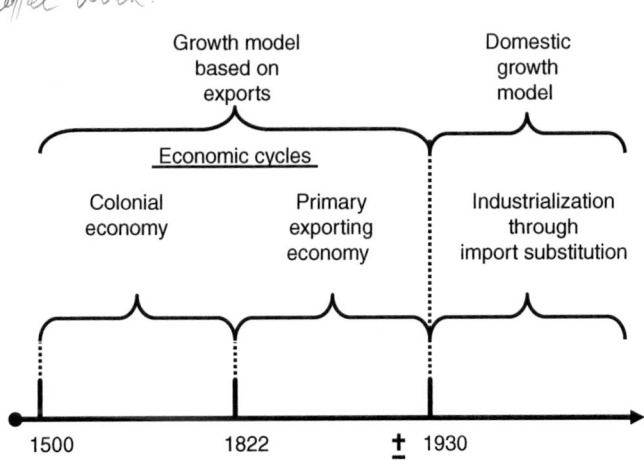

Figure 4.2 Economic and political development, Brazil, 1500–

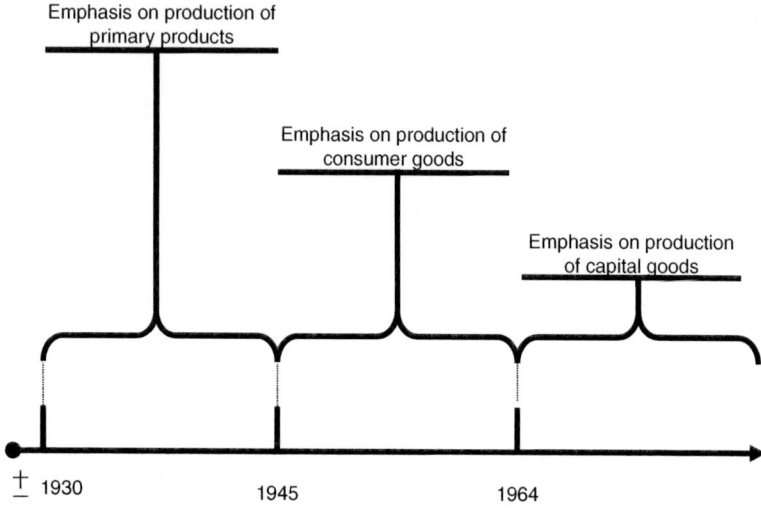

Figure 4.3 Evolution of industrial production, Brazil, 1930–

Portuguese America

The period between the discovery of Brazil in 1500 and the foundation of the first village (São Vicente) in 1530 is known as the pre-Colonial period. From this time until King D. Pedro's declaration of Brazil's national independence, Portugal occupied the colony, promoting colonization and creating domestic economic and financial mechanisms. In terms of cultural life, the system was designed to keep Brazil isolated and dependent and thus incapable of establishing any kind of independence from Portugal.

The colonial period was, therefore, marked by the conquest and control of the territory, as well as by exploration of the agricultural and natural resources. In the beginning, thanks to its immediate appearance, its abundance, and its easy exploration with a minimum of necessary investment, Pau-Brasil (Brazil-Wood) gave rise to the first economic cycle called the Cycle of Brazil-Wood. The most intense period of its exploration goes from Brazil-Wood's discovery until the middle of the sixteenth century.

Industry was developed along the coast, from the Rio Grande do Norte to the region of Rio de Janeiro, through a lease system between the state and particular companies which turned over one-fifth of their production to the Portuguese government. During this period, cutting and local haulage were done by Indians, under the control of administrators, traders, and colonists. Later, black slaves were used.

In the period between 1570 and 1650 another important cycle in the colonial period, known as the Cycle of Sugar, took place. The success of this crop was favored by the experience acquired by the Portuguese in the islands of the Atlantic Ocean, by the favorable climate and soil in the Northeast region, by the abundance of enslaved manpower, and by the expansion of the consumer market in Europe. Together with this activity, subsistence agriculture in the form of cattle grazing developed. Sugar production favored the occupation and colonization of the territory. These developments assured considerable profits to the aristocracy and to the Portuguese Crown. However, the decline in consumption in Europe and the competition from the production of sugar in the Antilles by the Dutch led to the end of the monopoly in sugar production in the second half of the seventeenth century.

Coincidently, with the beginning of the decline of the Cycle of Sugar, the colony of Brazil started to experience a new period of wealth and prosperity, which was confirmed at the turn of the eighteenth century by the discovery of gold in the region of Minas Gerais (at the time equivalent to what is today the state of Minas Gerais, Goiás, and Mato Grosso). This event sparked a shift in migratory streams coming from the Northeast region to the region of São Paulo, which led to the founding of new villages.

Estimates indicate that the population of Brazil in 1770 was around two million, with 20.5 percent in Minas Gerais, 18.5 percent in Bahia, and 15.4 percent in Pernambuco. In the mining regions society was already urbanized, with core populations and diversification of activities, functions, and jobs. In other regions, the population was organized around farms for cotton, tobacco, and cattle. Power was concentrated in the hands of the agricultural aristocracy who, in many cases, substituted for the public authorities, ordering the lives of the people around them. It was a patriarchal society.

A primary exporting economy

Imperial Brazil is the period extending from independence, on September 7, 1822, until the declaration of the republic on November 15, 1889. This period is marked by a centralized monarchy in conflict with rebellious liberal ideals and by the emerging economic diversification of the coffee expansion.

The second half of the nineteenth century was marked by diverse economic transformations. The influx of European immigrants was absorbed as qualified, wage-earning manpower. The immigrants began to consume national products, thus contributing to industrial and economic expansion. They also increased the hold of internal capital over the economy after the prohibition of the importation of slaves. Part of this capital found its way into the farming of coffee and commercial and industrial enterprises. Another part went into the constitution of companies, plants, railroads, and banks.

The crisis in the French colony of Haiti provoked a rise in the price of coffee on international markets and stimulated an increase in production in Brazil. Thus, coffee became the leading national export. The expansion started in the highlands near Rio de Janeiro, and took advantage of idle manpower from the mining areas. From there, the coffee culture spread to Minas Gerais and São Paulo, thus creating the main axes of production. With the prohibition of the Black slave trade in 1850, enslaved manpower was replaced by the contracting of European immigrants, attracted by the incentives offered by the Brazilian government.

The socio-economic transformations in this period led, in the middle of the nineteenth century, to conflicts of interests, which led in turn to the end of the monarchy.

On November 15, 1889, the republic was proclaimed, thus initiating a period of great social, economic and political change that has continued until the present. During the last decades of the nineteenth century and the first decade of the twentieth century, the Amazon region was transformed into the scene of the fastest economic cycle of Brazil – the Cycle of Rubber. The cycle began with the invention of the tire in 1890, and the expansion of the automobile industry, mainly in the United States.

These developments raised the demand for the product, increasing its price, and bringing prosperity to the main cities in the Amazon region. Production reached its peak in 1912 and began to decline with the arrival, in 1910, of the production of rubber in the British colonies in South-East Asia.

This period of the primary exporting economy was marked by a great boom in the economy, based on coffee. At the end of the nineteenth century, 70 percent of the worldwide production of coffee came from the coffee plantations of Brazil. The expansion of coffee farming created the conditions for the appearance of a consumer market and contributed to the accumulation of capital. This development was accompanied by further industrial development, particularly of the center-south region.

Until the time of the declaration of the republic, there were barely 600 industries in the country, which produced food, textiles, and clothes. The First World War changed this picture. With the disorganization of the worldwide economy, the Brazilian economy benefited thanks to the difficulties in importing certain products, such as food. The government tried to advance the industrialization process, granting financing for the importation of machinery and to stimulate immigration.

The result of these measures can be seen by the number of companies in 1920: more than 13,000 industrial establishments. During this period, much the same thing happened to the banking sector. Despite this industrial expansion, the dominant sectors of the Brazilian economy continued to be trade (importing and exporting) and the great coffee plantations. This picture remained basically unchanged up to 1929, when worldwide economic depression began. The crisis was reflected in Brazil, leading coffee producers to bankruptcy due to the fall in prices on the international market.

Industrial economy

The depreciation of the main export, coffee, contributed to successive record harvests. This fact generated a major crisis, beginning in 1930 and extending to 1944. Looking for a solution, the Brazilian government acquired and destroyed about 80 million bags of coffee.

The crisis led to the exploration of new products such as fruits, cotton, oil, and ore, and to the development of an economy based on the domestic market. The government granted funds to the credit system, set up safeguard tariffs, controlled prices, and established a policy of wage control. In the areas in which the private sector could not invest, the government built its own companies, such as the Companhia Siderurgica Nacional (National Steel Company), created in 1941. The Companhia Vale do Rio Doce was established in 1942 for ore mining.

Industrial growth suffered a decline during the Second World War because of the difficulty in importing machinery and industrial equipment. In 1944, the government devised a plan for infrastructure development and the creation of basic industries.

With the coffee crisis, the power of the coffee barons declined, and the social and political space for an industrial bourgeoisie and for the middle class increased, giving them more participation in political life. The laboring classes also grew considerably, but their expansion was controlled by government intervention mechanisms.

From the middle of the 1950s, the country lived through a phase of real economic progress, under the stimulation of the Plano Nacional de

Desenvolvimento (National Plan for Development). Industrial production grew by 80 percent. Basic industries expanded, and other projects such as the construction of hydroelectric plants and the construction of Brasília modernized the country. These events contributed to the increase in internal migration and an rise in the rural exodus.

The Brazilian economy opened to foreign capital, through the concession of special incentives to spur the input of equipment indispensable for industry. To the national private sector, the government offered advantageous credit policies that assured the expansion of internal demand. These strategies received favorable reactions from both national and foreign entrepreneurs. At this time the country reached self-sufficiency in certain key sectors, such as the automobile industry. However, at the beginning of the 1960s, the investment tax started to decline and inflation went up uncontrollably.

On March 31, 1964, the military regime began. It continued until the redemocratization of the country. For the economy, a new model was adopted to support income concentration and sacrifice low-wage earners. At the same time, the Brazilian government reopened the country to foreign capital and took on more external indebtedness to make investments in major public works projects.

Based on key security development, a new model for growth was undertaken to promote the growth of industrialization with resources drawn from foreign capital, national entrepreneurs, and the government as economic agent. The country's borders opened to multinational companies, which were attracted by the extremely favorable conditions to establish and expand their industries – especially the cheap price of manpower, because of government intervention limiting real increases in wages.

If these measures aggravated the income distribution imbalance, the results from the economic point of view were positive. From 1968 to 1973, GDP growth was around 10 percent annually. Added to the great public works projects, they characterized the "Brazilian Miracle".

However, from the second half of the 1970s, external indebtedness speeded up, inflation returned, the public sector went into crisis, and the economy as a whole started to plunge. In 1981, the economy's contraction reached depression levels, with a sharp fall in industrial production. In the following years, the crisis grew, with the external debt reaching US$80 billion in 1982 and US$100 billion in 1983. Consequently, the Brazilian government had to appeal to the International Monetary Fund (IMF). At this stage, the government could not even pay the interest on the debt.

From 1986, the government tried through successive economic plans (Cruzado, Bresser, and Verão) to control the high inflation, without success. Collor Plan #1 (1990) once more adopted the freezing of prices and wages. It also increased taxes and tariffs. This plan announced the privatization of state-owned companies, with the objective of containing public debt. It suspended tax incentives not guaranteed by the Constitution and created mechanisms to prevent tax evasion. Soon after its implementation, there was a drastic reduction in the productivity of the economy. After one year, the plan's impotence in the struggle with inflation was evident.

After difficult periods of contraction in the economy and the persistent growth of inflation, in July, 1994, a new plan was unveiled – The Real Plan. This solved the problem and led the Brazilian economy to a new phase, with low inflation and a steady currency. The role of the state was redefined. Protectionist laws were abandoned and market controls eliminated. Through this act, national industry became competitive with foreign industry on the domestic market. Moreover, national industry was forced to adapt to a global economy.

Recent trends

In the past three decades Brazil can be characterized as a developed center of agricultural and manufactured products and with a service sector in expansion. Thanks to these conditions, the Brazilian economy plays an important role in South America and its presence is growing in the world market.

After the financial crises suffered by the country in 2001–2003, the inflow of FDI returned to Brazil, and the currency (Real) rose against the US dollar. This Brazilian currency rise reduced the growth of the country's exports. Nonetheless, there was an increase in the employment rate and the real income of the population.

The inflow of FDI is summarized in Table 4.8.

The Brazilian economic recovery has been helped by a positive trade balance, led mainly by exports of commodities and a macroeconomic policy that endowed the country with historical levels of international reserves, a net public debt reduction, and a significant reduction in the interest rates. The adoption of floating exchange rates, the implementation of an inflation target, and a strict fiscal policy today represent the basis of the Brazilian economy.

The main products of the trade balance are in Table 4.9.

During his reelection campaign in 2006, President Luis Inácio Lula da Silva reinforced his commitment to fiscal responsibility, and promised to

Table 4.8 Foreign direct investments, Brazil, 2002–2008 (US$ millions)

	Inflows	Outflows	Balance
2002	26.460	9.870	16.590
2003	19.238	9.094	10.144
2004	25.801	7.655	18.146
2005	30.062	14.996	15.066
2006	32.399	13.577	18.822
2007	50.233	15.648	34.585
2008	71.836	26.776	45.060

Source: Banco Central do Brasil.

maintain the central government's surplus. At the beginning of his second term the president announced an economic reform program, with the aim of reducing the tax burden and increasing public investments. The public investment program is known as Programa de Aceleração do Crescimento – PAC (Growth Acceleration Program), that includes investments until 2010.

Despite the great inequalities and structural problems that still remain, and which the country has yet to solve, Brazil currently is quite different from 25 years ago. Three factors were essential for that transformation: (1) the democratization process, which took place during the 1980s; (2) the economic opening initiated by President Fernando Collor in the early 1990s; and (3) the monetary stabilization resulting from the Real Plan in 1994.

With the changes resulting from these three factors, the Brazilian image abroad has greatly improved. After years of a humiliating situation, when the country was considered one of the least recommended economies for FDI due to its high risk level, Brazil has moved beyond this image and become a country highly recommended for foreign investment, as illustrated by the achievement of its investment grade in 2008.

The new reality, characterized by increasing competition, has demanded from individuals and companies a new level of preparation. Individuals need better qualifications, including a spirit of creativity and leadership, while companies need enhanced efficiency and productivity – essential for the production of goods and services with the quality needed to survive in a more and more competitive world market.

Although the Brazilian economy has greatly improved over the last decades, the judicial sector has not followed. The instability of the

Table 4.9 Trade balance, Brazil, 2008

	Value (US$ millions FOB)	%
Main exported products		
Iron ore and concentrates	16,538.543	8.4
Petroleum oils, crude	13,555.608	6.8
Soybeans, including ground	10,952.197	5.5
Parts and accessories for automobiles	10,880.467	5.5
Passenger motor vehicles	8409.590	4.2
Meat and edible offal of chicken	5,821.977	2.9
Airplanes	5,495.248	2.8
Cane and other sugars	4,363.523	2.2
Coffee, not roasted	4,131.465	2.1
Meat of bovine animals	4,006.139	2.0
Others	113,787.686	57.5
Total	197,942.443	100.0
Main imported products		
Petroleum	16,390.893	9.5
Parts and accessories for automobiles	13,557.952	7.8
Passenger motor vehicles	6,865.314	4.0
Fuels	5,235.229	3.0
Pharmaceuticals products	3,916.658	2.3
Others	111,980.912	73.4
Total	173,196.634	100.0

Sources: Ministério do Desenvolvimento, Indústria e Comércio; Banco Central do Brasil.

enforcement of contracts, the current legal regulatory framework for some economic sectors, and the speed of court decisions still all need major improvements for the effective rule of law. These factors reduce the level of competitiveness of the country and impede the inflow of more constant investments that could be easily diverted to Brazil, if the country offered a better legal environment.

Such reforms still need to become a high priority for Brazilian policymakers, along with a reduction in the level of red tape that still exists in certain sectors, such as health and customs. To benefit better from the positive economic scenario the country has created, greater transparency, effective protection of private investment, and the use of arbitration as a tool for contractual security still need to be more widely used.

Note

We thank Professor Edson Canela for his contribution to the translation and revision of some parts of this chapter.

Bibliography

Caldeira, J. (1997). *Viagem pela História do Brasil*. São Paulo: Companhia das Letras.
Da Matta, R. Carnavais (1997). *Malandros e Heróis*. Rio de Janeiro: Rocco.
Food and Agriculture Organization of the United Nations (FAOSTAT), 2009.
Freire, G. (2000). *Casa Grande e Senzala*. Rio de Janeiro: Record.
Instituto Brasileiro de Geografia e Estatística (IBGE) (2001). *Brazil in Figures*.
Lucci, E. A. (2000). *Geografia. Homem e Espaço*. São Paulo: Editora Saraiva.
Maddison, A. (1989). "Desempenho da Economia Mundial desde 1870," in *Nova Era da Economia Mundial*. Gall, N. (ed.). São Paulo: Pioneira.
Nêumanne, J. (1992). *Reféns do Passado*. São Paulo: Siciliano.
Senna, J. J. (1995). *Os Parceiros do Rei. Herança Cultural e Desenvolvimento Econômico no Brasil*. Rio de Janeiro: Topbooks.
Skidmore, T. (1986). *Politics in Brazil, 1930–1964: An Experiment in Democracy*. Oxford: Oxford University Press.
Skidmore, T. (1990). *The Politics of Military Rule in Brazil, 1964–1985*. Oxford: Oxford University Press.

5
Chile

Hernán Felipe Errázuriz Correa

Chile is located in southwest South America. It is a narrow strip some 100–445 kilometers wide and 4200 kilometers long, located between the Pacific Ocean and the peaks of the Andean chain, running from the seventeenth parallel of southern latitude to Cape Horn. It is bordered by Peru to the north, Bolivia and Argentina to the east, the Drake Sea to the south, and the Pacific Ocean to the west, in which it possesses several islands and archipelagos. Chile also claims rights to over 1.2 million square kilometers on the Antarctic continent, where it maintains a number of bases. Excluding claimed Antarctic territory and including Easter Island, San Fernandez, and other islands, Chile has a land area of 756,566 square kilometers (see Figure 5.1).

Chile's capital is Santiago, with a population of 6,038,000 (2002). Administratively, Chile is divided into 15 regions and its principal seaports are Valparaíso, San Antonio, Iquique, Antofagasta, Talcahuano, San Vicente, Valdivia, Puerto Montt, and Punta Arenas. The official language of Chile is Spanish and its monetary unit is the peso (represented as CLP$), which floats freely against other currencies.

Chile's population totaled 16,933,141 inhabitants in 2009 with a population growth rate of nearly 1 percent (a projection made by the National Institute of Statistics and CEPAL (Comisión Económica para América Latina y el Caribe/Economic Commission for Latin America and the Caribbean). Women total 8,551,220 and men total 8,381,921 inhabitants. Therefore, 50.5 percent of the population are women and 49.5 percent men. This share has remained constant in the past few years. The urban population represents 87.5 percent, the largest concentration being in Santiago. In absolute terms urban and rural populations total 14,816,498 and 2,116,643 inhabitants, respectively. Between the 1992 and 2002 censuses, the urban population increased

Figure 5.1 Map of Chile

by 17.1 percent, while the rural population decreased by 9.1 percent. In 1992, the shares of urban and rural population were 82.45 and 16.5 percent, respectively. The average population density according to the 2002 census was 19.9 inhabitants per square kilometer, while in 1992 this figure was 17.7 inhabitants per square kilometer.

In terms of age structure, 22.6 percent of the population are between 0 and 14 years old, 68.4 percent are between 15 and 64 years old, and 9 percent are 65 years old and over. In 1992, this age structure was as follows: 30.1 percent were between 0 and 14 years old, 63.8 percent were between 15 and 64 years old, and 6.1 percent were 65 years old and over.

Life expectancy at birth is 74.8 years for men and 80.8 years for women. The birth rate is 15.1 per 1000 people and the death rate is 5.5 per 1000 people.

The total population's literacy rate is 96.5 percent. Chile's infant mortality rate is estimated to be 5.52 deaths per 1000 live births in 2010.

The vast majority of Chileans are of European or mestizo ethnic origin. Aboriginals represent only 3 percent of the population.

From 1987 to 2008, the workforce expanded at an annual average rate of 2.4 percent, well above demographic trends. Over the same period, jobs increased by an average annual 2.6 percent and unemployment dropped steadily from 10.9 percent in 1987 to 6.3 percent in 1998. As activity slowed and firms sought to counteract a contraction of domestic demand through productivity gains, unemployment rose to a peak of 11.5 percent in the winter of 1999. Ten years after the Asian crisis Chile has not recovered from the low rates of productivity observed in 1998. In 2008, the average was 7.8 percent. For 2009, the expected rate is over 10 percent as economic activity has been seriously damaged.

Table 5.1 summarizes indicators of housing and basic infrastructure in Chile, and Table 5.2 summarizes various indicators of health in the country.

Business

Chile has undergone substantial economic and social change since the mid-1970s, and the country has currently one of the most liberal, market-based economies in Latin America. Major structural reforms have been completed over the past decades.

Further changes in tax laws were introduced in 2001. Corporate income tax is currently 17 percent. Such income tax is treated as a credit toward the additional 35 percent tax for profit remittances abroad.

Table 5.1 Indicators of housing and basic infrastructure, Chile, 1970–2002 (%)

	1970	1992	2000	2002
Permanent housing	79.0	91.0	N/A	96.0
Owners of a house	54.0	68.0	72.5	73.0
Access to urban drinking water	67.0	N/A	99.6	99.6
Access to rural drinking water	N/A	86.0	N/A	77.8
Access to sewerage system	31.0	83.0	93.1	96.4

Source: CENSO 2002.

Personal income tax was reduced from 45 percent (top marginal tax) to 40 percent. In addition, since 1999 many law reforms have been approved, introducing additional restrictions to the regulation of labor contracts. Chile is also the most open economy to foreign trade and investment in Latin America. There are no restrictions for capital flows and foreign investment. Nontariff trade barriers are rare and customs duties are low (as an average, less than 5 percent) and nonselective. During 2002 Chile agreed to the terms of a free trade agreement (FTA) with the United States and in November of that year signed an Association Agreement with the European Union, which also eliminates most tariffs on bilateral trade.

Table 5.3 shows the annual growth rate of GDP in Chile from 1986 to 2008, and Table 5.4 puts per capita GDP in Chile since 1900 in the context of the rates for Argentina, Brazil, and Mexico.

Political system

The country's official name is the Republic of Chile. It is organized as a republic, and executive powers are invested in the president of the republic, legislative authority in the National Congress (bicameral: Senate and House of Representatives), and judicial power in the courts of law.

The head of state is Sebastián Piñera Echeñique (2010–), who was elected Chile's president in March 2010. Congressional elections held in December 2005 increased the percentage share of the opposition coalition Alianza por Chile to 38.8 percent.

Table 5.2 Health indicators, Chile, 1970–2010

	1970–1975	1980–1985	1990–1995	1995–2000	2000–2005	2005–2010
(a)						
Life expectancy at birth (years)	63.6	70.7	74.3	75.7	77.7	78.5
Infant mortality rate (per 1000 live births)	68.6	23.7	14.1	11.5	8.0	7.2
(b)	1970	1980	1990	1995	2000	
Undernourished (%)	15.5	11.5	7.4	5.3	N/A	
(c)	1970	1990	1994	1996	2000	2006
Average time in school (years)	4.5	9	9.2*	9.5	9.8	10.1
Time in school of children of the 20% lowest income families (years)	N/A	7.4	7.3	7.3	7.8	8.2
Children in high poverty without access to primary education (%)	43.0	3.6	4.1	3.0	3.0	3.2
Secondary education access (%)	40.0	71.5	74.9	77.9	81.0	83.1
Access to secondary education for children of the 20% lowest income families (%)	N/A	65.8	67.8	68.8	73.4	79.9

* Figure for 1992.
Sources: CEPAL; 1990–2006 CASEN surveys.

Natural resources

Chile is the largest exporter of copper in the world and its natural resources include timber, iron ore, nitrates, precious metals, and molybdenum. The central valley is very fertile and suitable for a wide variety of crops and fruit. Forestry, wines, fresh fruits, fish farming, and ocean fisheries are relevant sectors of the local industry. Domestic production of oil and natural gas is almost negligible.

Geography

Chile's national territory was formed by the elevation of the South American landmass through ongoing pressure from the Nazca plate in the Pacific, making it highly subject to earthquakes. It displays extremely diverse geographical and climatic characteristics.

In Chile's far northern reaches, called the Norte Grande or Great North, an arid climate prevails, with mountain ranges, salt flats, and

Table 5.3 Annual GDP growth, Chile, 1986–2008

Year	Growth (%)	Year	Growth (%)
1986	5.6	1998	3.3
1987	65	1999	–0.7
1988	73	2000	4.5
1989	10.6	2001	3.3
1990	3.8	2002	2.2
1991	7.9	2003	4.0
1992	12.2	2004	6.0
1993	7.0	2005	5.6
1994	5.7	2006	4.6
1995	10.5	2007	4.7
1996	7.4	2008	3.2
1997	6.6		

Source: Central Bank of Chile.

Table 5.4 GDP per capita growth, Argentina, Brazil, Chile, and Mexico, 1900–2007 (%)

	1900–1950	1950–1973	1973–2000	2000–2007
Argentina	1.2	2.1	0.4	2.5
Brazil	1.7	2.8	1.3	1.9
Chile	1.4	1.2	3.3	3.2
Mexico	1.2	3.1	1.8	2.0

Source: CEPAL, "Social Panorama of Latin America 2008."

the Atacama Desert, the world's driest desert. Below this area is the Norte Chico or Little North, with more abundant vegetation thanks to a greater number of rivers and streams.

Further south, lies Central Chile, which is also known as the Central Valley. This zone includes numerous transverse valleys, extending between the Andes chain and the coastal mountain range, carved by rivers surging from the high Andes to the sea. These rivers contribute to the creation of a moderately rainy Mediterranean climate, suited to a broad range of agricultural products. Below the Central Valley, the South begins, with its rainy and moderately cold climate, suitable for livestock ranching. Finally, in the continent's extreme southern reaches, toward

Cape Horn and Tierra del Fuego, lie the Austral Regions, presenting a rugged mixture of mountain and coastal landscapes, including the cold and windy Patagonian plains, massive forests, and torrential rivers, as well as numerous lakes, channels, ice fields, and glaciers.

Ethnicity and immigration

Upon the arrival of the first Spanish conquistadores in the mid-sixteenth century, indigenous people in the area numbered an estimated 500,000 and were distributed among more than 15 distinct ethnic groups.

The political and military influence of the Inca Empire predominated in the north, extending to the Maule River deep in central Chile. This Peruvian empire dominated numerous ethnic groups, the Picunches being the most prominent among them. The Picunches also occupied the lands southward to the Bío Bío River. After the Spanish conquest, they were assimilated within a short time, becoming the largest element of the colonial economy's workforce.

The Mapuches or Araucanos populated the lands between the Bío Bío and Toltén rivers. A few centuries before the European discovery of America, they had invaded Chilean territory from the east over the Andes mountains. With their warlike spirit, they continued to resist the Spanish invaders until the second half of the nineteenth century. Their descendents, although in part intermixed, make up Chile's only numerically significant original ethnic group today, comprising 3 percent of the population. In the Austral Regions south to Tierra del Fuego, small groups of indigenous peoples such as the Onas, Chonos, and Alacalufes roamed the islands and channels, fishing and hunting the llama-like guanaco. These groups are extinct today.

A special case is the Polynesian ethnic group, which colonized Easter Island or Rapa Nui in the Pacific, 3000 kilometers from the South American coast, in approximately AD 500. This territory was incorporated into Chile in 1888. Today, some 3000 people live on the island, mainly engaged in the tourist industry and with little agriculture, since most of the land remains under state control.

The surviving indigenous peoples have not been exempt from difficulties. The Andean communities (aymaras) in the country's north, estimated at 45,000 people, have been affected by water extraction by mining enterprises, as well as the urban and industrial enclaves that have sprung up in the great northern desert. The Mapuches continue to struggle for recognition of their culture and ownership rights to their ancestral lands. During the past ten years, Chile has created an institutional structure to address the problems of indigenous peoples, a long-term challenge which will involve measures to reduce poverty and improve health care and education.

The first Spanish settlers in Chile were single men, mostly soldiers. In 1541, 154 Europeans arrived. The number of European inhabitants was estimated at 25,000 in 1700 and 50,000 in 1800. A census in 1813 calculated the total population to be 521,175 whites, mestizos, and other mixtures; 80,000 peaceful Indians; and 150,000 rebellious Indians.

During the colonial period, Spanish legal barriers blocked immigration by other European nationalities. However, with the advent of the House of Bourbon on the Spanish throne in 1700, French settlers began to arrive in Chile. With independence (1810–1818) a free trade policy was decreed, paving the way for new waves of immigration from England, North America, and Italy. In the mid-nineteenth century, the government promoted the settlement of German and British immigrants in the southern Central Valley, Croats in Antofagasta and Punta Arenas, and finally Christian Arabs. In the Great North, a significant number of Peruvians and Bolivians became Chilean with the country's incorporation of the Tarapacá region after the War of the Pacific (1879–1883).

Political developments

Chile was "discovered" from the north by the frontier governor Diego de Almagro in 1536 who returned to Peru with the intention of organizing a new expedition. Earlier, in 1510, Chile had been "discovered" in the extreme south by the Portuguese explorer Ferdinand Magellan in the service of Spain. In 1541, Captain Pedro de Valdivia led an expedition into Chile and settled there on the order of the viceroy of Peru and in the name of Philip II of Spain. Valdivia was designated governor, founding Santiago as well as numerous forts and cities further south.

Indigenous resistance began, during which the governor was killed. The Spanish retreated north of the Bío Bío River, which constituted a sort of frontier, although it was not recognized by either side since the conquistadores extended as far south as Chiloé. The governors who succeeded Valdivia continued the war in sporadic battles; the area of La Araucanía was not pacified until 1860–1880. Meanwhile, the port of Valdivia and the main island of Chiloé remained under the direct control of the viceroyalty of Peru.

The colonial period

The Spanish royal government of Chile, under the authority of the viceroy of Peru, was organized in the late sixteenth and early seventeenth centuries. Executive authority was vested in the governor and the commander-in-chief of the armed forces, with legislative and judicial powers exercised by the Royal Tribunal and the city councils of the leading settlements, all dependencies of Peru and Spain. The Catholic church retained great influence which has been maintained over the centuries: 67 percent of the population is Roman Catholic, 14 percent Protestant, and 4 percent from other religions.

Chile's economic importance in this period was based partially on its provision of agricultural products to the viceroyalty and Spain, but more importantly on metals, including gold, silver, and copper. Its strategic significance derived from its possession of the only passage between the Atlantic and Pacific Oceans (the Strait of Magellan and Cape Horn) and from its status as the most intense focus of indigenous resistance, demanding constant reinforcements from Spain. Until the late eighteenth century, Chile covered not only the territory between the Pacific and the Andes, extending from the Atacama Desert in the north to the Strait of Magellan in the south, but also territories that are important provinces of Argentina today; the governor of Chile also controlled Tucumán, Mendoza, and other regions.

Independence

In 1700, the Spanish crown had passed from the Habsburgs to the House of Bourbon. In 1809, Napoleon installed his brother Joseph as king of Spain, replacing the Bourbon king Ferdinand VII. As in Spain itself, councils were organized in the Americas, and these pledged their allegiance to the Bourbon king. Chile formed its first governing council in 1810, installed its first National Congress in 1811, and attempted self-government on the basis of various constitutional texts. This gave the people of the New World an opportunity to gain their own experience in political affairs and promoted the spread of ideas of independence. When the Bourbon crown was restored in Spain, Ferdinand VII set out to recover his overseas dominions and sent ships and troops to Chile, sparking the wars of independence. In 1814, Spain reconquered Chile and reestablished European authority. This lasted only until 1818, however, when final independence was declared under the authority of General Bernardo O'Higgins as Supreme Director.

The period of anarchy

Chile attempted to reorganize its political system under several constitutions (those of 1818, 1822, and 1823), which did not adequately reflect the prevailing ideas and were unable to bring order to the country. After some attempts at federalism and the promulgation of a very liberal constitution for the time (1828), Joaquín Prieto was elected president of the republic in 1831. With the help of his minister Diego Portales, Prieto spearheaded the constitutional reform that culminated in the establishment of the 1833 Constitution.

The republic

Under the 1833 Constitution, the government was successfully organized, exercising strong authority vested in the president of the republic. Further attempts to overthrow the government by force fell into disrepute and ceased. The country's new political cohesiveness permitted the waging of two significant armed conflicts: against the Peruvian-Bolivian Confederation in 1837 and against Peru and Bolivia in 1879–1883.

The country's executive authority remained rooted in the president of the republic. Legislative power was vested in two parliamentary bodies, the Chamber of Deputies and the Senate. Judicial power was exercised by the court system, including lower courts, appeals courts, and the Supreme Court.

As a consequence of the 1833 constitution Chile became one of the most stable and institutionalized countries in Latin America. Democracy, law, and order have been shared and respected values by the population during most of Chilean history.

The rise of the pseudo-parliamentary system

In the 1860s, parliamentary rules allowed a certain number of deputies or senators to summon ministers of government for questioning. This led to the Congressional demand that a minister or cabinet who was subject to a vote of censure by the legislature should be dismissed, since the government must have the confidence of Congress. This practice gave rise to periodic disputes and a high turnover of ministers. The president found himself obliged to recall censured ministers, since if he did not, Congress would refuse to approve recurring measures such as those relating to the budget, taxes, and the armed forces. The president did not have the power to dissolve Congress and allow the voters to settle conflicts. This style of government became known as "pseudo-parliamentary".

The 1891 civil war

Because of disagreements over President Balmaceda's political and economic proposals, Congress refused to approve the national budget for 1891. The president, supported by the armed forces, responded by decreeing that the previous year's budget would remain in force for the current year. Congress accused the president of legislating by decree, declared him a dictator, and, calling upon the Navy for support, formed a parallel government in the north, financed with the proceeds from the area's rich nitrate mining operations. Hostilities broke out, and the war culminated in September 1891 leaving 10,000 dead. Finally, the parliamentary system was reestablished, with Congressional interference in executive affairs increasing until 1924, when the problem of ministerial turnover was exacerbated by social tensions, chiefly arising from the decline of the nitrate industry after the invention of synthetic nitrates.

The 1925 reform

In 1924, the military declared the political system inoperative and incapable of resolving the country's urgent social problems and forced Congress to approve social legislation such as the Labor Code. President Arturo Alessandri was deposed, but the military requested his return in 1925. He accepted on the condition that the Constitution should be reformed to allow ministers to serve solely at the president's discretion, to eliminate the need for recurring approval of some laws, and to provide that the previous year's budget would remain in force if a new one was not approved in a timely manner. The new Constitution was approved through a plebiscite.

Toward socialism

Between 1925 and 1932, popular protests and the country's economic crisis led to the dissolution of several governments. Two presidents were obliged to resign and were constitutionally replaced by military ministers; the country was even governed during a short period by military councils proclaiming a "socialist republic".

In 1932, President Arturo Alessandri again took office and established a fully constitutional government. In 1938, the Popular Front, which originally included the Communist Party, was elected to power. It launched an economic policy aimed at industrialization, autarky, and the protection of domestic industries, achieved through the creation of public enterprises, price fixing, exchange rate controls, and limits on imports and exports.

In 1958, Jorge Alessandri became president with the backing of a center-right coalition, pledging to introduce liberal reforms into the economy. However, he failed to achieve fulfillment of his program due to lack of support in Congress. In 1964, the Christian Democrats came to power and again increased state intervention in the economy, promoting their plans as a third option between the right and Marxism. Their policies included agrarian reform with land expropriations, state purchase of shares in the big privately owned copper mining companies, and the extension of state interference in all economic spheres.

In 1970, socialist President Salvador Allende took office and quickly nationalized all of the country's mining, agricultural, manufacturing, and financial activities, establishing fixed prices for products in all sectors. Many of these initiatives were contrary to the law and the Constitution, even violating the rulings of the courts. The country entered a state of crisis, with shrinking production levels, industrial paralysis, high inflation, shortages, exchange rate and balance of payments crises, and other difficulties. Allende tried to relieve the country's paralysis by designating active admirals and generals as ministers, but he sparked conflict with the judicial branch due to state officials' reluctance to abide by court decisions, as well as with Congress for his attempt to push through a constitutional reform creating three areas of the economy – state-held, mixed, and private without the approval of the legislature.

In August 1973, the Chamber of Deputies declared the government unconstitutional and called upon the military leaders serving as ministers to put an end to the illegalities, signaling that failure to do so would compromise the armed forces' professional and constitutional status. Days later, Allende declared that the country's food supply was sufficient for only three days.

The Pinochet government

In September 1973, in the midst of a full-fledged production crisis and with serious threats of civil unrest, a military council took power after a violent coup d'état. The aim of the military council was basic economic reorganization: reestablishment of the legal framework, the return of banks and businesses to their owners, price deregulation, and implementation of an economic policy allowing resources to be assigned by the market.

In 1982 and 1983, the balance of payments crisis came to a head, and Chile maintained a fixed exchange rate for four years, leading to an acute banking crisis and the renegotiation of the country's external debt. The country confronted this crisis by liberalizing currency markets, negotiating with foreign creditors to extend repayment periods, taking over and liquidating several banks, and strongly supporting exports, all of which led to a turnaround in the situation by 1986.

Starting in that year the country's GDP began to rise to unprecedented levels, thanks to far-reaching economic and social reforms, including tax and tariff reductions; the privatization of state-owned companies; the encouragement of international investment, capital, and trade; privatization of the social security system through individual savings accounts; the founding of private universities; the transfer of primary and secondary education to the municipalities, supported with subsidies; and administrative decentralization and regionalization, along with overall reductions in the size of the state. With moderate alterations, the country has continued to follow the main thrust of these reforms.

The government of Augusto Pinochet faced a hostile international climate, both within the Communist orbit – since it had deposed the first popularly elected Marxist head of government –and also in the Western world, which accused it of disrupting democracy and of serious human rights violations and restrictions on individual liberty.

Additional difficulties included tensions with Peru and Bolivia at the centennial of the Pacific War and disputes with Argentina over the Picton, Lenox, and Nueva Islands in the eastern mouth of the Beagle Channel, south of Tierra del Fuego, which were finally resolved through the mediation of Pope John Paul II. Under the military regime, Chile withdrew from the Andean Pact, which had fixed common external tariffs for its members (Chile, Peru, Bolivia, Ecuador, Colombia, and Venezuela) and regulated foreign trade and investment.

The new Constitution, approved in a plebiscite in 1980, reestablished a strong presidency, a bicameral legislature, and an independent judiciary. It also extended and strengthened individual rights, created new mechanisms for their protection, and accentuated the autonomy of the Constitutional Tribunal, the office of Comptroller-General, and the Central Bank.

The transition period

The 1980 Constitution gradually took hold in the political system during a long transition period in which the military council approved the basic laws complementary to the Constitution, in contrast with the country's experience in 1925 when the Constitution did not take full effect until 1932, since the laws established by Congress in the interim distorted and even contradicted constitutional provisions. The 1980 Constitution established a transition period lasting until 1989, when elections would be held to install the new National Congress. The presidency would be established through a plebiscite on General Pinochet's leadership in 1988, or if the result was negative through a presidential election in 1989. The negative result of the 1988 plebiscite led to free presidential elections in 1989, in which Patricio Aylwin was elected president.

The binomial system

The new electoral provisions established a so-called binomial system, in which all voting districts simultaneously elect two representatives. This system tends to favor moderate, centrist politics, both in the designation of candidates and the election of representatives. Extreme positions are rejected, resulting in the formation of two great coalitions or political movements, favoring the search for consensus and compromise.

In March 1990, in fulfillment of the Constitution's political plan, the military handed over legislative power to the new National Congress and executive authority to President Aylwin, who was elected by a majority of the parties opposed to the military regime, united in the Concertación coalition.

The Concertación administrations: Aylwin (1990–1994), Frei Ruiz-Tagle (1994–2000), Lagos (2000–2006), Bachelet (2006–2010), and Piñera (2010–)

With the advent of democracy, the country reestablished political normality under President Patricio Aylwin without crisis. The armed forces were gradually subordinated to civilian authority, and the country earned favorable recognition abroad. Aylwin's economic policies maintained the growth rate, budgetary discipline, and economic reforms achieved by the military government, and the new administration designated a special commission (the Rettig Commission) to investigate human rights violations during the previous regime. Aylwin also initiated negotiations for FTAs with Canada and Mexico, which were concluded successfully by his successor.

Arbitration commenced to resolve the outstanding border disputes with Argentina in the far south (at Laguna de Desierto and Campo de Hielo Sur). Diplomatic relations were normalized with Cuba and Russia, as they had been with Poland, Czechoslovakia, Hungary, and other Central European countries at the end of the military government, after the fall of the Berlin Wall.

During the administration of President Eduardo Frei Ruiz-Tagle, the trade negotiations initiated by Aylwin resulted in final agreements, and the border disputes with Argentina were resolved. Chile also became an associate member of Mercosur. President Frei's economic policies continued the trend initiated in the mid-1970s and achieved further advances in privatization with the sale of the state's minority shares in an electric company, the transfer to foreign investors of the principal state-held water utilities, the privatizing of the country's ports, and the initiation of roadway concessions to private enterprises. However, moderate budget deficits, higher taxes, and growing pressure for intervention in the labor market, combined with the Asian financial crisis, contributed to a gradual decline in the country's growth rate.

The presidential term of Ricardo Lagos began in March 2000, after a narrow victory over the mayor of Santiago, Joaquín Lavín. The new president began negotiations with the opposition for constitutional reforms to the electoral system, to increase the number of senators and eliminate the nonelected "institutional" Senate seats. Such negotiations continued in 2003. The unfavorable repercussions of a labor reform that added costs to the hiring or firing of workers, combined with slow economic growth, led Lagos, by the end of 2001, to announce measures favoring employment and private investment. At the beginning of President Lagos's term and the end of US President Clinton's, negotiations were initiated for an FTA between the two countries. In December 2002, an FTA was agreed to with the United States, while in November an Association Agreement was signed with the European Union. President Lagos maintained economic reforms and market-oriented policies although he stopped privatizations. Lagos's period ended in March 2006 when Michelle Bachelet became the first woman to obtain the Chilean presidency. During her presidency, she has maintained the main frame for the economic policy, including new FTAs.

Bachelet's administration has been affected by the implementation of the TranSantiago, a new public transportation system planned during Lagos administration, which has not given the expected results.

Nevertheless Bachelet maintained over 68 percent approval ratings, higher than any other Chilean president. Two of the most important reforms that she is leading are the reform of the pension system, which increased a social security pillar and validated the private pension system, and the reform of the educational system to increase the quality of education through a combination of public and private services.

Economic policies

The protectionism imposed by the Spanish colonial authorities was gradually eased during the establishment of the republic. The period from 1860 to 1897 saw significant trade liberalization. In the late nineteenth century, however, Chile's industries pressed for higher tariffs, organizing themselves into the SOFOFA (Sociedad de Fomento Fabril, or Federation of Chilean Industry), which remains the country's leading industrial association.

They pushed through a law empowering the president of the republic to impose tariffs of up to 35 percent by decree. Despite the increasing restrictions on international trade, however, the export sector represented 70 percent of GDP – thanks to the income from nitrate and copper mining – and continued to drive the country's economic growth until the 1930 crisis, which led to expanded state ownership and intervention in productive activities, as well as a new wave of trade protectionism. Both trends continued, until virtually all industries were in state hands and external trade was shut down in the 1970–1973 period. The situation has been reversed since that time through privatization and trade liberalization, as explained earlier.

To confront the 1930 crisis, the authorities opted for selective manipulation of the economy, with import reductions through higher trade barriers and the stimulation of internal demand in favor of domestic production. This policy continued unbroken until its fatal unraveling in 1973. Populist forces, industrial cartels, and labor organizations pressed for rising state intervention in manufacturing and service industries, reinforcing protectionist impulses and rejecting the trade liberalization opportunities arising from the creation of General Agreement on Tariffs and Trade (GATT) at the end of the Second World War.

Import substitution

Protectionism received strong support from the Economic Commission for Latin America and the Caribbean (ECLAC), created by the United Nations after a petition by Chile in 1950. ECLAC laid the conceptual basis for protectionism as a tool to confront falling prices for raw materials and to promote domestic manufacturing industries with a protected market.

Discrimination against the export sector led to export stagnation, the monopolistic domination of domestic markets by obsolete industries, increased external vulnerability, recurring balance of payments crises, currency devaluations, and high inflation rates. Chile's GDP growth rate for the period between 1930 and 1973 was approximately 1.2 percent per annum.

Regional integration

An attempt was made to correct the failures of the import substitution policy with the expansion of the limited internal market through

Chile 91

planned regional integration, which would permit economic competition on a larger scale. The first integration initiatives were undertaken in late 1960. The ALALC (Asociación Latinoamericana de Libre Comercio, or Latin American Free Trade Association), which included 15 countries, did not achieve significant advances, and the product-by-product tariff reduction negotiations, with producers in each member country enjoying voting rights, paralyzed the process. Meanwhile, through the Andean Pact, Chile, Peru, Bolivia, Ecuador, and Venezuela hoped that their relative similarities would permit a more rapid advance toward economic integration, but again, interminable discussions on the location of various industries, the application of protectionist measures and trade barriers, and discrimination against foreign investment led to the failure of the pact, from which Chile withdrew in 1976. In the mid-1970s, ALALC was transformed into Asociación Latino-Americana de Integración (ALADI), which favored the more modest objective of bilateral accords, rather than free trade among all its members. By refraining from insisting on the extension of bilateral accords to all other members, ALADI permitted moderate advances in integration.

Unilateral trade liberalization

Between 1974 and 1991, Chile opted for a strategy of unilateral trade liberalization, reducing its tariffs on all products from an average rate of 100 percent to some 10 percent, without negotiating reciprocal agreements. Its across-the-board tariff of 7 percent, with very limited exceptions (automobiles, milk, wheat, cooking oils, and sugar) would continue to fall each year, dropping to 6 percent in 2003.

Bilateral and regional free trade agreements

Since 1991, Chile has continued its unilateral trade liberalization process while promoting bilateral and regional FTAs. It has concluded bilateral trade agreements setting tariffs at zero for nearly all commercial transactions with Bolivia, Peru, Mexico, Canada, Ecuador, Venezuela, Colombia, Costa Rica, Central America, and Panama.

Mercosur

The high and variable external tariff levels (ranging between 0 and 20 percent during a ten-year period) of the Southern Common Market (Mercosur) treaty, to which Argentina, Brazil, Uruguay, and Paraguay were parties, along with the macroeconomic instability of its members and their policy of negotiating collectively with the European Union and the United States, led to initial resistance on Chile's part to joining this association. However, it entered into the special status of associate member in 1998, without applying the common external tariff, and with an agreement to reduce tariffs within the group and gradually eliminate other trade barriers, resulting in free trade for most transactions by 2008.

Association agreement with the European Union

In November 2002 the EU–Chile Association Agreement (the "EU Agreement") was signed. Although trade is an important part of the agreement, it goes far beyond this aspect. The EU Agreement is based on three pillars – political dialogue, cooperation and trade – thus covering the broad range of EU–Chile relations.

The trade part of the EU Agreement establishes an FTA in goods through the progressive and reciprocal liberalization of trade in goods over a maximum transitional period of ten years. At the end of the transitional period, full liberalization will have been reached for 97.1 percent of bilateral trade of CLP$7387 million (average 1999–2001), with, per sector, 100 percent full liberalization of industrial trade, 80.9 percent full liberalization of agricultural trade, and 90.8 percent full liberalization of the fisheries trade. In addition, for a number of agricultural and fisheries products other forms of tariff preferences are granted, such as tariff quotas, leaving only 0.4 percent of total bilateral trade not covered by any form of liberalization.

Table 5.5 details imports and exports between Chile and other countries, trade blocs, and regions in 2008.

Liberalization of trade in goods will thus take place consistently with Article XXIV of GATT, that is, involving substantially all trade liberalization and not excluding any sector.

The tariff elimination schedules are as follows:

- Industrial products: The European Union eliminates 100 percent of its tariffs for most imports from Chile at the entry into force (99.8 percent) and the rest in 2006. Chile equally eliminates all its industrial tariffs for most imports at entry into force (91.7 percent) and the rest in 2008 (4.5 percent) and 2010 (3.8 percent). During 2008 EU industrial imports from Chile amounted to CLP$3777 million.
- Agricultural products (including processed agricultural products): On the European Union side, tariffs will be eliminated for 97 percent of agricultural imports from Chile, relating mostly to full elimination of tariffs and in certain cases to elimination of ad valorem

duties only. This will be done at entry into force (33 percent), in 2007 (55 percent), in 2010 (12 percent), and in 2012 (0.2 percent). In addition, certain products will benefit from other forms of preferential treatment, including tariff quotas for products such as meat, cheese, certain fruits, and sugar confectionary. Agricultural products not benefiting from any form of liberalization represent 0.9 percent of total Chilean imports into the European Union. Chile eliminates tariffs for 81.9 percent of EU agricultural exports to Chile, at entry into force (61.5 percent), in 2008 (16.6 percent), and in 2012 (3.8 percent). In addition, Chile grants the European Union preferential treatment under tariff quotas for products such as olive oil and cheese.

During 2008 EU agricultural imports from Chile amounted to US$2054 million.

- Fish and fisheries products: The European Union eliminates tariffs for 90.8 percent of fish imports from Chile at entry into force (34.3 percent), in 2007 (39.6 percent), in 2010 (2.4 percent), and in 2012 (14.5 percent). Chile eliminates its tariffs for 97.6 percent of fish imports from the European Union at the entry into force of the EU Agreement. Both sides grant each other reciprocally tariff quotas for products such as tuna and hake.

Table 5.5 Exports and imports, Chile, 2009

	Exports		Imports	
	US$ millions (FOB)	%	US$ millions (FOB)	%
Mercosur	3958	7.4	7480	18.8
Argentina	733	1.4	4284	10.8
Brasil	2736	5.1	2699	6.8
Other Latin American (excl. Mexico)	4844	9.0	3323	8.4
NAFTA	8763	16.3	9079	22.8
European Union	9650	18.0	6426	16.2
Asia	24537	45.7	10891	27.4
Others	1984	3.7	2554	6.4
TOTAL	53735	100.0	39754	100.0

Source: Central Bank of Chile.

During 2008 EU fisheries imports from Chile amounted to US$515 million. The tariff elimination programs start from the tariffs as applied at the entry into force of the Agreement (the so-called base rates). In the case of Chile, this applied tariff was 6 percent for basically all products (an exception is information technology (ITA) products, for which the applied tariff was already at zero). In the case of the European Union the tariffs applied to Chile vary, depending on the product. As part of an overall package, the European Union agreed to start its tariff elimination from the rates effectively applied to Chile instead of the MFN (most favored nation) duties. In practical terms, these rates are those which the European Union unilaterally grants to Chile under the Generalized System of Preferences (GSP).

In order to benefit from preferential treatment under the Agreement, a product when exported must be considered as originating either in the Community or in Chile. For this purpose, it must comply with the origin rules established in a specific annex to the EU Agreement. In this respect, when the product exported is not entirely manufactured ("wholly obtained") in one of the two parties, goods imported from third countries must undergo sufficient working or processing in compliance with the specific origin rule set out for the final product to be exported.

The EU Agreement includes a standstill clause ensuring that neither side would increase its tariffs vis-à-vis the other party as from the entry into force of the EU Agreement.

Free trade agreement with the United States

The United States and Chile began bilateral negotiations on a free trade agreement (FTA) in December 2000. In December 2002, the United States and Chile reached an agreement on an historic and comprehensive FTA (the "US Agreement") designed to strip away barriers and facilitate trade and investment between both countries.

Trade Representatives and the Chilean Foreign Minister signed the US Agreement and submitted it to their Congresses for approval in 2003. The US Agreement is the first comprehensive trade agreement between the United States and a South American country.

The United States has only five other FTA partners: Canada, Mexico (within the North American Free Trade Agreement, or NAFTA), Israel, Singapore, and Jordan. US firms may offer financial services to participants in Chile's highly successful privatized pension system.

The US Agreement establishes a secure, predictable legal framework for US investors in Chile. Among the most important features of the US

Agreement is that both parties commit to enforce their domestic labor and environmental laws effectively. An innovative enforcement mechanism includes monetary assessments to enforce commercial, labor, and environmental obligations. Cooperative projects will help protect wildlife, reduce environmental hazards, and promote internationally recognized labor rights.

State-of-the-art protections and nondiscriminatory treatment are provided for digital products such as US software, music, text, and videos. Protections for US patents, trademarks and trade secrets exceed past trade agreements.

Free trade agreement with China

On the August 21, 2006, the FTA between China and Chile was enacted. This agreement is important because it allows Chile to establish an entire network with Asian partners as it also has agreements with the Pacific 4 and Japan. This FTA includes the following topics: institutions and administrations of the agreement, markets access and trade defense, origin rules, sanitary and phytosanitary actions, technical barriers to trade, controversy solutions, and cooperation between the labor and social securities authorities. There is also an environmental cooperation agreement, but it does not include commercial services.

From the first day, there was no tariff for 92 percent of Chilean exports (for example copper, other minerals, vegetables, pigs, and pork) or for 50 percent of Chinese exports. Other Chilean goods will have no tariff after one, five, and ten years, while Chinese goods will have no tariff from one, two, five and ten years. There are some products that are excluded from the agreement, for example wheat, sugar, and flour.

This FTA represents a clear benefit for Chilean consumers since the reductions in tariffs of around 6 percent will reduce the price paid by the consumers. It has also been noted that the FTA will encourage investment because it creates a secure and more favorable frame for business development.

Other free trade agreements

In recent years Chile has signed FTAs with other important economies like Australia (2008), Korea (2003), and EFTA (2003), and also with members of the South American region like Peru (2006), Colombia (2006), and Panama (2006) (see Table 5.6).

Table 5.6 International agreements, Chile

	Type of agreement	Date of signature	Date effective/status
Pacifico-4[a]	Economic partnership agreement	July 18, 2005	November 8, 2006
European Union[b]	Economic partnership agreement	November 18, 2002	February 1, 2003
Canada	Free trade agreement	December 5, 1996	July 5, 1997
Korea	Free trade agreement	February 15, 2003	April 1, 2004
China	Free trade agreement	November 18, 2005	October 1, 2006
TLC Chile-Centroamerica			
Costa Rica	Free trade agreement	October 18, 1999	February 14, 2002 (bilateral protocol)
El Salvador	Free trade agreement	October 18, 1999	June 3, 2002 (bilateral protocol)
Guatemala	Free trade agreement	October 18, 1999	Under parliamentary procedure (bilateral protocol)
Honduras	Free trade agreement	October 18, 1999	August 28, 2008 (bilateral protocol)
Nicaragua	Free trade agreement	October 18, 1999	Bilateral negotiation protocol
United States	Free trade agreement	June 6, 2003	January 1, 2004
Mexico	Free trade agreement	April 17, 1998	August 1, 1999
EFTA[c]	Free trade agreement	June 26, 2003	December 1, 2004
Panama	Free trade agreement	June 27, 2006	March 7, 2008
Colombia	Free trade agreement	November 27, 2006	May 8, 2009
Peru	Free trade agreement	August 22, 2006	March 1, 2009
Ecuador	Economic complementation agreement no. 32	December 20, 1994	January 1, 1995
Mercosur[d]	Economic complementation agreement no. 35	June 25, 1996	October 1, 1996

Continued

Table 5.6 Continued

	Type of agreement	Date of signatur	Date effective/ status
Bolivia	Economic complementation agreement no. 22	April 6, 1993	July 7, 1993
Venezuela	Economic complementation agreement no. 23	April 2, 1993	July 1, 1993
India	Partial scope agreement	March 8, 2006	August 17, 2007
Cuba	Partial scope agreement	December 2, 1999	August 28, 2008
Japan	Economic partnership agreement	March 27, 2007	September 3, 2007
Australia	Free trade agreement	July 30, 2008	March 6, 2009
Malaysia	Free trade agreement		Under negotiation
Thailand	Free trade agreement		Draft approved
Turkey	Free trade agreement		End of negotiations
Vietnam	Free trade agreement		Commencement of negotiations

[a] Pacífico-4 comprises Chile, New Zealand, Singapore, and Brunei Darussalam.
[b] The European Union comprises Germany, Austria, Belgium, Denmark, Spain, Finland, France, Greece, Italy, Ireland, Luxembourg, Netherlands, Portugal, the United Kingdom, and Sweden, and since May 1, 2004, ten new member countries: Cyprus, Slovakia, Slovakia, Estonia, Hungary, Latvia, Lithuania, Malta, Poland, and the Czech Republic, and since January 2007 Romania and Bulgaria.
[c] The European Free Trade Association comprises Iceland, Liechtenstein, Norway, and Switzerland.
[d] Mercosur comprises Argentina, Brazil, Paraguay, and Uruguay. Chile is involved as a partner country.

Ground-breaking anticorruption measures in government contracting

US firms guarantee a fair and transparent process to sell goods and services to a wide range of Chilean government entities, including airports and seaports. Traditional market access to services is supplemented by strong guidelines on regulatory transparency. Regulatory authorities must use open and transparent administrative procedures, consult with interested parties before issuing regulations, provide advance notice and comment periods for proposed rules, and publish all regulations.

Property rights

Under Chile's Constitution, expropriation can take place only where there is a law authorizing it in that specific case. Compensation is determined by mutual agreement or, in its absence, by the Chilean courts.

In general, property rights are strongly enforced. The Constitution expressly states: "in no case may anyone be deprived of his property, assets, or any of the essential faculties or powers of ownership, except by virtue of a general or a special law which authorizes expropriation for the public benefit or the national interest, duly qualified by the legislator."

The expropriated party may contest the legality of the expropriation before the ordinary courts of justice and, at all times, has the right to indemnification for patrimonial damage actually caused, which is to be fixed by mutual agreement or by a decision issued by the courts in accordance with the law. In the absence of an agreement, the indemnification must be paid in cash.

Material possession of the expropriated property will take place following full payment of the indemnification, which, in the absence of an agreement, must be provisionally determined by experts in the manner prescribed for by law. In the case of contestation regarding the justifiability of the expropriation, the court may, on the merit of the information adduced, order the suspension of material possession.

Therefore, expropriation requires indemnification on the basis of market value. In the event of a dispute, the Chilean government cannot take possession of the property until the courts issue a final decision on indemnification. As this may necessitate a long trial, the administration usually prefers to pay prices similar to the market value, or even higher.

Environmental regulations

The Chilean Constitution of 1980 grants to all citizens the right to live in an environment free of pollution. It further provides that other constitutional rights may be limited in order to protect the environment. One of the prime objectives of Chile's environmental policy concerning the introduction and development of investment projects hinges on reconciling the strategy for economic growth with proper environmental protection in the arena of public and private investment processes.

The Chilean Environmental Act, which is known as the "Environmental General Basis" law, Law No. 19,300, was promulgated in March 1994. The regulatory framework for its enforcement – in terms of considering environmental concerns in investment projects – includes, among other things, Environmental Impact Assessment System (EIAS). The purpose of Environmental Impact Assessment, applied to projects and/or activities performed by the public and private sectors, is to assure the environmental sustainability of such undertakings.

Certain projects or activities prone to generating environmental impact must be subjected to an Environmental Impact Assessment. Their specific effects, characteristics, or circumstances will determine whether an Environmental Impact Statement or an Environmental Impact Study should be filed.

The Environmental Act is to be conceptualized as a set of procedures designed to identify and evaluate positive and negative environmental impacts to be generated or presented by a given project or activity. The EIAs will then assist in designing measures aimed at abating the negative impacts and enhancing any positive effects. An important part of these procedures depends on the involvement of state entities with environmental jurisdiction and/or in charge of issuing specific sector environmental permits associated with the project or activity.

The Environmental Act has placed the burden of implementing and administrating the EIAs on the National Environmental Commission (CONAMA), which is an inter-ministerial commission. Within this institutional framework, CONAMA and the Regional Environmental Commissions (COREMAs) are in charge of coordinating the process whereby ratings are assigned to the Environmental Impact Study and Environmental Impact Statements are reviewed. The various state bodies with environmental competence participate actively in this process.

The Environmental Act provides that the projects or activities under its purview and further specified in the Regulations may be executed or revised only after an assessment of their environmental impact. Further, it stipulates that the environmental contents of all the permits and dictums to be issued by state entities must be analyzed and settled through the EIAS.

Since June 2007, Congress has been discussing a bill that promotes some significant modifications to the environmental institutional framework. This bill introduces changes to the Law (19,300), and creates new environmental institutions such as the Environmental Ministry (created in 2008), which will replace CONAMA, an independent Environmental Assessment Service, and an Environmental Supervising Agency.

Foreign investment, capital movements, and exchange rates

Starting in 1974, as trade liberalization progressed, restrictions on capital movements and transactions in foreign currencies were also gradually eliminated. Currently, Chile places no restrictions on the entry and exit of capital, and the nondiscrimination principle is applied to foreign investors, who may invest in all areas of the economy. Foreign investment, chiefly from the United States, Spain, Canada, and the United Kingdom, is concentrated in manufacturing, mining, electricity, fisheries, banks, and financial services.

Foreign investors are subject to a tax of 35 percent on the repatriation of their profits. Exchange rates are fixed freely by the market and without interference by the Central Bank. Capital movements to or from Chile do not require prior authorization. However, amounts over US$10,000 must be remitted through commercial banks, which must inform the Central Bank about the remittances.

Privatization

The state has privatized nearly all public enterprises, with the exception of BANCOESTADO, ENAMI and CODELCO (Chile's largest company and the world's largest copper producer) in the copper mining sector, along with ENAP, the National Oil Company, which maintains a monopoly in the area of fuel refining and oil extraction (the country's oil reserves are nearly depleted, and more than 90 percent of oil and gas supplies are imported). The state also holds shares in water and sewerage utilities.

Bilateral investment treaties

In 1991, Chile became a signatory of the Washington Convention of 1965 that created the International Centre for Settlement of Investment Disputes (ICSID). From then on, Chile began to negotiate bilateral investment treaties (BITs), agreements through which Chile provides additional protection both to inward and outward foreign investment flows. As of January 2002, Chile had negotiated 51 BITs, of which 35 were in force.

Under these agreements, each contracting state commits itself to providing fair and equal treatment to investments legally made in its territory by investors of the other contracting state. It also guarantees the principles of national treatment, nondiscrimination, and most favored nation status. Moreover, BITs usually grant private property rights through the establishment of basic principles and minimum standards in the case of expropriations. Likewise, they guarantee that any expropriation or measure with similar effect is adopted in accordance with a law based on the public good or national interest, in a nondiscriminatory manner.

Through BITs, the contracting states guarantee the free transfer of capital, of profits, or interest generated by foreign investments, and, in general, any transfer of funds related to investments. Additionally, these agreements establish a dispute settlement mechanism in case of controversies that might arise between an investor of one contracting state and the other. Basically, this mechanism assures that controversies will be settled through friendly consultations. If no agreement is reached, the investor will be entitled to submit the case to the domestic jurisdiction of the host state of the investment or to international arbitrage. This jurisdictional option is definitive.

As an additional guarantee for foreign investors, BITs allow access (if not full access, at least access with reasonable premiums) to insurance coverage against noncommercial risks offered by multilateral or governmental agencies such as the Multilateral Investment Guarantee Agency (MIGA) and the Overseas Private Investment Corporation (OPIC).

The aforementioned guarantee is reinforced by the principle of subrogation granted in BITs. This means that if one contracting state – or an agency authorized by it – grants any kind of insurance against noncommercial risks to an investment in the territory of the other contracting state, the latter shall recognize the rights of the former to subrogate for the rights of the investor in case it has paid the insurance. The protection provided by these agreements applies both to investments made after the agreement comes into force as well as to those made before that date.

Conclusion

Chile's trade agreements and reforms make its economy the most open to international competition in Latin America. To this is added almost 30 years of conservative balanced budgets, increased monetary stability with a growth rate that is declining. For more than a decade (1986–1998), Chile's GDP grew at an average annual rate of 7 percent, although in the following ten years, the average growth rate declined to 3.4 percent.

Thanks to these successes, a broad consensus prevails among both the government and opposition parties to maintain Chile's policies of openness to international trade, avoid budget deficits, keep inflation under control, and promote private investment. From a political perspective, during the past decade democracy and the rule of law have been expanded and stability is well established. Military subordination to the government has been reached, an independent judiciary is ruling without government intervention, and freedom of expression has been increased after a new press law was published.

Nowadays the difference, in terms of popular support, between "Concertacion" – the political coalition that conducts the government – and "Alianza por Chile" – the opposition coalition – has been reduced to very little. The last two presidential elections went into a second round. This year there is to be a presidential election. According to different opinion polls taken in the past two years, opposition leader Sebastian Piñera, ex senator from Santiago, appears to be the most likely successor to President Bachelet. The public agenda is concentrated on reforms of the corporate governance for the public enterprises and in environmental regulation, and in constitutional changes in order to change the voting and electoral registration systems.

Bibliography

Periodical publications

Banco Central. *Boletín Mensual* (Monthly).
Banco Central. *Cuentas Nacionales* (Annual).
Banco Central. Documentos de Trabajo.
Banco Central. *Indicadores de Comercio Exterior* (Monthly).
Centro de Estudios Públicos CEP. *Estudios Públicos* (Quarterly).
Centro de Estudios Públicos CEP. *Puntos de Referencia* (Monthly).
Instituto Nacional de Estadísticas INE. *Compendio Estadístico* (Annual).
Libertad y Desarrollo. Serie Informe (Económica; Política; Social) (Monthly).
Libertad y Desarrollo. *Temas Públicos* (Semanal).
Social Panorama of Latin America (2008). Institutional Periodical Reports, ECLAC. December
Universidad Católica de Chile. *Cuadernos de Economía* (Quarterly).
Universidad de Chile. Centro de Economía Aplicada CEA. Documentos de Trabajo. Serie Economía.
Universidad de Chile (2002). Centro de Economía Aplicada CEA. Análisis económico descriptivo de las regiones chilenas. Documentos de Trabajo. Serie Economía Agosto.
Universidad de Chile. Instituto de Estudios Internacionales. *Estudios Internacionales* (Quarterly).
Universidad de Chile. Facultad de Ciencias Físicas y Mátematicas. *Perspectivas en política, economía y gestión* (Biannual).
Universidad Gabriela Mistral. Report of Chile (Annual).

Books

Büchi Buc Herná (1993). *La Transformación Económica de Chile, del Estatismo a la libertad*. Editorial Norma.
Comité Inversiones Extranjeras. *Chile Inversión Extranjera en Cifras*. Período 1974–1999.
French-Davis, Ricardo; Stallings, Bárbara (2001). *Reformas, crecimiento y politícas sociales en Chile desde 1973*. CEPAL.
Góngora, E.; Robertson, R.; Vial, C. Gonzálo et al. (1984). *Dimensión histórica de Chile*. Revista Dpto. de Historia y Geografía de la Academia de Ciencias Pedagógicas.
Holt, Jocelyn; Correa, Sofía y Figueroa Consuelo (2002). *Historia del siglo XX chileno*. Editorial Sud Americana Chilena.
Lavín, Infante Joaquín (1988). *Chile a quiet revolution*. Editorial Zig Zag.
Libertad y Desarrollo Cristián Larroulet (ed.) (1991 & 2003). *Soluciones Privadas a Problemas Públicos*. Quebecor World Chile SA. 1991 1ª edición; 2003 2ª edición.
Lüders, Rolf; Ibañez, Pedro (1983). *Hacia una economía de mercado: diez años de Política económica*.
Márquez de la Plata, Alfonso (1992). *El salto al futuro*. Editorial Zig Zag.
Méndez, Juan Carlos (1979). *Chilean Economy Policy*. Calderón y Cia. Ltda.
Piñera Echeñique, Jóse (1997). *Chile 2010 Libertad, libertad mis amigos*. Economía y Sociedad Ltda.
Piñera Echeñique, Jóse (1992). *La Revolucíon Laboral en Chile*. Editorial Zig Zag.
Piñera Echeñique, Jóse (1993). *Camino Nuevo*. Economía y Sociedad Ltda.
Rojas Sánchez, Gonzalo (1998). *Chile escoge la libertad. La presidencia de Augusto Pinochet*. Santiago de Chile: Editorial Zig Zag.
Wisecarver, Daniel; Williamson, Carlos; Lüders, Rolf; Desormeaux, Jorge et al. (1992). *El Modelo Económico Chileno*. CINDE Centro Información para el Desarrollo Económico.

Public policies

Libertad y Desarrollo. Cristían Larroulet (1994). *Las Tareas de Hoy. Políticas Sociales y Económicas para una Sociedad Libre*. Editorial Zig Zag.
Libertad y Desarrollo. Cristían Larroulet (2002). *Chile 2010: el desafío del desarrollo*. Quebecor World Chile SA.

6
Costa Rica

Ricardo Monge-González and Ana Laura Torrentes-García

The Republic of Costa Rica is located in the Central American isthmus. With an area of 51,000 square kilometers (19,652 square miles), the country has two immediate neighbors, Nicaragua in the north and Panama in the south. In addition, it has ports on both the Atlantic and Pacific Oceans. Costa Rica is a country characterized by a traditional, established democracy, especially since its army was abolished in 1949. With elections held every four years, Costa Rica has stable political and economic environments. The business environment and legal framework are also designed to favor foreign investment.

Costa Rica has a population of about 4.5 million. This number includes approximately 320,000 foreigners, of whom nearly 230,000 are from Nicaragua (Chaves, 2008). The population density is 87.6 inhabitants per square kilometer, life expectancy is 79.0 years, the literacy rate is 95 percent, and 98 percent of the population is provided with potable water; living standards indicators are the highest in Central America. The percentage of people living under the poverty line is close to 18 percent, less than half of that in the rest of Central America. Compared with the rest of the world, Costa Rica's indicators are high. According to the United Nations 2007 Human Development Index (HDI), Costa Rica held forty-eighth place and has one of the highest rankings for the quality of human resources among developing countries.

Some of the differences between Costa Rica and its neighbors have been present since colonial times. They have survived through the years and have been important factors in the creation of the nation. Other differences are due to the many years of peace and democracy during the last half of the twentieth century, while other countries were exhausted by domestic and international conflicts.

Historical background

Pre-Columbian era

When Spanish explorers arrived in what is now Costa Rica on September 18, 1502, they found a region populated by several poorly organized, autonomous tribes – with around 20,000 indigenous people. Although human habitation can be traced back at least 10,000 years, the region had remained a sparsely populated backwater separating the two areas of high civilization: Mesoamerica and the Andes. High mountains and swampy lowlands had impeded the migration of these advanced cultures.

The region was a potpourri of different cultures. In the east along the Caribbean seaboard and along the southern Pacific shores, the people shared distinctly South American cultural traits. In the highlands, the Corobicís tribe arrived from Mexico around two centuries before Columbus. Trade in pottery from the Nicoya Peninsula brought the northern area into the Mesoamerican cultural sphere. A culture also developed among the Chorotegas (the most numerous of the region's indigenous groups) that in many ways resembled the more advanced cultures farther north such as the Mayans and Aztecs.

Colonial era

When Columbus arrived on the east coast of Costa Rica in the Bay of Cariari on his fourth voyage to the New World, he called the region La Huerta ("The Garden"). Starting in 1506, different expeditions tried to colonize the Atlantic coast of Veragua, but they failed. It was not until 1522 that an expedition under Gil Gonzalez Davila set off from Panama to settle the region. It was Davila's expedition, having found quantities of gold, that named the land Costa Rica ("Rich Coast"). Davila's Catholic priests also apparently managed to convert many Indians to Christianity. For the next four decades Costa Rica was left virtually untouched. The conquest of Peru by Pizarro in 1532 and the first of the great silver strikes in Mexico in the 1540s turned all eyes away from southern Central America.

Guatemala became the administrative center for the Spanish in 1543, when the captaincy-general of Guatemala, answerable to the viceroy of New Spain (Mexico), was created – with jurisdiction from the Isthmus of Tehuantepec to the empty lands of Costa Rica. By the 1560s, several Spanish cities had consolidated their positions farther north.

Spanish representatives in Guatemala thought it was time to settle Costa Rica and Christianize the natives. However, the epidemics of European diseases had already cut the Indian population. The survivors moved to the forests and eventually found refuge in the remote valleys of the Talamanca Mountains. Only in the Nicoya Peninsula did there remain any significant Indian population.

In 1562, Juan Vásquez de Coronado, the true conquistador of Costa Rica, arrived as governor. He treated the surviving Indians more humanely and moved the existing Spanish settlers into the Cartago Valley. Cartago was established as the national capital in 1563. The economic and social development of the Spanish provinces was traditionally the work of the soldiers, who were granted *encomiendas*, or land holdings, which allowed the use of indigenous serfs.

In the highlands, land was readily available, but there was no Indian labor to work it. Without native slave labor or the resources to import slaves, the colonists were forced to work the land themselves. Even Coronado had to work his own plot of land to survive. Without gold or export crops, trade with other colonies was infrequent at best. In fact, money became so scarce that the settlers eventually reverted to the Indian method of using cacao beans as currency. After the initial impetus given by its discovery, Costa Rica became the lowly Cinderella of the Spanish empire.

Intermixing with the native population was not a common practice. In other colonies, Spaniards married natives and a distinct class system arose, but mixed-bloods and mestizos represent a much smaller element in Costa Rica than they do elsewhere in the isthmus. Costa Rica became a traditional rural democracy with no oppressed mestizo class resentful of the maltreatment and scorn of the Creoles. Removed from the mainstream of Spanish culture, the Costa Ricans became individualistic and egalitarian.

Independence

The independence of Central America from Spain on September 15, 1821, came on the coat tails of Mexico's declaration earlier in the same year. Independence had little immediate effect, however, for Costa Rica had required only minimal government during the colonial era and had long since gone its own way. In fact, the country was so out of touch that the news that independence had been granted reached Costa Rica a full month after the event. A hastily convened provincial council voted for adhesion to Mexico.

In 1823, the other Central American nations proclaimed the United Provinces of Central America, with their capital in Guatemala City. After the declaration, effective power lay in the hands of the separate towns of the isthmus. It took several years for a stable pattern of political alignment to emerge. The local quarrels quickly developed into civic unrest and, in 1823, led to civil war. After a brief battle in the Ochomogo Hills between the republican forces of San José and the conservative forces of Cartago, the republicans were victorious. They rejected Mexico. Costa Rica joined the Central American Federation with full autonomy in its own affairs.

From this moment on, liberalism in Costa Rica had the upper hand. Elsewhere in Central America, conservative groups tied to the Church and the previous colonial bureaucracy spent generations at war with anticlerical and laissez-faire liberals, and a cycle of civil wars came to dominate the region. By contrast, in Costa Rica colonial institutions had been relatively weak and early modernization of the economy pushed the nation out of poverty and laid the foundations for democracy far earlier than elsewhere in the isthmus. While other countries turned to repression to deal with social tension, Costa Rica turned toward reform.

After 1824, the Costa Rican government guided the country, establishing a stable judicial system and founding the nation's first newspaper and public education. It also encouraged coffee growing and gave free land grants to would-be coffee growers. The nation, however, was still driven by the rivalry between the two main parties. In 1838, Costa Rica withdrew from the Central American Federation and proclaimed its complete independence. By 1849, a new elite had emerged. The growing prosperity of the coffee growers, or *cafetaleros*, led to rivalries among the wealthiest family factions, who competed with each other for political dominance. Thus began a small but constant tension between the coffee growers and the military.

Democracy

The shift to democracy came in 1889 through elections with popular participation. Women and Blacks, however, were still excluded from voting. During the course of the next two generations, militarism gave way to peaceful transitions to power. On the other hand, several presidents attempted to amend the Constitution to continue their rule and even dismissed uncooperative legislatures. Throughout this time the country had been at peace. In 1917, democracy faced its first major challenge. At that time, Costa Ricans had come to accept liberty as their due. They were no longer prepared to accept oligarchic restrictions.

Reform and civil war

The decade of the 1940s and its climax, the civil war, mark a turning point in Costa Rican history. From paternalistic government by traditional rural elites, Costa Rica turned to modernistic, urban-focused statecraft controlled by bureaucrats, professionals, and small entrepreneurs. In a period when neighboring Central American nations were under the repression of tyrannical dictators, Costa Rica promulgated a series of social reforms such as land reform (the landless could gain title to unused land by cultivating it), establishment of a guaranteed minimum wage, paid vacations, unemployment compensation, progressive taxation, and a series of constitutional amendments codifying workers' rights. The Catholic Church and the communists played important roles in these changes.

In 1948, after the association of different parties, the country was polarized and claims of fraud in the elections heightened the tension. This tension ended in revolution. The 40-day civil war claimed more than 2,000 lives, most of them civilians. After the war, a Junta of the Second Republic of Costa Rica was constituted as a government. During this period, the government consolidated the social reform program and added its own landmark reforms, banning the Communist Party, introducing suffrage for women and full citizenship for Blacks, revising the Constitution to outlaw a standing army, establishing a presidential term limit, and creating an independent Electoral Tribunal to oversee future elections.

Contemporary scene

Social and economic progress since 1948 has helped return the country to stability, and although post-civil war politics have reflected the play of old loyalties and antagonisms, elections have been free and fair. With only two exceptions, the country has alternated presidents between the two main parties, Liberación Nacional (PLN) and Unidad Social Cristiana (PUSC).

By 1980, Costa Rica was mired in an economic crisis reflected in inflation; crippling currency devaluation; soaring oil bills and social welfare costs; plummeting coffee, banana, and sugar prices; and the disruptions to trade caused by the Nicaraguan war. When large international loans came due, Costa Rica found itself burdened overnight with the world's greatest per capita debt. It required a great effort from all Costa Ricans to get the country out of this predicament.

In February 1986, Costa Ricans elected Oscar Arias as their president. Arias' electoral promise had been to work for peace in Central America. Immediately, he began working on resolving Central America's regional conflicts. He attempted to expel the Nicaraguan military forces located in the northern part of Costa Rica and enforced the nation's official proclamation of neutrality made in 1983. Arias' efforts were rewarded in 1987, when his Central American peace plan was signed by the five Central American presidents in Guatemala City: an achievement that earned the Costa Rican president the 1987 Nobel Peace Prize.

Abolition of the army and efforts made to maintain peace, not only within the country but also in the region as a whole, have given Costa Rica a reputation at a global level as a country of peace. Costa Ricans are characterized by their peacefulness, taking action only when necessary.

In the early twenty-first century, Costa Rica promoted the expansion of its exports and tourism. The promotion of export-oriented manufactured goods has taken the form of special fiscal regimes, especially for electronics, under the free zone regime. Despite efforts to generate linkages between export-oriented activities and the rest of domestic industry, spillovers have been limited. Apart from the special fiscal regimes, measures to promote industrial production have been focused on small and medium-sized enterprises (SMEs).

Tourism remains a major source of foreign exchange and investment. Inefficiencies in some other service areas imposed unnecessary costs on these activities until recently. Thanks to new liberalization efforts, the state no longer retains monopoly rights in insurance, telecommunications, and energy distribution. State-owned banks still dominate the industry despite considerable growth in the private sector (Monge-González, 2009).

Costa Rica has exploited its two primary resources – its biodiversity and its human capital. In the first case, the biodiversity has positioned Costa Rica as one of the top places to visit, attracting more and more people and investments every year. In the case of human capital, Costa Rica is characterized by a high level of knowledge, not just in the technical fields but also in English as a second language, which attracts considerable investment to the country.

The main destination of Costa Rican exports is the United States. Its share of Costa Rican exports is around 35 percent. The Asian market is the second destination for Costa Rican products, with close to 21 percent of all exports, while the European Union's share is 15 percent. It should be noted that the products traditionally exported to the European Union, coffee and bananas, have declined in relative importance compared with modular circuits and other nontraditional goods such as pineapples, ornamental plants and foliage, and melons. The main sectors that attract the greatest volume of foreign investment are industry, the property sector, tourism, and trade. The main source of investment is the United States (54 percent) followed by the Netherlands (13 percent).

Costa Rica is now promoting a new development scheme. The new plan provides incentives to SMEs, especially those that use high technology and those that focus on international markets. In this group are the companies that create new software and those dedicated to e-business.

Costa Ricans have recently confronted the need to adapt to the country's increasingly closer ties to a globalized world. For example, free trade agreements (FTAs) with Central American, South American, and Caribbean countries and with the United States demand active and dynamic citizens with the capacity to analyze situations and participate in decision making.

While in the past it was necessary to create the Caja Costarricense de Seguro Social (CCSS), the labor code, and social guarantees to reach a higher level of development, today it is necessary to create new institutions and rules of the game to successfully confront the challenges and take advantage of the opportunities offered by globalization.

International trade policy

In the early twenty-first century, the government tried to encourage the participation of Costa Rica in international markets. The objectives of the government can be summarized in five main points:

1. Improve and secure access of Costa Rican products to foreign markets.
2. Promote domestic changes necessary to develop more efficient production of exportable goods, including the use of new technology in the production process.
3. Defend Costa Rican trade interests against protectionist measures by other countries.
4. Fully involve all sectors of the country's economy in exporting.
5. Establish a legal framework for the proper management of trade relations.

These objectives are administered by the Ministry of Foreign Trade (Ministerio de Comercio Exterior, COMEX) and are directly tied to the activities of two institutions: the Foreign Trade Promotion Body (Promotora de Comercio Exterior, PROCOMER), which is responsible for promoting exportable products abroad, especially those of SMEs, and the Costa Rican Coalition for Development Initiatives (Coalición Costarricense de Iniciativas de Desarrollo, CINDE), a private organization whose object is to foster the conditions needed to attract domestic and foreign investment and at the same time establish investment programs. Costa Rica has continued to step up the process of enlarging its trade, above all because the national economy is not large enough to provide the growth opportunities that the country needs. Therefore, a trade policy has been followed on a sustained basis over several years that is designed to achieve the fullest integration of Costa Rica into the global economy. The success of this policy can be seen in the growth of exports, the diversification of products and markets, the increase in foreign direct investment (FDI), and the creation of employment.

The government has different instruments to achieve these objectives. Some of these instruments are participation in multilateral agreements, regional integration, negotiation of trade and investment agreements, and unilateral liberalization initiatives.

Multilateral system

World Trade Organization (WTO)

Costa Rica has always believed in the multilateral trading system and has supported all moves to buttress that system since the inception of the WTO. A strong multilateral system with clear and transparent rules is of enormous benefit to a small, international-trade-dependent economy such as that of Costa Rica.

Costa Rica has adopted different commitments that are consistent with the country's policy, including the Agreement on Information Technology Products (ITA), which is consistent with Costa Rica's effort toward development of the information technology industry. Costa Rica also welcomed the start of agricultural negotiations in the WTO. The nation's goal is the total abolition of agricultural export subsidies, which constitute the most unfair and trade-distorting mechanism in international trade. Costa Rica, with the Cairns Group, maintains that all forms of domestic aid that distort international agricultural trade should be eliminated.

Regional integration

Central America Common Market (CACM)

In 1963, Costa Rica became a signatory to the general Treaty on Central American Economic Integration, which established the CACM, which included El Salvador, Guatemala, Honduras, and Nicaragua. Over the years, different efforts have been made toward the economic integration of the Central American countries. Despite the fact that in the past few years the trade flows between Costa Rica and the CACM region have grown more slowly than overall flows, Central America continues to be an important destination for Costa Rican exports.

The region has developed the legal framework necessary for the regulation of relations between the countries in CACM. The regional trade rules are presently being aligned with the commitments of each Central American country in the WTO. By the end of 2000, nine new regulations had been approved in the following fields: origin of goods, unfair business practices, safeguard measures, standardization measures, and metrology and authorization procedures, as well as sanitary and phytosanitary procedures. Approval of a regulation on disputes settlement is pending and negotiations are under way to conclude a treaty on services and investment.

The region also has a common legal code for customs called Código Aduanero Común (CAUCA). Although Costa Rica has been using this legal code, it did not participate in the unification of customs until June 2002. The four other countries (Guatemala, Honduras, El Salvador, and Nicaragua) have been implementing a plan that creates a common customs zone permitting the free movement of products regardless of origin. The result would be the elimination of customs among those countries. This is not the only initiative toward integration in Central America in which Costa Rica has been cautious. Costa Rica has been wary of other integration initiatives, especially the Central American Parliament. This discretion does not affect the desire of Costa Rica to integrate with the markets of the four countries or the initiative of the Free Trade Area of the Americas (FTAA). The agreement of Costa Rica to join to the Central American common customs zone stems from the advantage of sticking together as a region in negotiations with other countries and economic blocs.

So far, all tariffs have been unified with the rest of Central America for 94 percent of products (Ministerio de Comercio Exterior, 2009).

Mercado Común del Sur (Mercosur)

In 1998, the presidents of the countries that form Mercosur and the presidents of the CACM countries signed an agreement about investment and trade. The agreement is to increase the integration and trade between the two blocs. The main objectives of the agreement are:

- Tightening economic relations, especially trade, investment, and the transfer of technology.

- Recognizing the way, and the specific actions that need to be taken, to deepen the relationship among the parties.
- Giving incentives to the free market economies and highlighting the importance of the private sector in the economic development of the countries.
- Finding the way to promote and protect investments.

The Caribbean Community (CARICOM)

The Central American countries have been talking, in the past decade, with CARICOM, the group of Caribbean nations, about different agreements. During this process topics such as technology, transport, the environment, tourism, development banks, and natural disasters have been the main interests.

This treaty was signed in Kingston, Jamaica, on March 9, 2004. Costa Rica, Jamaica, Guyana, Barbados, Surinam, and Trinidad and Tobago agreed on a free trade regime, with special treatment for some commodities, a four-year tariff reduction process, and seasonal tariffs for some agricultural goods. This agreement came into effect for Costa Rica on November 15, 2005.

Negotiation of trade and investment agreements

Bilateral FTAs and mutual investment promotion with other countries are the two main instruments used by the government of Costa Rica to achieve its objective in international trade: to become one of the pioneers in the region. These agreements make the rules clear to all economic agents involved in international trade. The improvement in access to new and larger markets is an important incentive in the attraction of new investment and the promotion of the export sector of the country. The eradication of the different barriers to imports generates greater competition within the country, forcing the improvement of the production process.

At the end of January 2001 Costa Rica had agreements on mutual investment promotion and protection with the following countries: Argentina, Canada, Chile, Chinese Taipei, the Czech Republic, France, Germany, the Netherlands, Paraguay, Spain, Switzerland, the United Kingdom, and Venezuela. Foreign investment is promoted mainly through the CINDE.

During 2009, Costa Rica was involved in negotiations with China and Singapore to reach a free trade agreement with each of these two countries. In addition, negotiations along with the rest of the Central American countries to obtain an association agreement with the European Union are under way.

Investment arrangements in Costa Rica are supplemented by bilateral, regional, and multilateral treaties providing guarantees and protection for foreign investment. Costa Rica has FTAs with the United States, Canada, Mexico, Panama, Chile, and the Dominican Republic.

Free trade agreement with Mexico

Since the entry into force of the FTA between Costa Rica and Mexico in 1995, trade flows between the two countries have increased significantly. Costa Rica was the first country of Central America to have this kind of agreement with Mexico. During this time, the FTA has had a positive impact by reducing and even beginning to reverse in Costa Rica's favor the limitations that have typified the historical pattern of trade flows between Central American countries and Mexico. Costa Rican exports to Mexico have increased three times as fast as imports.

With respect to FDI flows, Mexican investment in Costa Rica has increased significantly since 1994. Mexico became the second most important country as a source of FDI in Costa Rica at the close of the twentieth century. Over half of Mexican investment in Costa Rica is concentrated in the food industry and mines and quarries. The latter is the result of the recent entry into the domestic market of the main cement manufacturer in Mexico (Cemex).

Free trade agreement with Chile

In 1999, the countries of Central America and Chile signed an FTA. The CACM member countries and Chile agreed that market access would be negotiated bilaterally between each Central American country and Chile. Thus, Costa Rica and Chile bilaterally negotiated the entry of products into the Costa Rican and Chilean markets. In this agreement the majority of Costa Rican products entered Chile with zero tariffs. This agreement came into effect in February 2002.

Free trade agreement with Canada

This agreement was signed in Ottawa, Canada, in April 2001. However, the agreement came into effect only in 2002. The agreement is of great importance for Costa Rica to promote FDI inflows and tourism from Canada. Although the trade balance with Canada has been negative, the gap shows a declining trend. Most of the imports from Canada are related to raw materials. Thus, they do not compete with local goods but increase the competitiveness of goods using them as inputs.

Free trade agreement with Panama

Since 1973, the Free Trade and Preferential Trade Agreement has governed the trade in goods between Costa Rica and Panama. This agreement is rather more limited in scope than, for example, the agreement with Mexico. In 1998, Costa Rica, together with the other CACM countries, began negotiations with Panama with a view to establishing a new treaty that would not only cover a wider range of tariffs, but would also include provisions on rules of origin and customs procedures, investment, services, government procurement, antidumping measures, sanitary and phyto-sanitary measures, and dispute settlement. This agreement was reached in 2007. Exports to Panama show continued growth. Thus, in 2005, Costa Rica exported US$207.2 million, in 2006 US$268 million, and in 2007 US$327.2 million (Ministerio de Comercio Exterior, 2009).

United States–Dominican Republic–Central America Free Trade Agreement (DR-CAFTA)

The DR-CAFTA is a set of bilateral agreements among the United States, the Dominican Republic, and the Central American countries. This agreement came into effect for Costa Rica on January 1, 2009. It is considered a very important agreement since it consolidates the commercial relationship with Costa Rica's most important partners both in trade and in investment flows (Ministerio de Comercio Exterior, 2009).

The agreement represents a great opportunity for Costa Rican exports because it not only consolidates the access that some of these products have to the US market but also increases the amount of goods and services that can be exported under a free trade regime by Costa Rica to that market. At the same time, Costa Rica has significantly reduced the tariffs on US imports.

One of the most important results of the negotiation was the elimination of Costa Rican state monopolies on the insurance and telecommunications sectors.

Unilateral liberalization initiatives

This instrument is important since it has increased competition in the local market and has provided incentives for innovation and efficiency in companies that participate in international markets. A great deal has been done in the way of unilateral tariff rollback measures. Between 1995 and 2001, Costa Rica's average tariff decreased by 11.7 percent for the entire tariff framework. In the same period, Costa Rica lowered its tariffs by 48.2 percent. No further changes have occurred on tariffs since 2001. But there is still work to do, especially in the farm production sector. This sector is still subject to higher tariffs than those for other products. On average, tariffs for the farming sector are 13.72 percent, compared with 4.96 percent for the industrial sector.

Some characteristics of Costa Rican enterprises

Companies in Costa Rica face an increasingly competitive environment. The government's international trade policy attracts foreign investment and facilitates imports of goods that compete with domestic products. Often, some sectors in the country are discontent with this policy. The production sector in particular frequently tries to maintain some protection.

Businesses in Costa Rica have special characteristics. Some characteristics are similar to those of other businesses in Central America, but others are unique to Costa Rica. In Costa Rica, most businesses are SMEs. These businesses have fewer than 100 employees, less than US$500,000 in equipment, and annual income of less than US$1 million. These businesses represent 98 percent of industry and 80 percent of exporting companies. The majority of the SMEs are micro-enterprises. These businesses have up to ten employees (including the owner) and an annual income of less than US$150,000. Also, most Costa Rican businesses are family owned. Some other general characteristics of Costa Rican businesses are discussed in the following sections.

Short-termism

In general, most Costa Rican enterprises do not have a specific strategy, especially the smaller ones. These enterprises see strategy as an isolated event. They do not see strategy as a continuous process. Any efforts to establish strategy are seen as a waste of time. Therefore, the strategy is not properly communicated to all parts of the company. In many Costa Rican companies, especially the SMEs, communication is a major problem. There is no commitment to continuous improvement, and important changes are always delayed. These changes are proposed until they become imperative. This situation creates isolated and discontinuous improvements. The lack of strategy and the desire for action showing immediate results often generate short-term thinking and goals in the companies.

Culture and values

Some cultural characteristics can limit companies' performance. In general, Costa Rican firms do not devote enough time and resources to defining and instilling values aimed at improved performance. Key values are rarely stated, as opposed to what happens in large international corporations, whose global headquarters define values. Rapid changes do not allow for correspondingly rapid changes in companies' culture and values, which take more time.

However, a series of initiatives for fostering change does exist. For instance, the Ministry of Economy, Industry, and Trade (Ministerio de Economía, Industria y Comercio, 2006) prepared an SME Policy Proposal whose purpose is to "strengthen competitiveness of micro-, small and medium-sized Costa Rican businesses so they may integrate themselves into the national production network and take advantage of opportunities offered by the local market and national economic opening."

This proposal defines strategic areas, according to programs and laws, in which priorities are to be established that will allow SMEs to confront their principal problems. According to the Ministerio de Economía, Industria y Comercio (2006), as actions of the various programs are implemented, new actions will emerge that will enable the achievement of the other objectives of the SME Policy. It is still necessary for all sectors to make a commitment for this proposal to have an impact. For this reason, all institutions related to the SME Network play a defining role: Fundación Comisión Asesora en Alta Tecnología (CAATEC), Instituto Nacional de Aprendizaje (INA), Ministerio de Ciencia y Tecnología (MICIT), Fondo Especial para el Desarrollo de las Micro, Pequeñas y Medianas Empresas (FODEMIPYME), Promotora de Comercio Exterior (PROCOMER), financial entities, universities, and so on (see Table 6.1).

The greatest problems faced in doing business

According to the World Economic Forum (2008), great efforts are being made in Costa Rica to improve the ways in which business is done in the country. However, there are still problems that affect the country's competitiveness. The persons interviewed were asked to select the five most important problems for doing business in Costa Rica, and rank them on a scale from 1 to 5, with 1 being the most problematic.

Governmental bureaucracy is the principal problem faced in the country according to the respondents, and it affects not only Costa Rican businesspersons but also any other national or international businessperson who might want to establish some kind of enterprise in Costa Rica. Moreover, even though the government has made a considerable investment in infrastructure, the existing infrastructure is still

Table 6.1 Summary of strategies, programs, and actions involved in the SME Policy, Costa Rica

Strategic areas	Programs	Actions
Access to financial services	Guarantee fund	Extending access through amendments to Law 8262 and its regulations
	PROPYME	Information dissemination and aggressive positioning between businesses
	Risk capital	Proposal for creation and implementation
	Support for feasibility studies	Proactive inclusion in FODEMIPYME and other resources
Access to nonfinancial services	Costa Rica Emprende	Educating male and female entrepreneurs
		Strengthening of business incubation processes
		Business accelerators
	Technical training and assistance	SME Costa Rica Web portal
		Videoconferencing
		E-SME project
		Product design
Access to markets	Government purchasing	Junta de Administración Portuaria y Desarrollo Económico de la Vertiente Atlántica (JAPDEVA) pilot plan
		Caja Costarricense de Seguro Social (CCSS) integration
	Costa Rica Vende	Pilot plan with 20 businesses
	Provider linkages	Business round tables (San Carlos)
Production chains	Chaining and connectedness	CR-USA Project
		Strategic alliances within the SME Network
	Clusters	Identification of, and cooperation with, other programs
	Regional programs	Orienting training and technical assistance towards regional chaining
		Japanese cooperation
Quality and excellence	Costa Rica Compite	Regional diagnosis and development opportunities
	Costa Rica Califica	SME quality standards
		SME Corporate Social Responsibility standards
Simplification and formalition	PROEMPRESA	Integration with municipal services
	Costa Rica Simplifica	Agreements with the CCSS, Engineers and Architects Association, Secretaría Técnica Nacional Ambiental (SETENA) and Ministry of Health

Source: Ministerio de Economía, Industria y Comercio (2006).

considered to be insufficient for businesses' requirements. Both factors become even more important in the light of recently signed FTAs, which are intended to help new multinational companies establish themselves in the country.

Costa Rica has another series of problems or factors that hinder business performance, such as inflation, which has remained at double-digit levels (except in 2009), affecting production costs and long-term planning within the country.

In addition, although the Costa Rican labor force is considered to be well qualified, and nowadays a significant proportion of Costa Rican professionals are proficient in English, some businesses continue to encounter obstacles when trying to find qualified professionals to carry out necessary activities (lack of supply). For these reasons, it is imperative that universities and other educational centers increase enrollment in professions that are now being demanded by national and multinational companies.

According to the World Economic Forum (2008), other problems affecting the way of doing business in the country include:

- Restrictive labor regulations
- Tax rates
- Restricted access to financing
- Corruption
- Crime and theft
- Tax regulations

Structure

As mentioned before, many companies in Costa Rica are family businesses or are owned by relatively few people. This characteristic creates companies that can decide their own futures, in contrast with the branches of an international corporation that must obey guidelines from headquarters. This structure also generates some degree of informality in the decision-making process. In large Costa Rican companies, the structure is complex, creating difficulties in relations and in the flow of information. The management, in general, acts only in a crisis and concentrates decision-making power in the hands of the owner-manager, an attitude that may be perceived as autocratic. The owner-manager structure generates problems such as a lack of teamwork and a lack of management training stemming from the owner's fear of losing control. Given these structures, Costa Rican firms are still conservative, especially concerning decisions related to international markets.

Finance, technology, and infrastructure

SMEs have many problems of access to financial resources. The lack of capital produces delays in the adoption of technology even when the companies possess the human capital necessary to use the latest technology. This lack of capital combined with the lack of strategy generates unruly growth.

These characteristics give rise to some advantages and some disadvantages. Some of the disadvantages are that in many cases the companies lack the financial capital needed to make changes within the company. The management tends to be conservative, and in some instances decisions are subordinated to factors not related to the market, particularly in family businesses. Some of the advantages are the flexibility of Costa Rican companies and the capacity to absorb changes in know-how and technology, given the high educational level of the Costa Rican workforce.

Plans for the future

Costa Rica has an open economy in which foreign trade is of supreme importance. For this reason, the country will be pressing ahead with a foreign trade policy promoting greater and more secure access for Costa Rican products to international markets as a way of generating the growth and development opportunities that the country needs. Under this logic, Costa Rica wants to obtain the maximum benefits from FTAs and it will continue to favor initiatives for more trade links with other countries and regions.

The country recently engaged in a new FTA with the United States, the Dominican Republic, and the rest of the Central American countries (DR-CAFTA). In Central America, Costa Rica will continue to support the regional integration scheme and its implementation of the dispute settlement system as soon as possible.

At the multilateral level, Costa Rica will continue to support the launching of a broad round of negotiations to serve the interests of all members and thereby further advance the trade liberalization process. From Costa Rica's point of view, in addition to the ongoing negotiations on agriculture and services, the new round of the WTO should also encompass negotiations pertaining to the creation of a multilateral framework for investments, rules on trade facilitation, and commitments to electronic commerce.

Costa Rica will continue to support SMEs. Currently, the government program in this sector is improving access to the financial markets through cooperation with two state banks. This program is intended to create links between universities and companies. In so doing, the government wants to encourage the flow of technology and managerial skills. Costa Rica's government will also encourage the commercialization of products and participation in different events. The plan also includes training for those companies that want to export their products.

Conclusion

Costa Rica has its sights focused on international markets. It is convinced that to further economic development, the domestic market is not enough. The transfer of technology and knowledge is more likely to be possible with an open economy. Costa Rica is also conscious of the significance of its economic integration in the Central American region. This integration is the first step to enhanced access to markets such as the United States and the European Union. With such integration, the Central American countries as a whole would have more bargaining power and would be more attractive to investors.

Costa Rica is also convinced that future development will be achieved through SMEs. This scheme aims at cutting poverty levels and using all the human capital available in the country. Costa Rica is also placing a bet on innovation and technological development. The incentives given to the software sector, in addition to the development of an advanced Internet network and a national plan to improve English language instruction throughout the country, especially in technical areas, would be a great impetus to the high-technology sector and the rest of economy. In fact, Costa Rica boasts the highest-ranking innovation performance enablers from Central America for 2009–2013 (Economist Intelligence Unit, 2009).

Bibliography

Arias, C. (1999). *Análisis de Estrategias Gerenciales de Compañías Multinacionales Establecidas en Costa Rica*. San José: Universidad de Costa Rica.
Cámara de Industrias de Costa Rica (2002). *Guía Industrial 2002*. San José: Cámara de Industrias de Costa Rica.
Chaves, E. (2008). *Investigación de Campo: Aspectos Socioeconómicos de las Remesas Familiares en Costa Rica*. San José: Banco Central de Costa Rica.
Economist Intelligence Unit (2009). *A New Ranking of the World's Most Innovative Countries*. London: Economist Intelligence Unit Limited.
Jiménez, R. (2000). *Los Retos Políticos de la Reforma Económica en Costa Rica*. San José: Academia de Centroamérica.

Ministerio de Comercio Exterior (2004). *Tratado de Libre Comercio República Dominicana-Centroamérica-Estados Unidos: Documento Explicativo*. San José: Ministerio de Comercio Exterior.

Ministerio de Comercio Exterior (2009). Acuerdos Comerciales. http://www.comex.go.cr/ACUERDOS/Paginas/default.aspx. June.

Ministerio de Economía, Industria y Comercio (2002). *Informe Final Programa Impulso*. San José: Ministerio de Economía, Industria y Comercio.

Ministerio de Economía, Industria y Comercio (2006). *Política PYME Costa Rica 2006–2010*. San José: Ministerio de Economía, Industria y Comercio.

Monge-González, R. (2009). *Banca de Desarrollo y Pymes en Costa Rica*. Santiago de Chile: Comisión Económica para América Latina y el Caribe.

World Economic Forum (2008). *The Global Competitiveness Report 2008–2009*. Geneva, Switzerland: World Economic Forum.

World Trade Organization Secretariat (2001). *Trade Policy Review: Costa Rica*. Geneva, Switzerland: Trade Policy Review Body, World Trade Organization. http://www.comex.go.cr/acuerdos/OMC/Examenes%20Politicas%20Comerciales/G83-eng.pdf.

7
Dominican Republic
Roberto B. Saladín

Since 1492, the Dominican Republic, on the beautiful Caribbean island of Hispaniola in the West Indies, has been a bridge connecting Europe with North, Central, and South America. It was from Santo Domingo that the New World was discovered. It has now become a crossroads of migrants of different origins and cultures. Dominicans are proud of their history, from their pre-Columbian archaeological inheritance to their Spanish cultural roots. The Dominican Republic is a multiracial country, where the merengue is the national dance and baseball the national sport. The country has a diversified, fast-growing economy with links to the United States, Europe, Latin America, and the Caribbean region. The Dominican Republic is a country with a future.

The Dominican Republic, the second largest island in the Caribbean region, was discovered by Christopher Columbus in 1492. The explorer called the island "Hispaniola" on his arrival on December 5, 1492. Isabela was the first site of Spanish settlement in the New World. The capital city, Santo Domingo, was founded on August 4, 1496, by Bartolome Colon on the east side of the Ozama River; it was then moved in 1502 to the west side of the river.

A brief history

While ruled by Spain during the colonial period, the island was baptized the "Athens of the New World." It held the distinction in America of having the first cathedral, the first university, the first hospital, the first aqueduct, and the first engraving and printing of money and so on.

The Dominican Republic was ceded to France in 1797 and regained by Spain in 1808. In 1821, Jose Nuñez de Cáceres declared what was later called the "Ephemeral Independence", as he sought to be part of Greater

Colombia under the leadership of Simón Bolívar. From 1822 to 1844 the Dominican Republic was occupied by Haiti; it became a sovereign state in 1844. In 1860, the island was annexed again by Spain. After the War of Restoration, it again became an independent state in 1865 when Spain withdrew from the island, defeated. From 1930 to 1961 the Dominican Republic was ruled by the dictator Rafael L. Trujillo.

In 1962 free elections were held for the first time in 38 years. Juan Bosch, who returned from exile, won the election but was overthrown in September 1963. As a consequence of the coup d'état, a civil war in 1965 opened the doors to intervention by US armed forces, later to be replaced by the Inter-American Peace Force, supported by the Organization of the American States (OAS). Since 1966, the country has had free elections every four years, thus being the strongest Spanish-speaking democracy in the Caribbean region to date.

The land, people, and government

The Dominican Republic has a surface area of 48,511 square kilometers and shares the island of Hispanolia with Haiti, which is 27,750 square kilometers. The island of Hispanolia is situated in the Caribbean between Cuba to the west and Puerto Rico to the east. The Cordillera Central mountains cross the center of the Dominican Republic, rising to over 3100 meters, the highest altitude in the Caribbean. Peak Duarte, named to honor the father of National Independence, Juan Pablo Duarte, is found here. The country has 31 provinces and one National District, in which is located the national capital of Santo Domingo. The Dominican Republic has a population of around 9.5 million inhabitants. Among the principal cities of the country are Santiago de los Caballeros (second largest city), La Vega, Puerto Plata, Monte Cristi, San Cristóbal, Azúa, Barahona, San Pedro de Macorís, La Romana, and Higuey y El Seibo.

The Dominican Republic is a republic with separation of powers. The executive branch is headed by the President of the Republic, who is elected every four years. At present, the president is H.E. Leonel Fernandez Reyna (1996–2000; 2004–2012). The National Congress is divided into the Senate and the Chamber of Deputies, each having a president for the direction of the chamber. At the head of the judicial branch are the National Council of Magistrates and the Supreme Court of Justice. Judges for the latter are appointed and undergo examinations at public hearings.

The economy

The Dominican Republic can be considered a *"wirschafstwundert"* (economic miracle) in the Caribbean region and indeed in Latin America in the past two decades. Despite the fact that the world economy experienced a sharp deceleration in 2008, triggered by the subprime crisis in the United States and the collapse of its financial sector, the Dominican Republic has remained one of the most dynamic economies of Latin America in the past few years. In fact, the Dominican economy showed the second highest annual growth rate in the region. During the period 1990–2006, the country experienced a 5.5 percent growth rate – second only to Chile. This rapid growth rate was interrupted by the local financial crisis in 2002–2003; however after the election of President Leonel Fernandez Reyna (2004–2008) the average growth rate for the period 2005–2007 reached 9.0 percent. The GDP of the Dominican Republic in 2008 reached 5.3 percent according to the Central Bank (CBDR).

After 1992, the performance of the Dominican economy was very positive, taking into account the per capita income (GDP-PPP 1995) (see Figures 7.1 and 7.2).

Previously, in the 1990s, the key sectors of growth were tourism and industrial free zones (*"maquilas"*). But after the implosion of the Dominican financial system, economic growth was supported by nontraditional sectors such as construction and telecommunications. In the four years 2005–2008, the performances on growth and inflation were among the best in the Caribbean region.

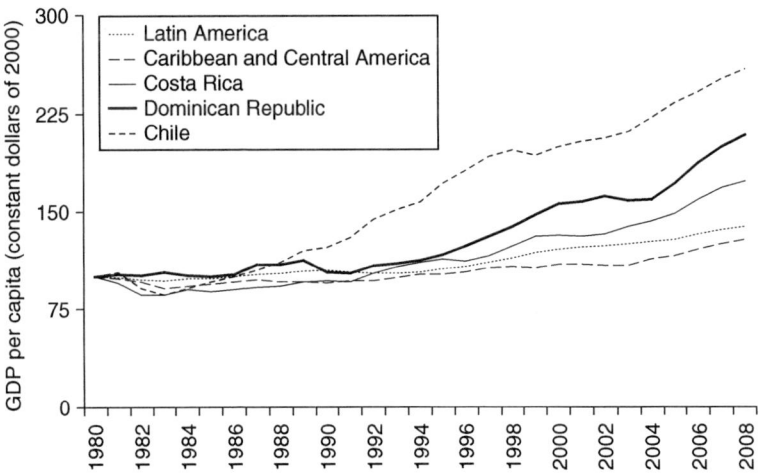

Figure 7.1 Economic growth, Dominican Republic and region, 1980–2008 (GDP per capita in constant dollars of 2000, 1980 = 100)

Source: Data from the World Bank, World Development Indicators, 2008.

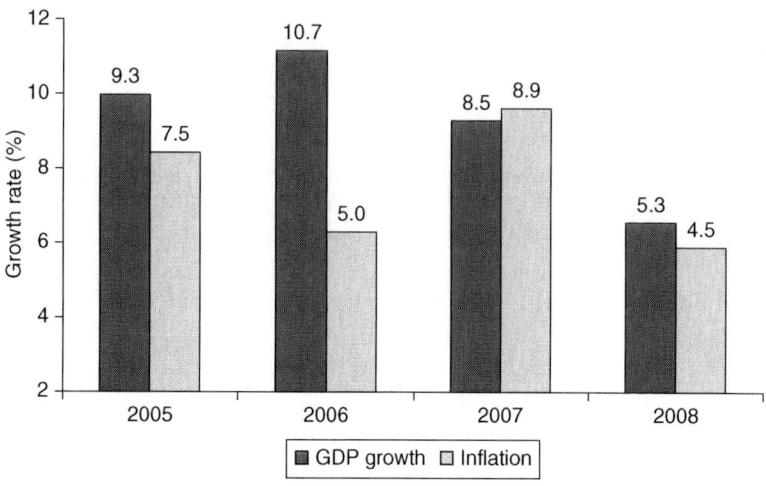

Figure 7.2 Growth rate of GDP and inflation, Dominican Republic, 2005–2008 (%)
Source: Economist Intelligence Unit and the CBDR.

The Dominican economy, like those of the other countries in Latin America and the Caribbean, began to suffer the shocks of the international financial crisis in 2008. Triggered by the subprime mortgage crisis in the US economy, the ensuing liquidity crunch, and the limited access to credit, a deceleration of economic activities at world level followed. In the first six months of 2008, the Dominican economy experienced strong inflationary pressure, pushed mostly by the increase in oil and food prices, in addition to an overheating of the internal demand, public and private. Moreover, the country was deeply affected by four severe tropical storms that flooded it.

The Dominican Republic, a full member of the Dominican Republic – Central America Free Trade Agreement with the United States (DR-CAFTA), achieved the second highest growth rate for the region in 2008 after Panama (9.2 percent).

Real GDP grew 5.3 percent during 2008, based on the performance of the following sectors: communications 19.9 percent, finance and insurance 13.7 percent, energy and water 10.3 percent, trade 5.0 percent, other service activities 4.8 percent, transportation 4.2 percent, and hotels, bars, and restaurants 3.4 percent. However, other specific sectors experienced a decrease in comparison to the 2007 performance, such as mining −30.3 percent, agriculture −3.4 percent, industrial free trade zones −1.1 percent, and construction −0.4 percent.

In 2008 (after August 16), the CBDR adopted a package of measures to preserve macroeconomic stability, with the aim of reducing inflation and internal demand. Among other measures, three increases in the interest rate (overnight rate) and a sell-off of international reserves explain how inflation closed at 4.5 percent for 2008, after reaching 10.7 percent in the first nine months of the year. The exchange rate remained relatively stable with a slight depreciation of 3.5 percent.

In this respect, for 2008 the balance of payments had a current account deficit of US$4436.8 million, equivalent to 9.7 percent of GDP. National exports fell US$231.0 million (–8.8 percent), caused by the fall of nickel exports. This deficit was financed by the financial and capital account, especially through foreign investment which reached an extraordinary level of US$2884.7 million. Gross international reserves at the end of the third quarter amounted to US$2643.5 million and net international reserves to US$2149.4 million.

The trade balance, including industrial free zones, closed 2008 with a deficit of US$9146.5 million, which was higher than the trade deficit in 2007 by US$2709.7 million (42.1 percent increase). Total imports of goods amounted to US$16,095.4 million, growing 18.4 percent in 2008. The oil invoice represented US$4241.3 million, an increase of US$1017.3 million (31.6 percent) above the amount registered in the 2007. Total exports dropped from US$7160.2 million in 2007 to US$6949.3 million in 2008. National exports decreased by US$231.0 million (8.8 percent) due in great part to the sharp drop in the exports of nickel, which were down US$606.4 million. On the other hand, exports from the industrial free zones registered a total of US$4544.8 million, similar to 2007.

By the end of 2008 the public external debt amounted to US$8322.8 million, representing an increase of 9.1 percent compared to the previous year. The external debt to multilateral institutions represented 28.8 percent, bilateral debt reached 44.7 percent, and private debt equaled 26.5 percent.

With regard to the fiscal sector, in the first semester of 2008, there was a deficit in the balance in the nonfinancial public sector (NFPS) of 3.4 percent of GDP. This deficit was due to the government's subsidies provided to the liquefied petroleum gas (LPG) sector, to the energy sector in general, and for food price stabilization. The quasi-fiscal deficit of the CBDR reached 1.3 percent of GDP, slightly below the level forecast in the Monetary Program for the year.

In 2000–2004, during the collapse of the local financial system that took down the country's three largest commercial banks (BANINTER,

BANCREDITO, and BANCO MERCANTIL), the authorities of the CBDR decided to avoid further systematic risk and thus honored all the deposits for these banks in the aftermath of the fraud. This act provoked the doubling of the monetary emission in less than a year (RD$35,328 million in January 2003 to RD$69,558 million to December 2003). Inflation reached double digits.

In 2004, when President Leonel Fernandez Reyna returned as President, the cost of the banking rescue amounted to RD$104,857 million. The CBDR had placed RD$89,438 million in certificates, at an average interest rate of 58.45 percent. Monthly interest payments amounted to RD$2973 million. At that time, the quasi-fiscal deficit of the CBDR fell from 4.0 percent of GDP in 2004 to 1.3 percent in 2008. The stock of certificates increased from RD$89,438 million in August 2004 to RD$206,944 million on July 22, 2009.

It is important to emphasize that the Dominican government assumed a commitment through the Law of Capitalization of the Central Bank, by which the government recognized all the losses of the CBDR since its foundation in 1947. The CBDR issued public annual bonds with payment interest (from 0.5 percent of GDP in 2007 up to 1.5 percent of GDP in 2008) for a period of ten years, allowing in 2016 the elimination of the quasi-fiscal deficit of the CBDR and thus a gradual decrease in the stock of certificates.

Investment climate

Since 1992, the Dominican Republic has strongly supported the creation of an attractive business climate for foreign investors through the implementation of its first generation of reforms based on its capacity to honor its financial commitments on time as well as a whole package of new laws in order to eliminate discrimination against foreign and particularly US investors. These reforms created equal treatment for national and foreign investors.

The new Foreign Investment Law (1995) eliminated any kind of discrimination against foreign direct investment, granting equal treatment to Dominican and foreign investors under national and international laws. Investors also have the right to repatriate up to 100 percent of the capital and profits, should they decide to do so.

According to the Foreign Investment Law, every investor has the right to make his investment in any of the following forms: (1) converting foreign currency at the official rate of exchange through a local bank;, (2) investing capital in the form of cash, goods or services, (3) using financial instruments approved by the Monetary Board, or (4) transferring technology by embracing technical licensing, technical assistance, "know-how", basic engineering, etc.

Tourism development

More than three decades ago, the country was a well kept secret, until the tourism sector of the Dominican Republic emerged as one of the strongest pillars of the economy. In 2008, there were some 66,116 hotel rooms, making the Dominican Republic the largest tourism destination among the Caribbean islands. Its development started with the Promotion and Incentive Law 153–71 for Tourism Development and the creation of the Department to Foster the Tourist Infrastructure (INFRATUR) of the Central Bank in 1971. The World Bank financed the development of the Puerto Plata resorts and airport, as well as the master plan for the development of the north cost.

In 1978 the Dominican Republic received 304,000 tourists, while in 2007 it received around four million. The impact of the tourism sector on the economy of the Dominican Republic reached 19.6 percent of GDP in 2007. For that year, tourism generated 190,259 jobs, representing 6.3 percent of the active population. Furthermore, the total income for tourism represented US$4064.2 million, and was the number one source of foreign currencies for the country, followed by remittances. For 2008, tourism generated 195,519 jobs. Tourism income for 2008 generated US$4176.1 million for the country (see Table 7.1).

The confidence of foreign investors is demonstrated by the fact that between 1993 and 2007, the foreign direct investment amounted to US$2766 million.

The geographical distribution of the tourism flows by region in the Dominican Republic is mainly concentrated on the east and north coasts (62.0 percent), given that hotels in the area operate mainly on the "all included" system. Around 72.0 percent of the hotel capacity is related to hotels with more than 300 rooms.

Alternative conflict resolution

Furthermore, another area in which the Dominican Republic has made important progress due to the development of its international trade is in conflict resolution. In this field and outside of the courts of the judicial system, a whole set of modern legislation has been adopted, leading

Table 7.1 Indicators for hotels, bars, and restaurants, Dominican Republic, 1980–2008

Period (annual)	Hotel rooms (units)	Hotel occupancy rate (%)	Tourist income (US$ millions)	Employment generated by the activity (persons)		
				Total	Direct	Indirect
1980	5,394	58.5	172.6	20,388	6,796	13,592
1981	6,132	59.5	206.3	23,180	7,727	15,453
1982	6,165	55.5	266.1	23,305	7,768	15,537
1983	6,527	60.3	320.5	24,693	8,231	16,462
1984	7,133	57	370.6	26,986	8,995	17,991
1985	8,562	61.8	451	32,364	10,788	21,576
1986	9,862	63.3	506.3	37,278	12,426	24,852
1987	12,043	74.1	571.2	45,522	15,174	30,348
1988	15,997	70.6	768.3	60,468	20,156	40,312
1989	18,478	70.7	818.4	69,846	23,282	46,564
1990	19,043	68.8	817.6	88,549	28,564	59,985
1991	21,510	64.5	840.4	97,871	27,963	69,908
1992	24,410	69.3	1007.1	111,066	31,733	79,333
1993	26,801	74.7	1223.7	112,564	32,161	80,403
1994	29,243	72.1	1428.8	122,821	35,092	87,729
1995	32,846	76.8	1570.8	126,458	36,131	90,327
1996	36,273	72.6	1780.5	126,956	36,273	90,683
1997	40,453	76.2	2099.4	155,744	44,498	111,246
1998	44,665	69.7	2153.1	156,328	44,665	111,663
1999	49,623	66.9	2483.3	159,786	45,653	114,133
2000	51,916	70.2	2860.2	167,170	47,763	119,407
2001	54,034	66.3	2798.3	154,106	44,031	110,075
2002	54,730	62.8	2730.4	157,388	44,968	112,420
2003	56,590	72.7	3127.8	164,694	47,055	117,639
2004	59,077	74.2	3151.6	171,478	48,994	122,484
2005	60,015	73.9	3518.3	172,116	49,176	122,940
2006	63,372	73	3916.8	188,289	53,797	134,492
2007	64,898	72.2	4064.2	190,259	54,359	135,900
2008	66,116	70.4	4176.1	195,519	55,863	139,656

Source: CBDR

to other methods of alternative conflict resolution, such as mediation, conciliation, and arbitration. Apart from the provision of the Civil Procedure Code and the Commercial Code a whole set of national and international procedures has been set up as, for example:

- Law No. 489-08 on Commercial Arbitration in the Dominican Republic, promulgated on December 30, 2008

- Adoption of the Guidelines of the Model Law of the United Nations Commission for International Mercantile Law (UNCITRAL)
- Law No. 50–87 on Official Chambers of Commerce, Agriculture, and Industries of the Republic and its modifications, opening the doors of the arbitrage to its members
- The Dominican Republic has representation in the International Court of Arbitration of the International Chamber of Commerce in Paris, France, while the Chamber of Commerce and Production of Santo Domingo hosts the National Committee of the International Chamber of Commerce.
- Simultaneously, close relations have been developed with the Inter-American Commission on Commercial Arbitration (CIAC) and the American Arbitration Association (AAA).
- The Convention on the Recognition and Enforcement of Foreign Arbitration Awards, known as the New York Convention was promulgated in the Dominican Republic by the Executive Power on November 8, 2008
- The Inter-American Convention on International Commercial Arbitration, which is known as the Panama Convention
- The Free Trade Agreement between the Dominican Republic, Central America, and the United States of America (DR-CAFTA), which allows party members to have access to the arbitration
- Ratification of the Multilateral Investment Guarantee Agreement (MIGA) of the World Bank for the resolution of differences among foreign investors

Finally, in the Dominican Republic, arbitration awards rendered in foreign countries are executed in compliance with the Arbitration Law and the treaties and agreements ratified by the country.

Foreign policy

The role played by the Dominican Republic is based on four fundamental axes: economic globalization, integration, cooperation, and the solution of conflicts. To this end, the Dominican Republic has set forth a plan to bolster its Foreign Policy agenda by emphasizing the following:

- Maximizing the benefits under the Free Trade Agreement between the US, Central America, and the Dominican Republic (DR-CAFTA) and more recently the Association of Economic Agreement (EPA) with the European Union

- Fostering economic and trade links with Central America and the CARICOM member states under the free trade agreements signed with those integration blocs
- Fully supporting the commitments agreed to by the Dominican Republic in the XIV Summit of Presidents (San José, Costa Rica, 19–20 November, 2004) under the program "Education for Progress"
- Fully supporting cybernetic programs at the national level to bridge the "digital divide" under the XIII summit of Presidents (Santa Cruz, Bolivia, November 14–15, 2003)
- Playing a role in regional conflicts as arbiter, such as the one played by President Leonel Fernandez Reyna at the XX Summit of Presidents of the Río Group (Grupo de Río) in seeking a solution for the differences between Ecuador, Colombia, and Venezuela (Santo Domingo, D.R. March 7, 2008)
- Improving and enlarging diplomatic links with the United States, Canada, the Caribbean Region, Central America, and South America through foreign policy, and expanding relations with the nations of Asia, Africa, and the Middle East
- Improving relations with Haiti, the neighbor of the Dominican Republic, progressing toward common goals, so as to keep responsible relations and respect between the two countries, and to foster a strong commitment by the international community to support the solidarity and the recuperation of Haiti

In the implementation of the above-mentioned strategy plan the Dominican Republic recently opened Embassies in South Africa, India, Egypt, Russia, Qatar, Palestine, Romania, Poland, Luxembourg, Hungary, Greece, and Andorra to attract new investment in the energy sector and to increase actions for the reduction of poverty.

Conclusion

Having a privileged position from a geographical viewpoint as a crossroads between Europe and America, the Dominican Republic is the natural technical landing point for all air and maritime traffic from the countries of the European Union and the United States and for all the New World. The Dominican Republic is trying to maximize this position by training the human resources needed. The country possesses one of the best communications systems in Latin America and the Caribbean region and has access to two major markets on both sides of the Atlantic Ocean.

The Dominican Republic is committed as a Caribbean country to fostering relations with Central America and the CARICOM countries, playing the role of a bridge among countries. To this end, it has signed free trade agreements with both regional economic blocks, and has requested to become a full member of CARICOM. Since March 2007, the Dominican Republic has been a member of DR-CAFTA, in addition to fulfilling all its obligations as a member of the World Trade Organization, and a recently becoming a member of the Economic Partnership Agreement with the European Union.

Bibliography

American Chamber of Commerce of the Dominican Republic (AMCHAM-DR) (2009). Investor's Guide 2009. Santo Domingo, DR.
Balaguer, Joaquín A. (1944). *Guía Emocional de la Ciudad Romántica*. Santo Domingo, DR.
Central Bank of the Dominican Republic (2008). Behavior of the Dominican Economy, January–December. Santo Domingo, DR.
De los Santos, Danilo (2003). *Memoria de la Pintura Dominicana, Raíces del Impulso Nacional*. Vols 1 and 2. Santo Domingo, DR.
Economic Commission for Latin America and the Caribbean (ECLAC) (2006). Preliminary Balance of the Economies of Latin America and the Caribbean (2006). Santiago de Chile: United Nations (ECLAC).
Economic Commission for Latin America and the Caribbean (ECLAC) (2008). Economic Study for Latin America and the Caribbean 2007–2008 (August).
Economic Commission for Latin America and the Caribbean (ECLAC) and the Pontifical Catholic University Madre y Maestra (PUCMM) (2000). Economic and Social Development in the Dominican Republic: Last 20 years and the Perspective for the XXI Century. 1st Edition. Santo Domingo, DR.
Inchaustegui, Aristides and Delgado Malagon, Blanca (1998). *Musical Life in Santo Domingo (1966–1996)*. Santo Domingo, DR: Banco de Reservas.
Nicasio R. Irma and Perez, Odalis G. (2007). *Migration, Identities and Culture in the Dominican Republic*. Santo Domingo, DR.
Palm, Erwin Walter (1955). *Arquitectónicos de la Isla Española*. Santo Domingo, DR.
Saladin Selin, R. B. (2002). Remarks on the Dominican Republic-United States Relations in the Political Economic and Social Context on the 21st Century by the Ambassador of the Dominican Republic to the United States of America. Athens, GA: The University of Georgia.
Sagas, Ernesto e Inoa, Orlando (2003). *The Dominican People: A Documentary History*. Princeton, NJ: Markus Wiener Publishers.
United Nations Development Program (UNDP) (2008). Report on Human Development in the Dominican Republic (2008). Santo Domingo, DR.

8
Ecuador

Luis Valencia Rodríguez

The Republic of Ecuador is situated in the northwestern part of South America, bordering the Pacific Ocean to the west, Colombia to the north and Peru to the east and south. Its total area is 256,370 square kilometers with the following borders: Colombia, 590 kilometers; Peru, 1420 kilometers; and the coastline, 2237 kilometers (see Figure 8.1).

The country is divided into three continental regions: the Coast (Costa), Highlands (Sierra) and the Amazon Jungle (Oriente) – as well as an insular region – the Galapagos Islands. Costa, located between the Pacific Ocean and the Andes mountains, consists of coastal lowlands and small mountains. Sierra is composed of two major chains of the Andes mountains, the Cordillera Occidental (Western Chain) and the Cordillera Oriental (Eastern Chain), and the intermountain basins or plateaus between the two chains. The Cordillera Occidental contains Ecuador's highest peak, Mount Chimborazo (6,268 meters), which is considered t the most distant point from the center of the Earth, given the oblate shape of the planet (wider at the equator). Mount Cotopaxi, in the Andes, is the highest active volcano in the world. The German explorer Alexander von Humboldt aptly dubbed this chain of mountains the Avenue of the Volcanos, for along it range most of Ecuador's 51 volcanic peaks, 21 of which are presently active. Many wear snowy crowns all year round.

Oriente (the eastern region) consists of Andean piedmont, eastern lowlands, and flat to rolling tropical jungle. The archipelago of the Galapagos is made up of islands of varied sizes located 1,000 kilometers west of the Ecuadorian coast. The Costa's climate is tropical, although variations in temperature and rainfall result from its proximity to warm and cool ocean currents (e.g. the Humboldt Current). The Sierra's climate ranges from tropical (in the lowlands and valleys) to freezing,

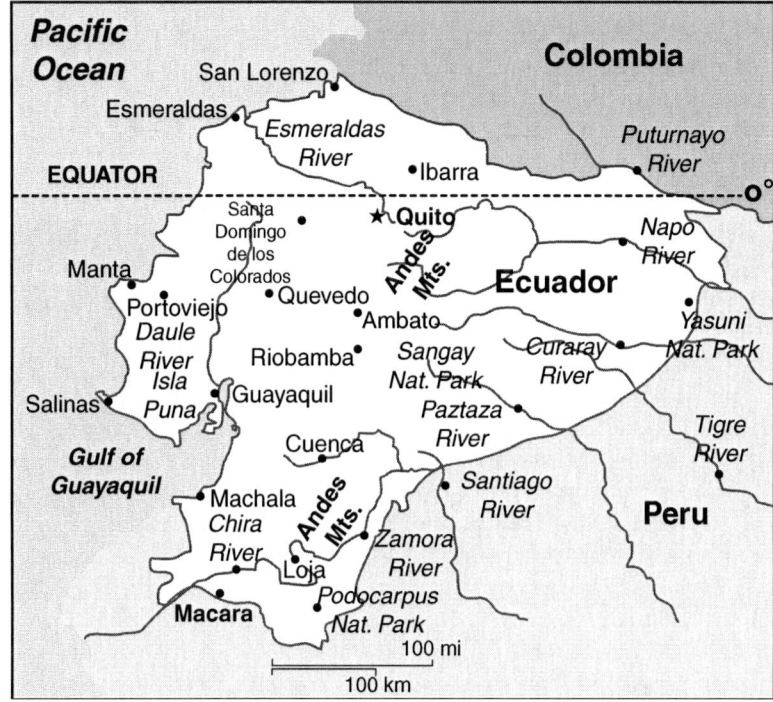

Figure 8.1 Map of Ecuador

depending on altitude. Notable rainfall variations also occur. Tropical climate and abundant rainfall prevail in the Oriente. The Galapagos' climate varies from tropical and desert-like at sea level to cool and wet at the highest point. Administratively, Ecuador is divided into 24 provinces with Quito as its capital.

Biodiversity

Despite its small territory Ecuador is one of 17 mega-diverse countries in the world according to the World Conservation Monitoring Centre. It has recorded 1600 bird species (15 percent of the world's known bird species) in the continental area, and 38 more endemic species in the Galapagos. In addition to 25,000 species of plants, the country has 106 endemic reptiles, 138 endemic amphibians, and 6,000 species of butterfly. The country presents an extraordinary biodiversity per square meter and a great concentration of rivers. The Galapagos Islands are well known as a region of distinct fauna, famous as inspiration for

Darwin's Theory of Evolution, and a Unesco World Heritage Site (1979 declaration). Despite being on the Unesco list, the Galapagos Islands at present are endangered by a range of negative environmental effects, threatening the existence of this exotic ecosystem.

The people

Ecuador's total population is 13,940,000 (March 2009; www.inec.gov. ec), giving a ratio of 54.3 people per square kilometer. The population growth rate is 2.1 percent (1990–2001). Life expectancy is 75 years. The infant mortality rate is 18.2 per 1,000 births (2006 estimate; www.siise. gov.ec).[1] The nominal GDP in 2008 was US$54,685 million (US$3,920 per capita).[2]

The population is ethnically mixed. The largest groups are indigenous, at around 25 percent,[3] and mestizos or cholos (persons of mixed Spanish and Indian ancestry) at 55 percent. Caucasian and others represent 10 percent of the population, and Africans[4] comprise the remaining 10 percent. Ecuador is a plurinational and multicultural state. In addition to the small number of whites, blacks, and Afro-Ecuadorians and the large numbers of mestizos, many Ecuadorians belong to indigenous nationalities, principally Achuar, Awá, Chachi, Cofán, Epera, Huaorani, Manta, and Quichua. The 2008 Constitution recognizes the right of people living in voluntary isolation to retain their ancestral territories and protects their right to self-determination.

Although Ecuadorians were heavily concentrated in the mountainous central highland region a few decades ago, today's population is divided almost equally between that area and the coastal lowlands. Migration toward cities – particularly larger cities – in all regions has increased the urban population to about 65 percent.[5] The Amazon tropical forest region to the east of the mountains remains sparsely populated and contains only about 3 percent of the population. Quito has 2,093,458 inhabitants and Guayaquil, the main port, 2,252,727 (2008 estimates).

The workforce is 4.4 million,[6] of which agriculture represents 42 percent; trade, 20 percent; services, 19 percent; manufacturing, 11 percent; and other, 8 percent. The main industries are petroleum, food processing, textiles, metalwork, paper products, wood products, chemicals, plastics, fishing, flowers, and lumber

The predominant religion is Roman Catholicism (95 percent), but religious freedom is recognized and other religions are practiced peacefully. In the rural parts of the country, indigenous beliefs and Catholicism are sometimes syncretized. Spanish is the official language. Quichua and shuar are official languages of inter-cultural relations. Other indigenous languages are recognized for official use by the corresponding indigenous peoples in the regions where they live.

The 2008 Constitution states that social policy should be directed primarily toward the poor in order to reduce the high percentage of Ecuadorians in poverty and to correct growing social inequalities. The public education system is fee-free including up to university, and attendance is mandatory from ages 6 to 14. In practice, however, many children drop out before age 15, and in rural areas only about one-third complete sixth grade.

Ecuador has 73 universities,[7] many of which offer graduate degrees. About 300 higher institutes offer two or three years of post-secondary vocational or technical training. In recent years, however, large increases in the student population, budget difficulties, and extreme politicization of the university system have led to a decline in academic standards.

The society and the environment

Spanish social structures and values took hold completely in the sixteenth century in the Sierra. Not by coincidence, the Sierra was also the Ecuadorian region where the Inca conquerors had been most successful 50 years earlier. Spanish officials adapted the prevailing Inca hierarchical social system and established a tripartite, semi-feudal structure consisting of small numbers of white elites (both peninsulares, Spanish-born persons residing in the New World, and criollos, persons of pure Spanish descent born in the New World), a somewhat larger group of mestizo artisans, and a large Indian underclass. Since Ecuador lacked the mineral riches found in other Spanish colonies, such as Peru and Mexico, land became the critical commodity. Through the encomienda system, elites received tracts of Sierra land along with the right to extract labor from Indians living on that land. Colonists also adapted the Inca concept of obligatory public service (mita) and required Indians to toil in textile sweatshops scattered through the highlands. Debts incurred through the Spanish mita often transformed what was supposed to be a transitory labor obligation into a peonage system transmitted across generations.

The Sierra, the region of earliest European settlement, was ruled for most of its history by a narrow rural oligarchy whose power base lay in the sizeable haciendas they controlled. The haciendas dominated both social and economic relations. Most of the population depended to a greater or lesser extent on the largesse of the white elite who controlled the land. This elite ruled virtually without challenge until the mid-twentieth century. Between this white elite and the mass of Sierra Indians were the mestizos or cholos. In values and identity, they were closer to the dominant whites. The Sierra Indians, at the bottom of the social pyramid, had limited opportunities for economic security and advancement. Both mestizos and whites regarded Indians as immutably inferior. The latter's only hope for improvement lay in assimilating the norms and values of the dominant ethnic groups, thereby changing their ethnic affiliation.

Like the hacendados of the Sierra, the elite of the Costa (coastal region) also had their roots in agriculture and the control of land, but their attention focused primarily on export crop production and commerce. Ethnically more diverse than the Hispanic elite of the Sierra, the Costa's upper class included successful immigrant families drawn over the years by the region's expanding economy. Most of Ecuador's blacks, the descendants of the small numbers of African slaves who came to work on the region's plantations, were also costeños (residents of the Costa).

The successful struggle for independence in the 1820s resulted in the transfer of power from peninsulares to criollos. It did little, however, to change other aspects of the social system, which by then had become dominated by haciendas with a resident Indian labor force. These Indian residents, known as huasipungueros, typically worked the hacienda fields for four days per week in exchange for the right to own a small plot of land (minifundio). The huasipungo system survived in isolated pockets of the Sierra until it was finally abolished by the 1964 Agrarian Reform Law. The state, according to the 2008 Constitution, is charged with promoting distributive policies allowing peasants access to land, water, and other productive resources.

The twentieth century saw the rise of an Ecuadorian middle class whose interests were genuinely distinct from the narrowly based rural oligarchy, and the demise of the self-contained, autonomous hacienda. Changes in the hacienda economy created a mobile, rural-based labor force, and by the end of the 1980s, society consisted of a small, privileged elite; a more numerous, diverse, and politically active middle class; and the mass of impoverished small-scale peasants, artisans, and wage earners. The middle class transformed Ecuadorian politics.

Like many other Latin American nations, Ecuador had enacted agrarian reform legislation in the 1960s and 1970s. These laws brought little substantive improvement in the lives of most peasants. In the early 1980s, only 5 percent of all farms exceeded 50 hectares, yet these same farms represented over 55 percent of land under cultivation. By contrast, 80 percent of all farms encompassed fewer than ten hectares and accounted for only 15 percent of farmland.

The Oriente was traditionally a neglected backwater, isolated geographically and culturally from the rest of the nation. Its population was limited to dispersed groups of indigenous tropical forest Indians who lived by slash-and-burn agriculture or by hunting and gathering. European intrusion was limited to the occasional missionary or trader. From the 1960s, however, the Oriente experienced colonization by land-poor peasants from the Sierra and exploration by oil companies. Both colonization and exploration have had a devastating impact on the indigenous population.

The migration process

Reflecting the economic crisis, unemployment in 1999 was at one of the highest levels ever in the country: 15.1 percent. Due to the acute banking crisis, many people lost their jobs. The rate of unemployed men increased from 7 percent in 1997 to 11 percent, while that of unemployed women increased from 13 to 20 percent. In 1999, poverty was 1.6 times higher than in 1995. The number of people living below the poverty line increased from 34 percent in 1995 to 46 percent in 1998 and to 56 percent in 1999. Extreme poverty also increased; from 1995 to 1999, it rose from 12 to 21 percent. Poverty was more acute in the countryside than in the cities. The Costa was most affected by this situation: its poverty level increased from 29 percent in 1995 to 56 percent in 1999. At the beginning, men were the principal flow of migrants, but later both men and women were looking abroad for work and subsistence.

The consequence of this situation was a massive migration of Ecuadorians, either legally or illegally. This migration produced serious socioeconomic consequences. According to the National Institute of Statistics and Census, the number of Ecuadorians who have migrated reached 1,571,450 people in 2007, while other calculations estimate two million.

Spain and the United States are clearly the principal countries of attraction. It has been estimated that approximately one million Ecuadorians are now residing in the United States. One may conclude that the rest are present under illegal conditions. The countries of Central America are used by migrants as a bridge to reach the "American dream". Most of them have to withstand very difficult and dangerous conditions in their journey to the USA, and if they succed in their attempt they will also have to face hardships in the host country before eventually being repatriated (sent back to Ecuador).

Migrants, especially those of low educational level, are often victims of traffickers who exploit them not only in Ecuador but also in other transit countries. As a consequence of the agreement of May 29, 2001, approximately 25,000 Ecuadorians residing illegally in Spain were legalized. The main purpose of the agreement is to select Ecuadorians to work legally in Spain and in this way to regularize the migration movement from Ecuador so Ecuadorian workers can enjoy the same rights as Spanish workers. Efforts continue to be made by the governments of Ecuador and Spain to regularize this situation.

To confront the problem created by migration, the Ecuadorian government has established a special high administrative body at ministerial level, the National Secretariat for the Migrant, which is in charge of giving advice and assistance to prospective migrants, monitoring compliance with international agreements on migratory problems, and combating the illegal traffic in migrants. At the Foreign Ministry there is also a body charged especially with coordinating these efforts at the international level. The government has also established a National Plan for Ecuadorians Abroad, the main purpose of which is to protect migrants residing abroad and to assist their families in Ecuador.

Conscious of violations of human rights against Ecuadorians abroad, the government has undertaken a process of providing information on the human rights of migrant people in order that all Ecuadorians are duly informed of their rights in the country and abroad. One important chapter of this national plan is the promotion among migrants of a return to Ecuador, which includes three aspects: (1) a voluntary decision by the migrant to return when he or she is abroad more than one year, (2) respect for human rights and development of personal initiatives to facilitate his or her readaptation, and (3) generation of the on-going development of returning migrants.

The Ecuadorian economy has been a great beneficiary of the remittances made by migrant workers. In 2007 they reached US$ 3 billion, but declined systematically in 2008 and 2009 due to the effect of the international economic crisis, particularly in the United States and Spain. As a result in 2009 they only amounted to US$ 2,5 billion. Figures of the first half of 2010 show a further contraction of 5 percent with respect to the same period of the previous year.

Ecuador is also a receiving country for migrants. As a consequence of the long subversive conflict in Colombia, Ecuador has received almost 500,000 Colombians as displaced persons or asylum seekers. Most of these persons are living near the border. Some of them have been regularized but others are still illegal. The Office of the High Commissioner of the United Nations for Refugees is helping the government of Ecuador to look for solutions to this problem. In the southern part of the country there is also a large number of Peruvians – around 200,000 persons – who have entered Ecuador, attracted by the dollarization process. This migration is mainly seasonal. Ecuador and Peru have come to an understanding to regularize the presence of these migrants.

History

Advanced indigenous cultures flourished in Ecuador long before the area was conquered by the Inca Empire in the fifteenth century. The most ancient artifacts – remnants of the Valdivia and Machalilla cultures found in the coastal region – date from as early as 3500 BC By 3,200 BC three distinct agricultural-based cultures had emerged, producing some of the hemisphere's oldest known pottery. Other archaeological sites in the Sierra date from 2,000 years ago. The Inca expansion met with fierce resistance by several Ecuadorian tribes. In 1463 the region became part of the Inca Empire. The influence of these conquerors based in Cuzco (modern-day Peru) was limited to about a half century, and even less in some parts of Ecuador. The invading Incas recognized the technological advancement of the people they were conquering.

In 1534, the Spanish arrived and defeated the Inca armies. The indigenous population was decimated by the Spanish forces and by diseases in the first decades of the new rule – a time when the natives also were forced into the encomienda, the labor system for the Spanish landlords. In 1563, Quito became the seat of a royal audiencia (administrative district) of Spain. The legacy of three centuries of Spanish colonial rule is also pervasive and includes a social inequality that largely coincides with race, rural land tenure patterns, and the nation's dominant European cultural expressions.

After nearly 300 years of Spanish colonization, Quito was a city of some 10,000 inhabitants. It was there, on August 10, 1809 (the national holiday) that the first call for independence from Spain was made in Latin America ("Primer Grito de la Independencia"), under the leadership of the local criollos. Quito's nickname "Luz de América" ("Light of America") comes from the idea that this first attempt produced the inspiration for the rest of Spanish America.

After independence forces defeated the royalist army in 1822 at the Battle of Pichincha (in front of the city of Quito), Ecuador joined Simón Bolívar's Republic of Gran Colombia, only to become a separate republic in 1830. The first president of Ecuador was the Venezuelan-born Juan

José Flores. Independence did little, however, to change other aspects of the social system, which by then had become dominated by haciendas. The nineteenth century was marked by instability, with a rapid succession of rulers. The conservative Gabriel Garcia Moreno unified the country in the 1860s with the support of the Catholic church and with the fierce imposition of his will in all the domains of the public and even private life of Ecuadorians. In the late 1800s, world demand for cocoa tied the economy to commodity exports and led to migrations from the highland to the agricultural frontier on the coast.

A coastal-based liberal revolution in 1895 under Eloy Alfaro reduced the power of the clergy and opened the way for substantial reforms of the state especially in the political and economic fields. The end of the cocoa boom produced renewed political instability and a military coup in 1925, which resulted in important reforms in political and social life. The 1930s and 1940s were marked by populist politicians such as five-time president, Jose M. Velasco Ibarra. After the Second World War, a recovery in the market for agricultural commodities and the growth of the banana industry helped restore prosperity and political peace. From 1948–1960, three presidents – beginning with Galo Plaza – were freely elected and completed their terms.

Recession and popular unrest led to a return to populist and domestic military interventions in the 1960s, while foreign companies developed oil resources in the Ecuadorian Amazon.

In 1972, a nationalist military regime seized power and used the new oil wealth and foreign borrowing to pay for a program of industrialization, land reform, and subsidies for urban consumers. With the oil boom fading, Ecuador returned to democracy in 1979, but by 1982 the government faced a chronic economic crisis, including inflation, budget deficits, a falling currency, mounting debt servicing, and uncompetitive industries. On three occasions in the twentieth century – 1925, 1963, and 1972 – the military seized direct political control. The last period of military rule was 1972–1979. Although one of the motivations for intervention was to prevent civilian politicians from dissipating the new-found petroleum wealth, the military's principal legacy was that of ever-increasing foreign debt obligations. On April 29, 1979, under a new constitution, Jaime Roldós-Aguilera was the first constitutionally elected president after nearly a decade of civilian and military dictatorships.

In 1984 Leon Febres-Cordero of the Social Christian Party (PSC) won the presidential election. In the first years of his administration, Febres-Cordero introduced free market economic policies and took a strong stand against drug trafficking and terrorism. Rodrigo Borja of the Democratic Left (ID) party won the presidency in 1988. His government was committed to improving human rights protection and carried out some reforms, notably the opening of Ecuador to foreign trade. The Borja government concluded an accord leading to the disbanding of the small revolutionary group "Alfaro Live", whose declared objectives were to promote better living conditions for the impoverished masses.

In 1992, Sixto Duran-Ballen, a rightist politician, won the presidency and his government's popularity suffered from tough macroeconomic measures, but it succeeded in pushing a limited number of modernization initiatives through Congress. A war with Peru erupted in January 1995 in a small region where the boundary prescribed by the 1942 Rio Protocol was in dispute.

Abdala Bucaram, a populist politician from the Guayaquil-based Ecuadorian Roldosista Party (PRE), won the presidency in 1996 on a platform that promised populist economic and social reforms and the breaking of what Bucaram termed the power of the nation's oligarchy. During his short term in office, Bucaram's administration drew criticism for corruption. Bucaram was deposed by Congress in February 1997 on grounds of alleged mental incompetence. In his place, Congress named interim President Fabian Alarcon.

In 1998, Jamil Mahuad of the Popular Democrat Party (center-left) took office as president. On the same day, Ecuador's new constitution came into effect. Mahuad concluded a general peace agreement with Peru in October 1998, but increasing economic, fiscal, and financial difficulties drove his popularity steadily lower. To avoid a banking collapse, large amounts of public funds were transferred to certain private banks as an emergency measure but with no positive results. President Mahuad then resorted to an unpopular measure to try to stop the transfer of funds abroad, freezing bank deposits for one year, which was later prolonged to three years.

During a night of confusion and negotiations President Mahuad was obliged to flee the presidential palace for his own safety. Vice-President Gustavo Noboa took charge. Congress met in emergency session in Guayaquil on January 22 and ratified Noboa as president of the republic in constitutional succession to Mahuad. Noboa implemented the dollarization of the economy that Mahuad had announced just days before his fall, and obtained congressional authorization for the construction of Ecuador's second major oil pipeline.

On January 15, 2003, Noboa turned the government over to his successor, Lucio Gutierrez, a former army colonel who first came to public attention as a member of the short-lived "junta" of January 21, 2000. Gutierrez's campaign featured an anticorruption and leftist, populist platform. However, Gutierrez adopted relatively conservative fiscal policies and defensive tactics, including replacing the Supreme Court and declaring a state of emergency in the capital to combat mounting opposition. The situation came to a head on April 20, 2005, when political opponents and popular uprisings in Quito prompted Congress to strip Gutierrez of the presidency for allegedly "abandoning the post". When the military withdrew its support Gutierrez went into temporary self-exile. Congress declared Vice-President Alfredo Palacio the new president. A semblance of stability returned, but the Palacio administration failed to achieve the major reforms that the Ecuadorian people were expecting.

In presidential elections on October 15, 2006, Rafael Correa, Palacio's former Finance Minister, running on an antiestablishment reform platform in line with the so-called "Socialism of the 21st Century" won the presidency. Correa's Proud and Sovereign Fatherland Alliance movement did not field any congressional candidates. Traditional parties saw their congressional representation cut in half. Correa was sworn in as president on January 15, 2007, and one of his first programs of government was to convene a constitutional assembly to prepare a new constitution. In March 2007, 57 members of Congress were dismissed on the grounds that they had violated campaign and electoral laws. Following that, the Congress was largely deadlocked. Correa, taking advantage of this situation, insisted on his political proposals to introduce substantive changes in the political structure of the country. The constitutional assembly was inaugurated on November 29, 2007, and on July 29, 2008, adopted the text of the new constitution, which was later approved by the people in a referendum on September 28, 2008.

As contemplated by the new constitution, new general elections took place, with the results that Correa was reelected for a new term (2009–2013).

Government

As a consequence of constant political instability, Ecuador has had 20 constitutions since the establishment of the republic in 1830. The current one is derived from the constitutional assembly gathered at the end of 2007. The major objectives that guided the work of the assembly were: (1) political reform aimed at resolving the governance problems of the democratic system; (2) economic reform directed toward the creation of institutions capable of responding to a new international environment and to the need for national development; (3) enlargement of the scope of human rights, making them enforceable by the judiciary; (4) assurance of effective control of civil society by the administration; (5) maintenance and strengthening of the powers of the executive branch.

Ecuador is a social, democratic, multicultural, plurinational, and unitary state with a republican, presidential, elected, responsible, and representative government. The constitution provides for concurrent four-year terms of office for the president, vice-president and members of Congress. The president and vice-president may be reelected only once, and legislators may also be reelected to a consecutive or later mandate only once. Suffrage is universal, and obligatory for literate citizens of 18–65 years of age and optional for other eligible voters. Military personnel on active duty may vote, as well as people between 16 and 18 years of age and Ecuadorians residing abroad. Foreigners residing in Ecuador for five years or more also have the right to vote.

The principle of "legislative co-participation" allows the president to share in the development of laws as well as in their execution and application. The Unicameral National Assembly (Congress) (124 seats; 15 members are popularly elected at large nationally, 103 members are elected by province, and six are elected by Ecuadorians residing abroad). Judges of the National Court of Justice are appointed by the Judiciary Council for a term of nine years with no possibility of reelection. The Constitution prescribes the independence of the judiciary and prohibits any other arm of the state to interfere in the exercise of judicial tribunals and judges.

Political conditions

Ecuador's political parties have historically been small, loose organizations that depended more on populist, often charismatic, leaders to retain support than on programs or ideology. Frequent internal splits have produced extreme factionalism. Persistent regional rivalries between Quito and Guayaquil (Sierra and Costa) have also contributed to the organization of administrations from the center-left which alternate with those from the center-right.

The new constitution strengthens the executive branch by eliminating mid-term congressional elections. However, Congress has the power to challenge cabinet ministers and eventually dismiss them from public office. It also empowers the president to dismiss the National Assembly (Congress) if it assumes powers not provided for in the Constitution or obstructs the National Development Plan. This presidential right can be exercised only once during the first three years of his mandate. The National Assembly is also empowered to dismiss the president when he has assumed powers not provided for in the Constitution or in case of severe political crisis or internal disorder. Similarly, this power can be exercised only once during the first three years of the Assembly's mandate. In both cases, the president and members of the Assembly finish their mandates and new elections take place. Party discipline is traditionally weak, and many deputies routinely switch allegiance during each term of Congress.

Beginning with the 1996 election, the indigenous population abandoned its traditional policy of shunning the official political system and participated actively, and it has established itself as a significant force in Ecuadorian politics, as shown by the selection of indigenous representatives to Congress. One of those who led the indigenous political party, Pachakutic, was second vice-president of the 1988 Congress.

Perhaps the most consistent element of Ecuador's republican history has been its political instability. Over a period of some 35 years (1925–1948 and 1996–2007), there have been no fewer than 80 changes of government, making for an average of less than two years in power for each regime. The long periods of civilian constitutional rule were from 1912 to 1925, from 1948 to 1961, and the longest, from 1979 to the present.

Combating corruption

Corruption constitutes an obstacle to the progress of Ecuador. It increases the cost of goods purchased and of public works, drives away investment, weighs negatively on the national budget, and causes serious damage to the national economy. The first signs of corruption, public and private, were present with the discovery of petroleum and the ensuing increasing indebtedness.

Ecuador has been regarded as one of the most corrupt countries in the world. According to Transparency International[8] it ranks 151st of 180 countries (2008). Only Venezuela and Haiti have a worse position in Latin America. This has led to the inclusion of severe measures in the text of the Constitution text to prevent, fight, and punish corrupt acts. Incompatibilities were established between economic interests and the performance of public functions, and authorities (including the police and the military) were required to present sworn declarations of their material possessions before taking public posts and upon concluding their functions. Furthermore, according to the 2008 Constitution, a new state organ, considered to be the fifth power of the state, the Council of Citizens' Participation, and Social Control, – autonomous and politically and economically independent – has, among other duties, that of investigating complaints about illicit acts or omissions committed by state institutions or officials. The council is in charge of submitting reports on its findings and determining responsibility for these situations and, if the complaints are well founded, transmits the reports to the courts. There are many cases under consideration by the judiciary, among them some involving high-ranking officials. The national courts, under the authority of previous legal provisions, have already pronounced some sentences on these matters.

Combating terrorism

Ecuador has always taken measures to combat terrorism both internally and internationally and has energetically condemned terrorist activities, whether directed against government officials or private citizens. Ecuador is a party to 12 out of the 13 international conventions adopted by the General Assembly of the United Nations on these matters.

It also has signed the Inter-American Convention against Terrorism of 2002. According to the Constitution, international instruments ratified by the country have the same level of enforcement as domestic laws. In 2005, Ecuador enacted the law to punish money laundering, which is frequently associated with terrorism. It established the National Council against Money Laundering and the Unit of Financial Intelligence, and counts on a permanent inter-institutional working group in charge of monitoring the application of these measures and suggesting new actions.

As a consequence of the terrorist attacks of September 11, 2001, in the United States, Ecuador has reinforced measures in the administrative, police, and military spheres to control any vestiges of terrorist activities, especially at its land, maritime, and aerial borders. It has increased its cooperation with other governments and international organizations (in particular the UN Security Council and the Organization of American States) to exchange information in order to combat terrorism or prepare new instruments for that purpose.

Foreign relations

Ecuador has always placed great emphasis on multilateral approaches to international problems. It is a charter member of the United Nations (and most of its specialized agencies) and a founder member of the

Organization of American States (OAS). It also is an associate of the Nonaligned Movement, G-77 and many regional groups, including the Rio Group, the Latin American Economic System, the Latin American Energy Organization, the Organization of Petroleum Exporting Countries (OPEC), the Latin American Integration Association, and the Andean Pact (Andean Community).

Ecuador's border dispute with Peru, festering since the independence era, was the nation's principal foreign policy issue up to 1998. For more than 50 years, Ecuador maintained that the 1942 Rio Protocol of Peace, Friendship and Boundaries, signed after a short war that meant a substantial loss of territory, left several issues unresolved. For example, it asserted that geographical features in the area of the Cenepa River valley did not match topographical descriptions in the protocol, thus making demarcation of the boundary there "in-executable". The long-running border dispute occasionally erupted into armed hostilities along the un-demarcated sections. The most serious conflict since the 1941 war occurred in January–February 1995, when thousands of soldiers from both sides fought an intense but localized war in the disputed territory in the upper Cenepa valley. A peace agreement brokered by the four guarantors of the Rio Protocol (Argentina, Brazil, Chile, and the United States) in February 1995 led to the cessation of hostilities. On April 15, 1997, Ecuador and Peru began a series of substantive negotiations in Brasilia, Brazil, to resolve the dispute.

Those talks were successful and provided a framework for resolving the major outstanding issues between the two countries through four commissions. The commissions prepared the Treaty of Trade and Navigation and the Comprehensive Agreement on Border Integration, to set the common land boundary and established the Bi-national Commission on Mutual Confidence Measures and Security.

The commission on border demarcation failed to produce an agreement by the May 30, 1998, deadline. Presidents Mahuad (Ecuador) and Fujimori (Peru) established direct communication through meetings and phone calls in an effort to overcome the two countries' remaining differences. In October 1998, after asking for and receiving a boundary determination from the guarantors (Argentina, Chile, Brazil, and the United States), the two presidents reached agreement. On October 26, 1998, at a ceremony in Brasilia, the presidents of Ecuador and Peru and their foreign ministers signed a comprehensive settlement.

According to this agreement, Ecuador obtained from Peru two sites at the far limits of the Amazon River to become navigation and trade centers. Peru also ceded to Ecuador, as a private property, a parcel of land of one square kilometer in the Cenepa Valley known as "Tiwinza." After the first ten years of enforcement of the treaty (1998–2008), the peace agreement has marked important results: (1) Ecuador has invested around US$1,620 million in development projects in the frontier zone, producing substantial benefits to 500,000 inhabitants of the region; (2) while the trade between the two countries in 1988 was nearly US$300 million, it increased to around US$2,200 million in 2008; (3) five bilateral land axes will establish an interconnection of routes of nearly 2,176 kilometers and Ecuador will allocate US$315 million in the next two years for the construction of these routes; (4) the humanitarian removal of land mines in the frontier zone is an important task in which both governments are involved and for which international support is essential – Ecuadorian troops have destroyed 4,775 land mines adding 122,000 square meters into the safe areas.

While relations with Peru have improved since the peace agreement, those with Colombia have deteriorated. On March 1, 2008, the Colombian air force fired bombs into a camp of the narco-trafficking Revolutionary Armed Forces of Colombia (FARC) 1.8 kilometers inside the border in a difficult jungle area of Ecuador known as Angostura. The target of the attack was long-time FARC leader – second in command – Raúl Reyes (nom de guerre for Luis Edgar Devia Silva), who was killed along with 24 others (including four Mexicans and an Ecuadorian). Colombia and other governments consider FARC a terrorist group. Ecuador considers FARC a revolutionary insurgent group.

Nine hours after the strike, President Alvaro Uribe of Colombia called to inform President Rafael Correa, who was caught totally unaware of the situation and even of the camp's existence. Indeed the attack had been prepared. Colombia was able to fix the location of Reyes at the camp, which had been in existence for at least three months without the knowledge of Ecuadorian authorities.

The reaction of President Correa was firm. He accused Colombia of violating Ecuador's territorial sovereignty and on March 3 broke off diplomatic relations. On March 5, the Permanent Council of the OAS considered the situation and established a fact-finding commission headed by the Secretary-General of the organization, to visit both countries and the site of the attack, and present a report with recommendations for a settlement. On March 8, the Summit of the Group of Rio meeting in the Dominican Republic unanimously "rejected" the violation of the Ecuadorian territorial integrity. President Uribe apologized for the attack. On March 17, the Consultative Meeting of American Foreign Ministers considered the report of the fact-finding commission, reaffirmed the declaration of the Summit of the Group of Rio, reiterated the principles of international law inscribed in the Charter of the OAS, and "rejected" the attack by military forces of Colombia on Ecuadorian territory.

In compliance with the resolutions of the OAS, the Secretary-General and other high-ranking personalities have endeavored to settle this situation and to restore diplomatic relations between the two countries. However, public statements made by Presidents Correa and Uribe and other high officials of both countries have not contributed to creating the appropriate political climate to achieved positive results and solve this difficult problem. For the reestablishment of diplomatic relations, President Correa has requested, among other things, that Colombia should: (1) stop the campaign to implicate Ecuador in connection with FARC, on the basis also of the recent statement made by the OAS Secretary-General that the Ecuadorian government is free of these connections (February 28, 2008); (2) maintain regular and efficient military vigilance of its frontier; (3) provide all information used by the Colombian military units for the attack of March 1, 2008, including the information from the computers supposed to belong to FARC leader Raúl Reyes and found in the camp at Angostura; (4) compensate the Colombian refugees and displaced persons, including Ecuadorians who have been forced to abandon their homes given the danger to their lives; and (5) compensate Ecuador for the attack of March 1 and all the consequences it has engendered.

At present, following a decision by the two presidents, the Ministers for Foreign Affairs of Ecuador and Colombia are maintaining conversations in order to restore diplomatic relations. They announced that during October 2009, chargés d'affaires in Quito and Bogotá would be appointed as the first step toward the full diplomatic relations. The Secretary General of OAS and the Carter Center are participating in facilitating these efforts.

Union of South American Nations (UNASUR)

The UNASUR Constitutive Treaty was signed on May 23, 2008, at the Third Summit of Heads of State, held in Brasilia, Brazil. It is an intergovernmental union integrating two existing integration systems: Mercosur and the Andean Community, as part of the continuing process of South American integration. The leaders announced their intention to model the new community on the European Union. According to the Constitutive Treaty, the Union's headquarters will be located in Quito, Ecuador. The participating states are: (1) members of the Andean Community of Nations (CAN) – Bolivia, Colombia, Ecuador, and Peru; (2) members of Mercosur – Argentina, Brazil, Paraguay, and Uruguay; and (3) other countries – Chile, Guyana, Suriname, and Venezuela.

At the moment the main structure of the UNASUR is as follows:

- The presidents of all the member nations have an annual meeting, which will be the highest political mandate. At the meeting of May 23, 2008, the president of Chile, Michelle Bachelet, was appointed president pro tempore (one year). The presidency will rotate among the member countries. At the meeting of August 10, 2009, the president of Ecuador succeeded to the presidency.
- The ministers of foreign affairs of each country will meet once every six months. They will formulate concrete proposals for action and executive decision.
- A secretary-general will be elected by the presidents of the member states. He or she is the top administrative official. The permanent secretariat will be in Quito.
- Sectorial ministers' meetings will be called by the presidents. The meetings will be developed according to Mercosur and CAN's mechanisms.
- On March 10, 2009, the ministers of defense of the 12 participating states met in Santiago (Chile) and established the UNASUR Defense Council, the main function of which will be to promote cooperation among the armed forces of the member states, and generate joint peace operations and transparency of military expenditures. Its decisions will be made by consensus. The presidency of the Council will be exercised by the president of UNASUR.

UNASUR foresees many important objectives. There is an Initiative for Infrastructure Integration of South America (IIRSA) underway, and this has received the support of the Inter-American Development Bank and the Andean Development Corporation. UNASUR has also plans for integration through infrastructure cooperation with the construction of the Interoceanic Highway, a road that it is intended will more firmly link the Pacific coast with Brazil and Argentina by extending highways across the continent.

Control of illegal drugs and related offenses

While Ecuador is not a drug producer, it is a significant transit country for cocaine and derivatives of coca originating in Colombia and Peru. Because of its geographic location between two major drug-producing countries in the Andean region, Ecuador has been an invaluable partner to other states in the fight against drug trafficking. Ecuador was one of the first Latin American countries to ratify the 1988 UN Convention Against Illicit Traffic in Narcotics and Psychotropic Substances. It has also implemented comprehensive antidrug legislation based on the UN convention. However, as a result of the implementation of the Colombia Plan, the northern Ecuadorian frontier is a vulnerable territory where Colombian traffickers have found refuge and assistance. This section of the Ecuadorian territory is economically depressed.

The original Andean Trade Preference Act (ATPA) in 1991 and its extension in August 2002 as the ATPDEA to Bolivia, Colombia, Ecuador, and Peru strengthened trade relations between the Andean countries and the United States. The first act granted preferential access to the US market for 5,600 products over a ten-year period, in order to promote exports from beneficiary countries and provide them with better trade alternatives for coping with illegal drug trafficking. In this way, drug crops were eradicated through movement to other crops or industrial sectors, which, in turn, had a positive social and economic impact on a population which is particularly vulnerable to drug trafficking and production.

The Andean Trade Promotion and Drug Eradication Act (ATPDEA), grants benefits to almost 700 additional products, such as apparel, petroleum and derivatives, tuna, footwear, and leather apparel. The ATPDEA expired at the end of 2006 but has since been renewed for short periods of time.

The ATPDEA has also been positive for Ecuador exports. Since this act was enacted, US exports to Ecuador have grown 30 percent and over 100 percent since the implementation of the Andean Trade Preference Act in 1991. Ecuador is also the primary exporter to the US under ATPDEA.

Economy

The Ecuadorian economy is still highly dependent on its petroleum resources, which accounted for about half of the country's export earnings during the period 2002–2008, reaching 57 percent in 2008[9] due to the very high international oil price that peaked around mid-2008. Oil export revenues are also particularly important in financing the public budget, accounting for nearly 25 percent of total revenues (2002–2007). The oil contribution to the public budget peaked in 2008 when it represented more than 40 percent.

This dependency on oil exports makes Ecuador's economic growth volatile in correspondence to the oil price. In 1999, after a widespread financial, fiscal, and external crisis, in which the country had to default on its public external debt, the economy shrank 6.3 percent in real terms. This crisis also led to the abandonment of its national currency for the US dollar. Since then, the economy has been growing continuously at an average real annual rate of 4.6 percent (2000–2008). GDP growth in 2008 reached a relative high rate of 6.52 percent according to the Central Bank of Ecuador, thus more than doubling the 2007 figure.

Ecuador is a relatively open economy: exports and imports of goods in 2008 reached the equivalent of 68.7 percent of its GDP. Total exports in 2008 added US$18.5 billion. Three-quarters of exports are concentrated in primary products: crude oil US$10.5 billion, bananas US$1.7 billion, seafood US$850 million, fresh flowers US$565 million, and cacao US$200 million. The main industrial exports are: refined oil products US$1.1 billion, processed tuna US$825 million, metal manufactures[10] US$726 million, and other products such as medicines, textiles, panama hats, etc. The United States (45 percent), the Andean Community, including Venezuela (17 percent), the EU (11 percent), and Chile (8 percent) are the main markets for Ecuador's exports (2008 figures).

Imports were worth US$17.6 billion in 2008. About 33 percent of all imports are made up of raw materials and intermediate goods; 26 percent are capital goods, and nearly 20 percent are fuels. Only one fifth of all imports are consumer goods (durables and non durables) which stresses the importance of a high level of imports to stimulate the economy.

The main origins of Ecuadorian imports are the United States 19 percent, the Andean Community 27 percent, Mercosur 9 percent, the EU 9 percent, and Asia – China, Japan, Korea –22 percent.

Both exports and imports have been growing very rapidly since 2000 and therein lies a structural weakness in the Ecuadorian economy. Even though the total trade balance has been positive in the past few years, this has been due to the growing oil export revenues as oil prices boomed. The non-oil trade balance is highly negative and declining at an alarming speed. In the period 2006–2008, it moved from 9 to 14.5 percent of GDP, which is clearly nonsustainable in a scenario of plummeting oil prices.

From October 2008 to February 2009, the total trade balance was negative at about US$500 million per month (1 percent of GDP). This phenomenon caused the government first to increase duties (on imports), which had little effect (as 40 percent of imported consumer goods come from countries with which Ecuador has trade agreements and therefore not subject to duties), and second to impose, from January 2009, balance of payments safeguard provisions to restrict certain imports.

The trade imbalance cannot be financed easily. Foreign direct investment is scarce. Ecuador does not have a record for attracting FDI in other sectors of the economy than oil exploration and exploitation. There was high interest among foreign mining enterprises in starting activities in Ecuador on a big scale but the government put these on hold. The new mining law, recently approved by the government, has opened new expectations in this field. The big oil companies that have been operating in Ecuador have not kept to their investment programs due to uncertainties in their contractual relationships with the state.

Another main item in the balance of payments is the remittances of Ecuadorian migrants. Unfortunately, due to the international crisis, this source of revenue has been affected. It reached US$2.8 billion in 2008 (5.3 percent of GDP), which is less in absolute and relative terms than the 2007 figures (US$3.1 billion, 6.7 percent of GDP).

Besides the oil dependency factor, during 2008 the government dramatically increased public expenditure, using up all the revenues of the oil boom. Several stabilization funds, were scrapped in 2005[11] and 2008, as well as macro-fiscal rules that put some restriction on fiscal expansion.

As a result, the government did not have any savings to face the impending crisis as oil prices declined. Furthermore, access to external financing, which potentially could be quite large due to the relatively small public external debt (about 20 percent of GDP), has been severely restricted because, in late 2008, the government went into default on some external debt tranches, claiming these debts were illegitimate[12] and managed to buy them back at a third of their price value (July 2009) Previously it had questioned a bilateral debt granted by Brazil, expelled the representative of the World Bank, and repeatedly declared that it would have nothing to do with the International Monetary Fund (IMF). The only external finance flowing in during 2009 came from the Andean Development Corporation (ADC); the Latin American Fund of Reserves (FLAR), both regional institutions of which Ecuador is a Charter Member; and from the Inter-American Development Bank (IADB). The government is also counting on financial assistance from friendly countries (such as Venezuela, Iran, China, etc.). It recently obtained from China an advanced payment of US$1 billion in a long-term oil export contract.

This gloomy panorama for 2009 was accentuated by the fact that Ecuador's private investment has been rather low and there is little, if any, confidence in the economic policies of the incumbent government which, in its first two years, pursued an unsustainably aggressive expansion of public expenditure, more subsidies, higher marginal income and inheritance taxes, an erratic trade policy, the introduction of capital controls, and higher labor costs.

It should be noted as well that the dollarization of Ecuador (2000), while helping the economic expansion of the country, poses restrictions on the options for economic policy (exchange rates), and means that the effects of severe liquidity reductions are transmitted directly to the real sector (thus causing unemployment). The vast majority of the population supports the dollar as the national currency as it clearly has contributed to preserving the real value of workers' incomes and savings while opening credit access to vast segments of the population.

Undoubtedly, Ecuador will face a very tough economic situation in the short and mid terms if oil prices do not rebound from their low levels.

Efforts of integration: the Andean Community

Ecuador has participated in all efforts at regional and subregional integration. It was a party to the Treaty of Latin American Association for Free Trade (ALALC), Montevideo, 1960, replaced by the Treaty of Montevideo, 1980, which established the Latin American Association of Integration (ALADI). It is also a party to the Treaty of Panama, 1975, that created the Latin American Economic System (SELA), and to the Treaty of Amazonian Cooperation (Brasilia, 1978). In the subregional sphere, Ecuador is a party to the Agreement of Cartagena (Andean Pact, Bogotá, 1969). It has also participated in and subscribed to various declarations and other instruments promoting integration, among them the Free Trade Area of the Americas (FTAA), which at present has no chance of success.

During 2009 Ecuador became a member of the Bolivarian Alternative for Latin America (Alternativa Bolivariana para las Américas, ALBA). Before that, President Correa had attended various meetings of ALBA and on these occasions he praised this initiative and stated that this proposal could eventually satisfy the aspirations of the Latin American peoples.

The Andean Community is the most advanced integration process in which Ecuador participates. It has a highly developed institutional framework. Its main purpose is to "promote a balanced and harmonious development" of the participating states through an "equitable distribution of the benefits derived from integration". The principle of solidarity is based on preferential treatment for the relatively less developed economies (Bolivia and Ecuador). Its founding members are

Bolivia, Colombia, Ecuador, and Peru. Venezuela joined in 1973 and charter member Chile withdrew in 1976.

In April 2006, Venezuelan President Hugo Chávez announced the withdrawal of his country from the Andean Community after stating that, as Colombia and Peru had signed free trade agreements (FTAs) with the United States, the community was "dead". According to preestablished procedures, Venezuela should respect the free trade provisions in force within the Andean Community for a transitional period of five years (up to 2011). This has not fully occurred because Venezuela has imposed trade restrictions.

During its 40 years of existence, the Andean Community has had periods of expansion and others of stagnation. At the present time systems of open regional integration like the Andean Pact afford an economic and political space for countries to adapt to globalization and emphasize its positive aspects while reducing the negative effects.

A considerable expansion of inter-community trade has occurred since the beginning of the 1990s as a result of the new openness of the economies and of the free trade zone that started to operate in 1992–1993, as well as the implementation, since 1995, of the Common External Tariff – CET – applied by Ecuador, Colombia, Venezuela, and to a lesser degree Bolivia.

Although the expressed intention was to broaden the CET to encompass Peru, this instrument was finally suspended in late 2007, thus abandoning de facto the goal, stated by the Andean presidents on various occasions during the late 1990s and early 2000s, of moving toward economic union. In reality, if some years ago the Andean Community had been described as an imperfect trade union, now it has regressed to being a mere free trade area.

The suspension of the CET was inevitable because the bilateral trade agreements the Andean countries entered into with third countries rendered it ineffective. There was also no objective basis on which to pursue the CET as trade within the Andean Community is relatively small with respect to the total external trade of its members.

This liberalization of trade in the subregion has produced systematically large trade deficits with Colombia, which peaked in 2008 at US$1 billion. It should be noted this trade is composed of non-oil products, which is why Ecuador's US$780 million exports to that market accounts for more than 11 percent of its total non-oil exports and a much higher percentage of its manufactured exports.

Ecuador has also maintained smaller trade deficits with Venezuela, which reached a record of US$354 million in 2004 (declining during

2005 and 2006). Yet, even as Ecuador started to import oil derivatives (gasoline, diesel, etc.) from Venezuela in 2007, by 2008 its trade balance was in the red by US$1.9 billion. Ecuador's exports to Venezuela, too, are manufactured goods.

Peru is the only country within the Andean Community with which Ecuador has a positive and increasing trade balance, which reached US$1.1 billion in 2008 (in 2009 it declined slightly to US$1.03 billion). However, in contrast with the nature of trade with Colombia, Ecuadorian exports to Peru are mainly crude oil. Trade with Bolivia is almost nil.

Thus the importance of the Andean market for Ecuador is reflected in its exports to Colombia and Venezuela, which are principally manufactured goods with a high aggregate value. In this sense, the core of Ecuadorian exports to the subregion is substantially different from the core of its exports to the rest of the world, where commodities and basic products (petroleum, bananas, shrimp, and flowers) represent almost 90 percent of the total.

Another interesting aspect of the Andean integration scheme, is that very early on it established financial cooperation, with its own development bank (Corporación Andina de Fomento – CAF – Andean Development Corporation) and the founding of the Andean Reserve Fund (Fondo Andino de Reservas), which later transformed itself into the Latin-American Reserve Fund (Fondo Latinoamericano de Reservas FLAR), and has the objective of supporting its members that are in balance of payments difficulties.

The CAF underwent a great expansion after 1990. Ecuador became its main debtor in 2007. Its outstanding debt reached US$2.0 billion (September 2008), far beyond what it owed to the World Bank and about the same as it owed to the IADB.[13] Similarly FLAR has always supported Ecuador. In fact, it has been the main recipient, and for many years was the only country to request credits from FLAR. The last credit of US$400 million was disbursed in January 2006 and paid back in full in January 2008.

Other trade negotiations

Despite the United States being Ecuador's main trade partner, Ecuador has not been able to negotiate a permanent commercial treaty. The FTAA initiative launched in 1994 came to a standstill from 2001 onward. Then bilateral negotiations between Bolivia, Colombia, Peru, and Ecuador started with the United States. Bolivia and Ecuador were hesitant to continue these negotiations.

Huge movements have opposed the FTAA at every stage of its development. A coalition of senior citizens, labor groups, environmentalists, and human rights and peace advocates as well as concerned citizens protested at both major meetings of the FTAA. The reality is that FTAA missed the target deadline of 2005. This event followed the apparent failure of the WTO Doha round. The failure of the Mar del Plata summit – November 4–5, 2005 – to set out a comprehensive agenda to keep the FTAA alive has meant that there is little chance for a comprehensive trade agreement in the foreseeable future.

A vocal critic of the FTAA is Venezuelan president Hugo Chávez, who has described it as an "annexation plan" and a "tool of imperialism" for the exploitation of Latin America. As a counterproposal to this initiative, Chávez has promoted ALBA, based on the model of the European Union, which stresses energy and infrastructure agreements that are gradually extended to other areas finally to include the total economic, political, and military integration of the member states.

Over time, some governments, not wanting to lose a chance of hemispheric trade expansion, have moved in the direction of establishing a series of bilateral FTAs. The present Ecuadorian administration has suspended negotiations in course of negotiating a trade agreement with the United States and in general is opposed to this kind of arrangement.

However, after a process of consultation and exchange of opinions, on January 23, 2008, Colombia, Peru, and Ecuador began negotiations in Brussels for a trade agreement with the European Union. Ecuador expressed its preference that these negotiations be conducted "bloc to bloc". However, if this approach were not possible due to lack of consensus within the Andean Community, Ecuador would be ready to negotiate bilaterally a "trade agreement for development" with the EU. This possible agreement would imply the enhancing of institutional capacities to facilitate the application of fair and equitable development policies. In July 2009 Ecuador abandoned these talks arguing they would conduct to the free trade agreement without addressing development issues. Colombia and Peru successfully concluded their negotiations in March 2010.

Ecuador and banana negotiations

Bananas are the world's most exported fresh fruit in terms of volume and value. Developed countries accounted for approximately 84 percent of world banana imports in 2001–2003. Until recently, the United States was the leading importing country, followed by the EU and Japan. Following its enlargement to include ten more countries in May 2004, the EU has now become the largest banana import market in the world. With 27 member states and a population of 450 million consumers, most of whom have high purchasing power, the EU market is important to banana exporting countries both for the large quantities it imports and for its high prices. Ecuadorian banana exports in 2008 represented 8.5 percent of the total exports of Ecuador.

This background explains why the negotiations on banana prices with the EU are so important for Ecuador. These negotiations began practically as soon as Ecuador became a member of the WTO in 1996. For many years the European Community (EC) has maintained an import, sales, and distribution regime for bananas outside its obligation to the GATT-WTO that favored the ACP (African Caribbean and Pacific) countries, thus illegally discriminating against third countries. This situation has seriously affected the trade of Ecuador's main export commodity (after oil). Many Latin American banana exporters had contended for years that the EU routinely gave preferential treatment to the former colonies (ACP countries) and kept import tariffs artificially high on the fruit originating in Latin America. During this time, the GATT and the WTO determined, on seven occasions, that the EC maintains a banana import policy that violates several of GATT's provisions.

Ecuador has made significant efforts, insisting that the EC comply with its obligations and commitments and discontinue discrimination against banana exports from Ecuador. The Ecuadorian position in the controversy with the EU has always been fundamentally the same: the latter should remove access restrictions and promote liberalization of the EC market in order to import the greatest amount of fruit. In this sense, Ecuador has favored a transitory tariff system consistent with the regulations of the WTO, which takes into account the interests of the fruit producers and distributors.

Ecuador sought concessions corresponding to the value of the damages it suffered, which have been estimated at $450 million per year. As was foreseeable, the EC questioned this amount and, at a meeting held by the Difference Solution Organization (OSD), resorted to arbitration in order to establish the amount of concessions to be paid. The EC recognized the existence of a prejudice against Ecuador and stated that it would respect the arbitration findings.

On March 17, 2000, the OSD, in an historic sentence, authorized Ecuador to impose sanctions on the EU for a yearly amount of US$201.6 million in retaliation for the restrictions imposed by the EC on Ecuadorian banana imports. In this way, Ecuador has become the first developing country to invoke the regulations of the Examination of Difference Solutions (ESD) on the imposition of sanctions. In the meantime the EU has continued imposing limits on the banana imports through a system of tariff quotas, the very situation to which Ecuador has been opposed. The process of negotiations aimed at replacing this system with a system based on a single tariff for MFN bananas and a duty-free quota for ACP bananas. As a result of these long negotiations, at the end of July 2008 the EU submitted a proposal to reduce the tariff in two stages: first, to reduce it starting in 2009 from €176 per tonne for most favored nations (MFN) to €148 and to maintain that level for ten years, and second, after that period the tariff would be €114. Ecuador submitted a counterproposal: to reduce the tariff from €176 to €114 until 2016. The EU proposal being accepted in principle by some Latin American producers, the ACP countries immediately denounced the deal as unacceptable, threatening to block the whole negotiation unless they saw changes. Under these circumstances, no agreement was possible and the EU has maintained its system of tariff quotas.

Conclusion

Despite being a small country Ecuador has three different geographical regions and an insular territory – the Galapagos Islands. It is one of the richest countries in the world for its biodiversity, and these characteristics give Ecuador different climates and landscapes which afford the development of increasing international tourism.

The Ecuadorian people present a wide range of composition. The majority of the population is ethnically diverse, with persons of mixed Indian ancestry and Spanish conquerors, who arrived in the country at the beginning of the sixteenth century. Many indigenous nationalities exist and as a result, profound regional, ethnic, and social divisions have continued to characterize Ecuadorian society.

Despite this, Ecuadorian people have always demonstrated their belief in democracy and the respect of human rights. The nineteenth century witnessed the struggle to establish the structure of the state, and during the following century Ecuadorians tried to consolidate these ideals and endeavored to diversify its exports. The consequence of these efforts was political instability – mostly with populist leaders rather than well structured political parties. At present, the main concern of the government and people of Ecuador relates to the present economic situation and to promoting better living conditions to the vast majority of the population.

When in 1998 the long-standing territorial problem between Ecuador and Peru was settled, the benefits for the two countries were of decisive importance. Ecuador has also been making substantive efforts to combat corruption and terrorism. All these endeavors have promoted the economy, especially toward the strengthening of the integration schemes with other states. Ecuador has not entered into trade agreements with other countries because it has advocated agreements on development. The problem of migration of thousands of Ecuadorians is still an issue of deep concern both for the government and the society as well.

Notes

1. A system of demographic and mother and infant health indicators, 2008. This indicator shows the percentage of children who died aged 0 to 59 months, in the year, in relation to the number of births.
2. http://www.bce.fin.ec, Información Estadística Mensual, September 2009.
3. It is difficult to establish a precise figure for the indigenous population. Some people consider that they make up only the 5 percent of the total population, while others think that they represent 40 percent. The 2001 census showed a figure of 6.83 percent, but it is possible that many mestizos declared themselves as white-mestizos and not indigenous. The figure of 25 percent is perhaps more realistic.
4. The ancestors of the Afro-Ecuadorians were introduced into the territory by the Spanish colonists during colonial times.
5. Estimates of the Centro Latinoamericano y Caribeño de Demografía, http://www.eclac.cl/celade/proyecciones/basedatos_BD.htm.
6. INEC, Encuesta Nacional, Empleo, Desempleo y Subempleo, December 2008.
7. http://www.conesup.net/lista_universidades.php.
8. http://www.transparency.org/policy_research/surveys_indices/cpi/2008.
9. Central Bank of Ecuador, Información Estadística Mensual, January 2009, http://www.bce.fin.ec/docs.php?path=/home1/estadisticas/bolmensual/IEMensual.jsp.
10. This figure includes cars assembled in Ecuador that are exported to neighboring countries under a particular trade agreement.
11. By initiative of President Correa of Ecuador, who in 2005 was Minister of Finance.
12. A presidential committee produced a report with these conclusions. The report has been branded as political and nontechnical by various analysts.
13. It should be noted that CAF credits have a higher cost than those of the IADB or the Word Bank.

Bibliography

Asociacion de Funcionarios y Empleados del Servicio Exterior – AFESE (2006). *Ecuador en el Mundo, 1830–2006*. Quito.
Ayala Mora Enrique (2004). "Ecuador Patria de todos," Edif. Universidad Andina Simón Bolívar, Quito.
Comunidad Andina (2000). "Evolución del Proceso de Integración, 1969–1999." 28 January.

Gómez Gil Patricio, Coordinador, Megadiversidad (1998). Los países biológicamente más ricos del mundo. Monterrey, México: CEMEX.

Hurtado, Osvaldo (1985). *Political Power in Ecuador.* 2nd Edition. Nick D. Mills, Jr. (Trans.). Boulder, CO: Westview Press.

Instituto Geográfico Militar del Ecuador. http://www.igm.gov.ec

Marcella Gabriel (2008). "War Without Borders: The Colombia-Ecuador Crisis of 2008." http://www.strategicstudiesinstitute.army.mil/pdffiles/PUB891.pdf

Ministerio de Relaciones Exteriores, Comercio e Integración – Ecuador (2007). Plan Nacional de Desarrollo, 2007–2010 – Protección de migrantes en el exterior. Quito.

Valencia Rodríguez, Luis (1982). "Visión del Ecuador." Imprenta del Ministerio de Relaciones Exteriores.

Valencia Rodríguez, Luis (2007). "Ecuador and Racial Discrimination," in AFESE No. 46, Quito.

Valencia Rodríguez, Luis (2008). Migración de ecuatorianos y corrientes de inmigración. Sus efectos. Una Vision del Ecuador. Ensayos Universidad Internacional de Ecuador. September.

9
Mexico

Mercedes Delgado and Bobby J. Calder

One thing is certain about Mexico. It has never been predictable. The history of modern Mexico began with a small army of conquistadors that conquered the flourishing Aztec Empire. They succeeded in part because the Aztec Emperor Moctezuma (Montezuma) mistook the Spanish leader Hernán Cortés for the returning Aztec god Quetzalcoatl. During the colonial period of the next 300 years, the economy was based on the exploitation of native Indian labor. Beginning in 1810, a revolution resulted in independence from Spain in 1821 under Emperor Agustín de Iturbide. The post-colonial period pitted the colonial economic model against a variety of new sources of political power. During this turmoil, symbolized by the multiple presidencies and military campaigns of Antonio de Santa Anna, Mexico lost much of its territory, including Texas and California.

In 1858 another revolution, La Reforma, yielded some economic and political change. Benito Juarez expelled the French under Maximiliano (Maximilian). The economy was still not organized around business firms. The three-decade long dictatorship of Porfirio Díaz finally resulted in economic progress, but was followed by further political upheaval with the Mexican Revolution in 1910. This culminated in the promulgation of the 1917 Constitution, by which Mexico became a federal republic. The new republic was representative and democratic, and made up of 31 autonomous states (and a Federal District). Eventually, a period of relative political stability emerged with the one-party rule of the Partido Revolucionario Institucional (PRI) in 1929.

We now turn to the Mexico of today, a country with a promising but, as ever, uncertain future.

Endowments

Mexico is rich in endowments, including inherited natural resources, geographic location, and a large population. Its land area covers 1.96 million square kilometers, ranking it as the fifteenth largest country in the world. Mexico and the United States share a common border, one of the longest in the world, with a length of 3118 kilometers, stretching from the Pacific Ocean to the Gulf of Mexico. Mexico is bounded to the south by Guatemala (943 kilometers) and Belize (249 kilometers); the western limit is the Pacific coast (7360 kilometers) and its eastern limit is the Gulf of Mexico and the Caribbean coast (2780 kilometers) (CIA, *The World Factbook*).

Much of the country is dry and water is unevenly distributed. Forest and woodland cover about 17 percent of the land. Mexico also has abundant mineral resources, and ranks as the largest producer of silver in the world (with mines mainly based in the states of Chihuahua and Zacatecas). Importantly, Mexico ranked as the sixth largest world oil producer in 2009.

Although Mexico enjoys a great abundance of natural resources, it has taken neither full, nor sustainable, advantage of them to date. Mexico has been slow to enact environmental standards. The General Law of Ecological Balance and Environmental Protection (LGEEPA, Ley General de Equilibrio Ecológico y Protección Ambiental) was not enacted until 1988. As a consequence, the country suffers severe air and water pollution, deforestation, and the depletion of natural resources. In response to the North American Free Trade Agreement (NAFTA), Mexico has enforced stringent environmental regulations. Although the concept that "polluters should pay" was enacted into law in 1996, enforcement is still very low. Nevertheless, the government has taken some measures, especially in Mexico City. Heavy industries have been moved outside the city and power plants have switched to natural gas. Standards for automobiles have been made tighter since 1997. Even so, severe traffic congestion and air pollution is a persistent problem in Mexico City and in other large cities.

Another important endowment that could contribute to the prosperity of Mexico is the *size of the home market*. The population of Mexico reached more than 106 million people in 2008 (the eleventh most populous country in the world and the largest Hispanic country) (IMF, World Economic Outlook Database). The rate of population growth has decreased significantly in the past three decades, from more than 3 percent per year in the early 1970s to 1 percent in the mid-2000s (Instituto

Nacional de Estadística, Geografía e Informática, INEGI). The economically active population is expected to increase further from 44 million in 2007 to 69 million by 2030 (*Plan Nacional de Desarrollo, 2001–2006*). Over the next three decades, the challenge will be to create millions of jobs and generate enough savings to improve the retirement contribution system.

The population distribution in Mexico is polarized. While 25 percent of Mexicans live in localities with 2500 inhabitants or fewer, more than 26 percent live in localities with more than 500,000 inhabitants. The average population density of 50 inhabitants per square kilometer is not representative. While entities such as Distrito Federal and Estado de Mexico have a density of 5643 and 611 inhabitants per square kilometer, respectively; Chihuahua, Sonora, Campeche, and Durango have a density of 12 inhabitants per square kilometer (INEGI). The heavily populated industrial cities of Mexico City, Guadalajara (Jalisco), and Monterrey (Nuevo León) reflect the important internal migration from rural to urban areas experienced during the twentieth century.

The percentage of urban population falls to less than 59 percent for the Mexican population living in the southern states. The two states with the lowest proportion of urban population are Chiapas (46 percent) and Oaxaca (45 percent). Rural areas show the highest levels of population dispersion, and many villages suffer from extreme poverty. The native Indian population (more than 9 percent of the total) is concentrated in rural areas (*Plan Nacional de Desarrollo (PND), 2007–2012*). The indigenous groups differ greatly in customs and languages, but they have all suffered from poverty. A rebellion in 1994 increased awareness of the poverty of the Mexican indigenous population.

To offer a complete picture of the Mexican population, we turn to the people of Mexican origin living in the United States. Many Mexicans started seeking work there more than half a century ago. A record 12.7 million Mexican immigrants lived in the United States in 2008 (32 percent of whom entered in 2000 or later; Pew Hispanic Center, 2009). On average, Mexican immigrants have lower levels of education, lower incomes, larger households, and higher poverty rates than other immigrants and US-born people (Borjas, 2007; Pew Hispanic Center, 2009). For example, in 2008 the estimated percentage of the population age 25 and older with at least a high school education was 39 percent for the Mexican immigrants versus 82 percent for other immigrants. However, this low percentage is above the level of education of Mexico's population.

Economic performance overview

Structure of the economy

The GDP per capita adjusted for purchasing power parity (PPP), is one of the best measures of country prosperity. Mexico's GDP per capita (PPP) was US$14,560 in 2008, the highest in Latin America, yet 69 percent lower than in the United States (IMF, World Economic Outlook Database; see Table 9.1). Mexico's GDP per capita experienced a relatively low annual growth rate of 4.6 percent in 2000–2008, lower than for the BRIC countries (Brazil, Russia, India, and China, India; with an average of 12 percent growth during this period), and lower than other peer Latin American countries (Chile, Argentina, and Venezuela). Similarly to other developing economies, the size of the national output is significantly larger if we take the informal economy into account. Mexico's estimated informal activities added some 30 percent to the gross national product in 2000 (Schneider, 2002). The large size of the shadow economy is both the result of, and a factor behind, the recurrent

Table 9.1 Comparative economic indicators, Mexico and selected countries, 2008

	Mexico	United States	Canada	Argentina	Brazil	Chile	Venezuela
GDP (US$ billions)	1,088.1	14,264.6	1,511.0	326.5	1,572.8	169.6	319.4
GDP per capita (PPP adjusted; US$)	14,560.4	46,859.1	39,182.9	14,413.2	10,325.8	14,510.2	12,785.1
Trade 2005–2007 (% of GDP)	64.5	27.3	71.2	44.8	25.8	76.2	56.4
FDI inflows (US$ billions)	21.9	316.0	45.0	8.8	45.0	16.8	1.7
Unemployment rate (%)	4.0	7.2	6.2	7.9	7.9	7.8	7.4
Inflation rate (%)	5.1	3.8	2.4	8.6	5.7	8.7	30.4
Government debt (% of GDP)	19.3	38.1	63.8	48.4	36.8	5.2	20.4
Current account balance (% of GDP)	−2.5	−2.8	−0.9	1.0	−1.8	−4.8	−0.4

Sources: International Monetary Fund, World Economic Outlook Database (GDP indicators, inflation, and current account balance); World Trade Organization (trade, 2005–2007); UNCTAD (2009) (FDI inflows); CIA World Factbook (unemployment); Economist Intelligence Unit (public debt).

economic crises. The job losses suffered during crises and excessive labor regulations have pushed people into informal activities (e.g. as street vendors), hindering the growth potential of the country.

The *GDP distribution across sectors* captures the core competitive activities of a country. The main generator of GDP and employment in Mexico is the service sector, accounting for around two-thirds of GDP during the past two decades. The top five activities in the service sector (by percentage of total GDP in 2007) are trade services (16.3 percent), real estate (10.9 percent), logistics and transport (7.4 percent), educational services (4.7 percent), and financial and insurance services (4.1 percent).[1] The service sector is comprised of many informal activities, especially in commerce and restaurant services. Indeed, more than 70 percent of the total informal employment is concentrated in the service sector (Alcaraz et al., 2008).

Tourist services are a key source of government revenue and foreign reserves (the third largest source after oil and foreign remittances), accounting for approximately 8 percent of GDP (Banco de Mexico). Mexico is the eighth largest tourist destination in the world by number of international arrivals (World Tourism Organization; Acevedo *et al.*, 2008). Perhaps not surprisingly, the main origin of tourists is the United States (which accounts for around 68 percent of full-time tourists) (Secretaría de Turismo). These figures are relatively small given Mexico's abundance of tourist destinations (two very long coasts, archeological resources, forests, etc.). Safety and security concerns contribute to explaining its underperformance in the tourism industries (World Economic Forum, 2009).

The industrial sector is the main source of growth in the Mexican economy. It generates more than 30 percent of GDP and absorbs almost the same percentage of the working population, offering higher wages than in many activities in the service sector. The largest industrial sectors are manufacturing (more than 18 percent of GDP and over 75 percent of total exports) and construction services (with almost 7 percent of GDP). Although Mexico has abundant mineral resources, mining activities account only for just over 5 percent, and electricity, water, and gas-related industries generate less than 2 percent of total GDP.

The main manufacturing activities in terms of output include metal products, machinery, and equipment; food, beverages, and tobacco; and chemicals, petroleum products, rubber, and plastic. A high proportion of manufacturing activities takes place in the *maquiladora* sector (in-bond assembly plants for reexport). These activities are mainly the assembly of vehicles and electronic goods, and the production of textiles and furniture. The manufacturing sector is concentrated in high-tech clusters strategically located on the northern border with the United States, especially in the western city of Guadalajara (which touts itself as "Mexico's Silicon Valley"), and in the Southern Yucatán, which is a short distance from the United States by sea (e.g. see Arber *et al.*, 2009). The primary sector (agriculture, fishing, and forestry) generated around 3.8 percent of GDP in 2007. These natural resource-intensive activities have underperformed. Lack of investment to modernize the production process explains this poor output. An additional problem in the agricultural sector is land reform (Warman, 2003; The Economist Intelligence Unit, 2001). Also, excessive exploitation and fires are other factors explaining the poor performance of forestry. In 2000 the Federal Office for Environment Protection (Procuraduría Federal de Protección al Ambiente) reported that forestry areas in 23 states were in severe danger. To address the deforestation problems, the National Forestry Commission was created in 2001 (Comisión Nacional Forestal; CONAFOR).

So far, we have examined the GDP generated by different economic sectors. In order better to understand the performance of Mexico's economy, we must also look at the GDP distribution across states (Figure 9.1). The main finding is that it is extremely uneven. The top two industrial states (Distrito Federal and Mexico) contribute more than 27 percent to total GDP. Other states (especially in the south) seem isolated from

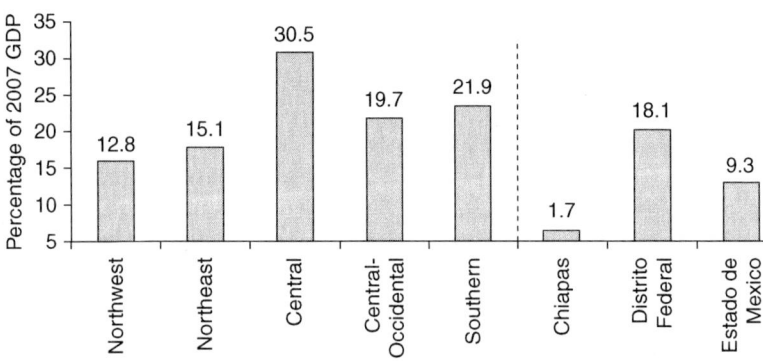

Figure 9.1 GDP distribution by region and selected states, Mexico, 2007 (at constant 1993 prices)

Source: Instituto Nacional de Estadística, Geografía e Informática, *Dirección General Adjunta de Cuentas Nacionales*. Following the classification in Mexico's National Development Plan, 2001–2006, we group the Mexican states into five regions.

the considerable growth experienced by the manufacturing sector. For example, the southern states of Chiapas, Guerrero, and Oaxaca, and the central state Hidalgo suffer from extreme poverty, generating only 6 percent of GDP, although they account for some 13 percent of the Mexican population. The lack of proper infrastructure helps to explain the disintegration of the economy.

Unemployment and labor productivity

A great challenge and opportunity for Mexico is to provide jobs for its growing economically active population. The unemployment rate was 4 percent in 2008, lower than in many Latin American countries and lower than in the United States (see Table 9.1). However, this rate is optimistic. The percentage goes up to some 25 percent if we also consider those employed for fewer than 35 hours per week – the underemployed (CIA, *The World Factbook*). The percentage increases further when we consider those employed who earn less than the minimum wage. A striking feature of the labor force is that more than 40 percent of urban employment is informal, with lower wages than in the formal economy (Alcaraz *et al.*, 2008). Furthermore, the distribution of jobs across genders is very uneven, and the participation of women in the labor force remains low (around 35 percent) (World Bank, 2009).

In addition to a high rate of underemployment, Mexico has a low labor productivity per hour worked of US$16.1 in 2008 (70 percent lower than in the United States, and lower than in some South American countries, such as Argentina, Chile, and Venezuela) (Conference Board, 2009). Mexico has experienced low labor productivity growth, with an annual average growth rate of 0.7 percent in 2000–2008 – lower than in Argentina (2.3 percent), Chile (1.4), and Brazil (1.2). One of the reasons for the low productivity growth is that the labor force is not sufficiently educated to take advantage of the technological changes that took place during the 1990s. The innovation infrastructure is lagging and the poor social infrastructure and political institutions hinder the productivity of businesses. Furthermore, the emphasis that Mexico has placed on improving its macroeconomic management is still insufficient, and the high cost of access to financing for the private sector remains a major problem. These and other factors that influence Mexico's competitiveness are discussed below.

External sector: trade indicators and foreign investment

Mexico's external sector is shaped by its relationship with the United States. A famous saying about Mexico and the United States has been attributed to Porfirio Díaz, the dictator who ruled Mexico from 1877 to 1910: "Poor Mexico: so far from God and so close to the United States!" (Fuentes, 1996).

The integration of Mexico into North America was consolidated with the North American Free Trade Agreement (NAFTA) that came into effect in January 1, 1994. It created the largest free trade area (FTA) in the world, including Canada, the United States, and Mexico. Some tariffs and nontariff barriers were eliminated immediately, and others were phased out gradually through 2008 (like corn, sugar, beans, etc.). In response to environmental concerns in the United States, several agreements were added to enforce environmental law in Mexico.

The benefits from NAFTA become obvious when all member nations grow. During NAFTA's infancy, Mexico suffered a severe recession. NAFTA helped Mexico recover from the recession sooner than in the previous external debt crisis (1982–1983). Mexico is especially sensitive to shocks from the United States, as demonstrated by the 2009 US crisis, since exports and foreign direct investment (FDI) are key drivers of employment and the United States is its main export destination and source of FDI. Although NAFTA helps sustain Mexican stability and growth, commercial integration is not enough. There are other crucial competitiveness factors, which will be discussed later on.

Mexico enjoys close integration with the rest of the world. It has been a World Trade Organization (WTO) member since January 1995, and implemented much of the Trade-Related Aspects of Intellectual Property Rights (TRIPS) agreement by January 2000 (World Trade Organization). In addition, the country was admitted to the Asia-Pacific Economic Cooperation forum in 1993 and to the OECD in 1994. The Fox administration (2000–2006) favored an activist foreign policy, entering into FTAs with Israel and the European Union (2000). Other recent FTAs have been started with Uruguay (2003) and Japan (2004) (World Trade Organization, Trade Profiles). While the greater openness of the Mexican economy has improved the quality of the business environment by facilitating better access to inputs and technologies, the country also faces increasing competition from other WTO-member countries, including China, Japan, and the Republic of Korea.

In the past decade, there has been a renewed effort to improve integration with South America. The Fox administration expressed interest in reaching agreements with the Mercado Común del Sur (Mercosur), although similar intentions have failed in the past, due to trade conflicts with Brazil. Furthermore, a Puebla-to-Panama Plan was initiated in 2001 to increase integration between southern Mexico and Central

Mexico 171

America. The goal was to link nine states in southern Mexico to the isthmus with new roads and electrical and telecommunication links, but little progress has been made.

Mexico's goods and service exports have been increasing in the past decade (reaching 2.5 percent of world exports in 2007). Exports are led by manufactured goods (above 75 percent), followed by fuels and mining products (18 percent of total exports). Apart from the United States, which accounts for roughly 82 percent of Mexican exports, other main export destinations are the European Union (EU) and Canada (World Trade Organization, Trade Profiles).

Figure 9.2 documents the export performance of Mexico across 43 clusters of related and complementary industries using a unique dataset developed by the International Cluster Competitiveness Project.[2] The analysis of the Mexican export portfolio and its changes over 1997–2007 reveals emerging patterns and strengths in the nation's competitive

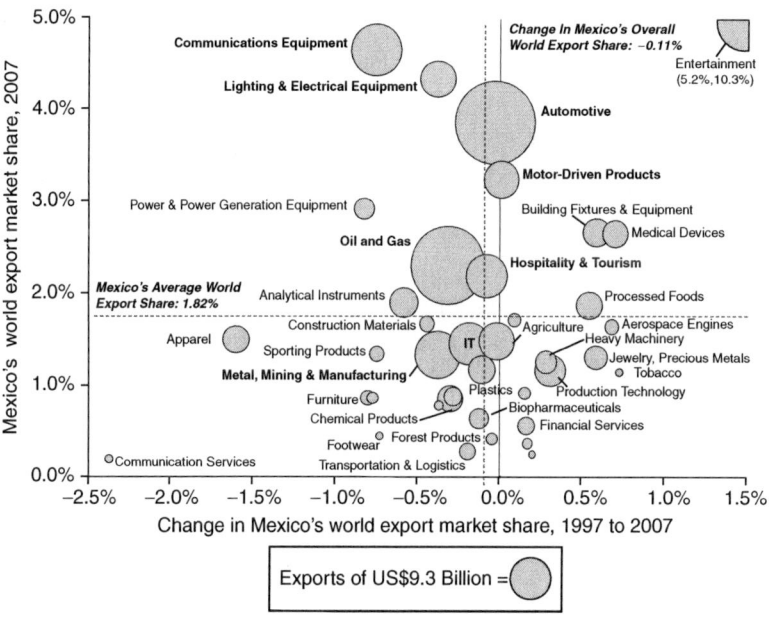

Figure 9.2 Cluster export portfolio, Mexico, 1997–2007

Source: Prof. Michael E. Porter, International Cluster Competitiveness Project (ICCP), Institute for Strategy and Competitiveness, Harvard Business School; Richard Bryden, Project Director. Underlying data drawn from the UN Commodity Trade Statistics Database and the IMF balance of payment statistics.

trade position. Specifically, Mexico's top six clusters by value of exports are automotive (US$49.7 billion), oil and gas products (US$42 billion), entertainment and reproduction equipment (US$24.1 billion), communications equipment (US$19.1 billion) and metal mining and manufacturing (US$15.6 billion). The three clusters that have experienced the greatest increase in their share of world exports in 1997–2007 are entertainment and reproduction Equipment (reaching 10.3 percent of world exports by 2007), tobacco, and medical devices; the activities that have experienced the largest decline in world market share include communications services, apparel and power generation equipment.

Imports to Mexico have also been increasing (to 2.8 percent of world imports in 2007). Intermediate goods are the main imports, mainly because Mexican assembly plants rely heavily on imported inputs. The top sources of imports are the United States (almost 50 percent), followed by the EU (12 percent) and an increasing presence of imports from China (10.6 percent), Japan (5.8 percent), and the Republic of Korea (4.5 percent) (World Trade Organization, Trade Profiles).

The trade balance has become increasingly negative since 1998, as a result of strong internal consumption, trade liberalization, and the strong peso. Transfers received have been increasingly important (US$25 billion in 2008 – made up primarily of remittances from migrant workers). Adding up the balance of trade, services, and transfers, we obtain the current account balance, whose deficit has been growing in the past decade (–2.5 percent of GDP by 2008; see Table 9.1). The current account deficit has been balanced in part by FDI followed by portfolio investments.

In the rest of this section, we explore another important performance indicator: the inflow of FDI and its distribution across sectors (Figure 9.3). The Foreign Investment Law enacted in 1993 stimulated FDI flows, which reached more than US$21 billion by the year 2008. Not surprisingly, the main source of FDI is the United States with more than two thirds of the total.

Foreign investment promotion is the task of Nafin (Mexico's development bank) and Bancomext (the foreign trade bank). The investment rules vary by sectors. For many activities, 100 percent foreign investment participation in the equity of Mexican firms is allowed. Other activities, including oil, hydrocarbons, basic petrochemicals, energy transmission, and distribution, are reserved exclusively for the State. Additionally, other activities, such as development banks, services of radio and television broadcasting (other than cable television), and domestic land transport of passengers, tourist, and freight are reserved for Mexican investment. Finally, foreign participation in other areas is

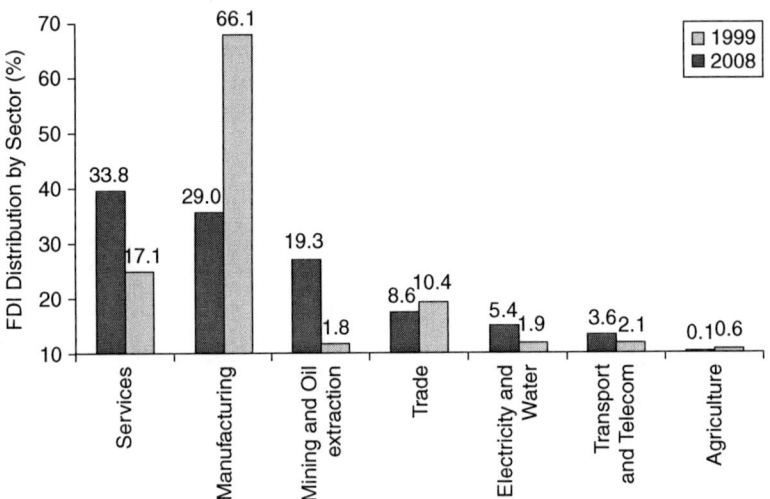

Figure 9.3 Inflows of foreign direct investment by sector, Mexico, 1999 and 2008

Source: Secretaría de Economía, Dirección General de Inversión Extranjera (DGIE). The reported total FDI inflows are US$13.8 billion (1999) and US$22.5 billion (2008).

limited to neutral investments (i.e., nonvoting equity). Examples are certain activities in finance, communications, and transport.

Importantly, the FDI distribution across sectors has changed significantly over time (see Figure 9.3). The relative FDI participation in manufacturing industries declined from 66 percent to 29 percent by 2008, while FDI flows into mining and oil extraction and into services increased sharply.

The presence of FDI in primary sectors has been relatively low (less than 1 percent of total FDI). These sectors suffer from low investment and productivity. However, given Mexico's abundance of natural resources and the great potential of both internal and external demand, they represent an important investment opportunity.

While construction-related products (cement, glass, etc.) are mainly provided by large Mexican firms, the construction sector received almost 4 percent of FDI flows in 2008. The potential of the consumer market plays a crucial role in this sector, as the supply depends on housing demand and infrastructure development.

Retail and wholesale commerce has received extensive FDI during the past decade, (8.6 percent in 2008). The retail market in particular has faced major changes in the past decade. Large foreign companies have entered the market, such as Wal-Mart de México. The intense competition has pushed leading Mexican firms to modernize, reduce costs, and increase their presence in smaller cities. Another major change in the retail sector has been the recent development of large shopping centers, but small family-run firms still account for more than half of retail sales (Economist Intelligence Unit, 2001).

Financial services have experienced a large increase in FDI. The participation of foreign firms in the banking sector is significant, driven by the removal of all limitations on the foreign ownership of banks in 1998. Acquisitions by foreign banks have created some of the country's largest financial institutions (including BBVA-Bancomer and Banamex). By 2000, there were more than 34 commercial banks, but the sector is still small in terms of credit opportunities. As a result, larger companies have found it cheaper to borrow from foreign banks and to raise money by issuing foreign bonds.

Another financial sector with potential is the stock market. The Bolsa Mexicana de Valores (BMV, Mexican Stock Exchange) is governed by the 1975 Mexican Securities Law, and opened to foreign traders just over a decade ago. Foreign capitalization of the stock market has been increasing, but it seems that the BMV is not able to attract many firms. One factor behind the small size of the stock market (Bolsa Mexicana de Valores, with 130 firms listed in 2009) is that big firms have access to the New York Stock Market through American Depositary Receipts (for example Telmex, and Cemex, SA). Besides, the requirements to access the BMV take time, and many firms do not want to provide the detailed information required. Due to the lack of dynamism in the stock market, domestic savings and remittances are mostly channeled through the banking system.

Crises and economic policies

From 1929 to 2000, Mexico was governed by the Partido Revolucionario Institucional (PRI; Institutional Revolutionary Party). For many years high economic growth ensured strong popular support for the PRI. The deterioration of the economy in the 1970s precipitated an external debt crisis in 1982. In response to this crisis, the administrations of President Miguel de Madrid (1982–1988) and Carlos Salinas de Gortari (1988– 1994) started a major structural economic reform, including the liberalization of the economy.[3] The economy was opened to market forces and the role of the state was reduced considerably. The liberalization process was consolidated with FTAs, most notably NAFTA, and more attractive investment rules.

During this period, the inflation rate decreased from 52 percent in 1988 to 7 percent in 1994 thanks to a pegged exchange rate. Lower inflation led to lower interest rates, which helped to reduce the cost of domestic debt. The government also took advantage of the corporatist structure of the PRI to enforce difficult austerity measures (wage restraint, for example). The liberalization of the financial sector also contributed to reducing interest rates. The government privatized its commercial banks in 1991–1992, and allowed the establishment of foreign banks in 1994. The Banco de Mexico (the central bank) became independent in 1994, but the government retained control of exchange rate policy.

Mexico faced another deep crisis in 1994. The current account deficit was too large due to overvaluation of the peso and increasing trade, and the government had to issue US$29.2 billion worth of *Tesobonos* (US dollar-dominated bonds) to deal with domestic debt and stop the loss of reserves. Furthermore, in 1994, the uprising of the Ejército Zapatista de Liberación Nacional (EZLN) weakened investor confidence. The government of Ernesto Zedillo Ponce de León (1994–2000) was unable to sustain the exchange rate band system and the peso collapsed by the end of 1994.

In January 1995 the government agreed to an emergency plan, as it lacked the funds to pay the *Tesobonos*. The plan included the devaluation of the peso, credible austerity measures, and a bank bailout to avoid the collapse of the banking system, which faced huge external debt servicing costs and bad debts. The government secured financial support from the United States, the Bank for International Settlements, and the International Monetary Fund (IMF). Over time, reserves were restored, and the peso remained relatively stable.

Two external shocks impacted Mexico's economy in 1998 that increased the deficit: lower oil prices and the loss of confidence in emerging markets due to the crisis in South-East Asia. However, depreciation of the peso helped exports and – together with the recovery in oil prices – kept the public debt under control. During the year 2000, the strength of the US economy, domestic demand, government consumption, and gross fixed investments, increased the annual GDP growth rate to its highest level of the 1990s (almost percent).

In December 2000, the political system changed after the PRI was defeated by the Partido Accion Nacional's (PAN: National Action Party) candidate, Vicente Fox Quesada. The transition to a more democratic multiparty system has been slow, as Mexico lacks the proper institutions. The country continues shaped by the system inherited from the PRI party. Therefore, negotiations are crucial to implement the necessary social and economic reforms (*The Economist*, 2000).

The PAN administrations of President Vicente Fox (2000–2006) and President Felipe Calderón (2006–2012) have faced major socio-economic challenges. The government needs to take care of the deep-rooted conflicts over land, religion, and politics, which most affect the poorest southern states of Mexico, and which provoked the uprising by the Zapatistas in 1994. To support the middle class and reduce social inequalities, the government must continue with the reform of social institutions (education, health, and infrastructure). The government has initiated fiscal reform to generate more funds to improve the social infrastructure. The inflow of private and foreign investment and transfers will continue to play a crucial role as a source of funds to improve the infrastructure of the country. While the PAN administrations promised long-due reform of the energy sector, little progress has been made in the past decade in opening the state-run energy sector to private investment and to the development of this sector. The telecoms and petrochemical sectors are two other crucial ones for increasing domestic and foreign competition.

While there has been considerable continuity in policy since 2000, the current administration of Felipe Calderón has put new emphasis on the important task of fighting organized crime, with strong support from the Mexican population. Surprisingly, after the July 2009 midterm elections, the PRI made a comeback (with almost 50 percent of the seats in the Chamber of Deputies), dramatically increasing its role in governing Mexico. It seems that this shift has been the result of a weakening economy, as Mexicans are worried about the consequences of the slowdown of the US economy induced by the 2009 sub-prime mortgage crisis (*The Economist*, 2009). Hopefully, the clear symptoms of low productivity and growth in the Mexican economy will not be ignored, and the reforms of the social and political institutions will remain a priority in the next decade.

In the rest of the chapter, we pay closer attention to the competitiveness of the Mexican economy, contending that the potential of consumer markets is contingent on the competitiveness of the country. Then, we will close the chapter with an analysis of the emergent consumer market, and alternative marketing strategies to exploit this changing market.

Assessing the competitiveness of Mexico

Is the Mexican economy ready to take advantage of growing domestic and international demand? We will address this question using the new country competitiveness framework developed by Porter *et al.*,

(2008). The authors identify two overall building blocks of country competitiveness (i.e. the productivity with which a country's endowments are used): *macroeconomic competitiveness* and *microeconomic competitiveness* (see Figure 9.4). Building on Porter's (1990) diamond framework and the foundations laid in the business competitiveness index of recent years (e.g. Porter *et al.*, 2008), there are two main areas of microeconomic competitiveness: the sophistication of *company operations and strategies* (COS) and the quality of the *national business environment* (NBE). Based on the literature on country productivity, the authors distinguish two broad areas of macroeconomic competitiveness: *macroeconomic policy* (MP) and *social infrastructure and political institutions* (SIPI). While the macroeconomic factors are the focus of central governments' actions, the microeconomic factors are influenced by multiple stakeholders (government, companies, academic institutions, business associations, etc.).

The main source of data to measure country competitiveness is the Executive Opinion Survey (EOS) developed by the World Economic Forum in collaboration with the Institute for Strategy and Competitiveness, at the Harvard Business School. An important attribute of the survey is that the respondents are executives of companies, who report their perceptions about a variety of country competitiveness factors (see Browne *et al*, 2009).[4] In what follows, we examine the competitiveness of Mexico in 2009, comparing its performance to a constant sample of 94 countries.

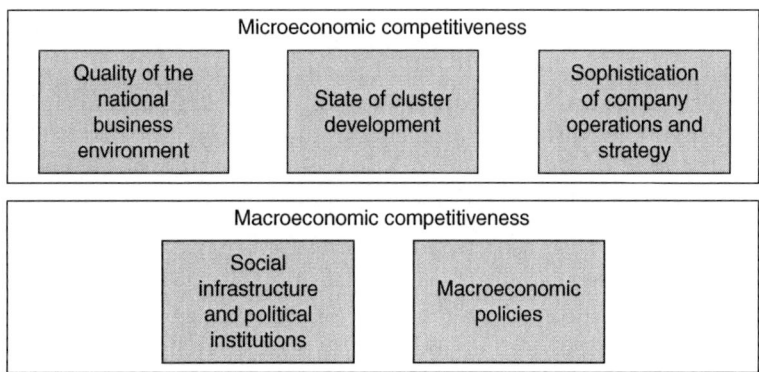

Figure 9.4 Foundations of a country's productivity
Source: Porter, *et al.* (2008).

Microeconomic competitiveness

Mexico ranked fifty-eighth in *microeconomic competitiveness* in 2009, significantly behind some South American countries (Chile and Brazil) and other large emerging countries (India and China), but with a much healthier microeconomic area than Argentina and Venezuela.

The weakest indicators of *companies operations and strategies* (COS) include limited reliance on professional management, a low orientation to innovation, and the lack of breadth of international markets for Mexican companies (the latter may simply reflect the fact that Mexico's main trade effort is heavily concentrated on the US market). In the next section, we address how companies could develop sophisticated marketing strategies that take into account the potential of the emergent consumer market.

Based on Porter's (1990) diamond framework, the quality of the *national business environment* (NBE) in a country can be understood in terms of four interrelated dimensions: the quality of factor (input) conditions, the context of rules in which firm strategy and rivalry take place, the quality of local demand conditions, and the presence of related and supporting industries and clusters. In terms of the NBE, Mexico lags in innovation and administrative infrastructure and domestic credit for firms, and suffers serious market distortions. A more detailed picture of the quality of the business environment is offered below.

A country's *factor (input) conditions* directly affect the productivity of companies and the country's prosperity. While it is a challenge to provide adequate infrastructure in a developing nation with 106 million people that ranks as the fifteenth largest country, the benefits from improved infrastructure are large. In the past decade, the process of privatization and liberalization of many infrastructures, including ports, railways, airports, and communications networks, has facilitated development of these facilities. NAFTA and the development of the tourism sector have both accelerated this process. The new administration has to improve the liberalization strategy in order to attract increased private and foreign investment, especially in the energy and communications sectors.

While the soundness of banks has been improving, domestic credit to the private sector is very limited, making firms dependent on foreign resources, and increasing the external debt. For example, the rate of domestic credit to private sector (as a percentage of GDP) is only 22 percent, significantly lower than in Chile, Brazil, and China (World Bank, 2009).

The administrative and innovation infrastructures are also lagging. While the number of days to start a business dropped from 58 in 2005 to 27–28 afterward (World Bank, *Doing Business*), the perception by business leaders of the difficulty in opening new businesses continues to be very negative (ranking below seventieth in the EOS indicators).

Mexico enjoys a very large population, but this great asset is underused due to the low quality of the educational system and, in particular, of math and science education. Enrollment in tertiary schools is low (around 26 percent, versus 64 percent in Argentina or 47 percent in Chile) (World Bank, 2009). Due to the poor innovation infrastructure, Mexico's international innovative output (as measured by patents per capita registered in the US Patents and Trademarks Office) is far behind many Latin American and BRIC countries.

Mexico's *context for firm strategy and rivalry* has some aspects with great strengths and others with serious weaknesses. After the liberalization process initiated in the 1980s, today's Mexico enjoys greater trade openness, stronger investor protection, increased foreign ownership, and better access to foreign technology. However, as mentioned earlier, some key sectors are state run or do not allow the participation of foreign firms, greatly distorting the market and access to these inputs. Taxation and subsidies also hinder competition.

Specifically, the telecoms sector is dominated by the former state monopoly, Telmex. Both domestic and foreign investors are awaiting the planned reform of the 1995 Mexico Federal Telecommunications Law. Another related issue is the liberalization of the state-run energy sector. The energy sector is on the agenda of the current administration, but any proposal of foreign involvement in the traditionally "nationalistic" energy sector, which includes one of the oldest Mexican labor unions, will be hard to negotiate. In order to meet the increasing demand, the government needs to invest in electricity and natural gas development. However, it lacks the funds to do so. FDI is required to take advantage of the full capacity in this sector. In addition, new investments will decrease unemployment, the biggest challenge to populous Mexico. The reform will not be easy, as it must guarantee that the government does not lose a crucial source of revenue and that Mexican firms remain able to compete.

Demand conditions have improved with the emergent middle class and the role played by Mexican immigrants in the United States, who bring additional income and new products to their relatives in Mexico. However, buyer sophistication remains relatively low compared to China and India. Furthermore, the government has played a poor role in promoting the demand and use of advanced technologies.

The component of the NBE for which Mexico has the best performance is the *strength of related and supporting industries and clusters* (ranking forty-seventh in 2009). This measure refers to the attributes of "clusters" – geographic concentrations of interconnected companies and institutions in a particular field. These attributes include the prevalence and depth of clusters; the collaboration within clusters among suppliers, partners, local customers, and institutions; and the quality and quantity of local suppliers. While Mexico has developed a stronger network of suppliers since NAFTA, it continues to rely heavily on imports of intermediary goods. Mexico's manufacturing and service industries are highly concentrated in certain geographic areas, but lack, in many cases, a favorable environment for innovation. Examples of strong clusters in Mexico are the electronics cluster in the state of Jalisco (near Guadalajara), the tourism cluster in Baja California Sur, and footwear in Mexico State and Jalisco (Ketels *et al.*, 2006; Arber *et al.*, 2009; Acevedo *et al.*, 2008).

Macroeconomic competitiveness

Mexico's *social infrastructure and political institutions* (SIPI) form the competitiveness area with the worst performance (ranking sixty-fifth in 2009), far behind Chile (twenty-seventh) and some BRIC countries (China and India). However, Mexico performed better than other peer Latin American countries (such as Brazil, Argentina, and Venezuela). Important factors behind this result are crime, lack of trust in politicians, and corruption, which hinder the competitiveness of companies and the overall prosperity of the country. There are three dimensions of SIPI that we will examine below: *basic human capacity, political institutions*, and *rule of law*.

While primary education enrollment is relatively high (ranked twenty-second), the quality of the primary education is very poor (seventy-fourth), and enrollment in secondary education is significantly lower (forty-eighth). Around 9 percent of the population of 15 years or over was illiterate in 2009 (World Bank, 2009). Better education services require not only higher education spending, but also better training of teachers, as well as addressing child malnutrition and other health problems, which are especially serious in rural areas.

The main health care providers in Mexico are the Instituto Mexicano del Seguro Social (IMSS, the Mexican Social Security Institute) and the Instituto de Seguridad y Servicios Sociales de los Trabajadores del Estado (ISSSTE, the Social Security Institute for Public Sector Workers). The portion of the population that does not contribute to the national social security system or to private plans can obtain free healthcare from the Ministry of Health or the IMSS-Solidaridad (EIU). With a very small percentage of the population paying contributions, the challenges to provide high quality health care services are huge. According to the EOS, the quality of the Mexican health care ranks fifty-third, lower than in Argentina, but better than in other Latin American countries.

The SIPI dimension with the weakest performance is the *rule of law* (ranking seventy-second), far behind other large emerging economies such as China and India. This poor position reflects the opinion of the business community as concerns the severe organized crime, poor control of corruption, and lack of reliability of policy services. The *quality of the political institutions* is also lacking, especially in terms of the effectiveness of law-making bodies and the public trust in politicians.

Recent literature has put increasing emphasis on the role of institutions in country productivity and growth (Hall and Jones, 1999; Acemoglu *et al*, 2003). The role played by the social infrastructure and the political institutions in country competitiveness is especially important in developing countries (Porter *et al*, 2008). Without proper institutions the potential for sustainable long-run growth is seriously limited. Thus, Mexico cannot delay the necessary reforms in the political system, rule of law, and educational and health institutions. All these reforms require government funds, and so the government has to reduce wasteful spending and continue with the fiscal reform to guarantee enough funds.

Regarding the *macroeconomic policy* area, since 2000 Mexico has implemented a successful monetary policy, keeping inflation and interest rates relatively low. Entrepreneurs consider inflation as an obstacle to business growth because high inflation increases uncertainty about prices and leads to high interest rates, increasing the investment costs for the private sector. Economic policies have been very successful in decreasing the inflation rate, which averaged over 19 percent during 1996–2000 and fell to 5.1 percent by 2008 (Table 9.1), a relatively low level compared to other Latin American countries.

A big concern for the fiscal policy is the sustainability of government financing. A persistent problem is the low tax base in the country, with most of the government income based on oil revenues (and so subject to oil prices). Mexico has one of the lowest tax-collection rates in Latin America. One challenge is to improve the efficiency of tax collection and enforcement, without worsening the low income of many Mexicans. A major problem is that the size of the shadow economy is very large, and concentrated in sectors that are crucial for government revenues, such as tourism. In addition, high-tech sectors have lobbied to obtain fiscal incentives and avoid high value added taxes that could damage domestic demand. The fiscal reform enacted by President Calderón has increased tax revenues through higher taxes, but further reforms are needed to improve collection.

During the twenty-first century government debt (as a percentage of GDP) has been low, but the total external debt continues to be high since the private sector has relied heavily on foreign borrowing due to the limited availability of domestic credit. As an indicator of improved debt management, since 2002, Mexico's long-term foreign debt has maintained a credit rating of investment grade (Standard & Poor's). Mexico should continue to benefit from lower borrowing costs, greater inflows of investments and consolidation as a place for safe investment in Latin America.

Overall our analysis suggests that Mexico's standard of living (measured by income per capita) seems higher than would be justified by its competitiveness. This discrepancy could be explained by its abundance of natural resources and favorable geographical location in comparison to other nations, in particular, its close geographic and commercial relation with North America. The main competitiveness strengths of Mexico are the openness to trade and to foreign investments (with exceptions in some sectors) and the presence of a strong network of related and supporting industries and clusters. The main weaknesses of the Mexican economy are the very poor social infrastructure and political institutions, which seriously hinder the country's prosperity.

In developing countries, competitiveness relies on the ability to produce efficiently to international standards of technology and quality, which consequently raises productivity and income. Additionally, in today's global world, a key factor for future competitiveness is the ability to innovate, that is, to create and commercialize new products and processes (Porter and Stern, 2001). In order to improve the innovation infrastructure in Mexico, the government needs to improve the quality of education and the incentives for students to stay in school, to reduce the cost of and unstable access to financing for the private sector, and to further liberalize of the economy.

Emergent consumer market

We now turn to examine the potential of the Mexican consumer market, which must provide goods and services to more than 106 million people. The potential of the market is driven by private consumption, which, in turn, relies on job creation and real earnings.

While Mexico's economic accomplishments are indisputable, with one of the highest incomes per capita in Latin America, wealth inequalities between families are extreme. The wealthiest 10 percent of families account for almost 40 percent of total income, while the poorest families in the bottom decile account for 1.6 percent.[5] The growth potential in the southern states is hindered by severe poverty conditions, as they have not benefited from the centers of growth in northern and central Mexico. The integration of the market through improved education, health, transportation, and communications infrastructures is a crucial factor in order to generate millions of jobs all over Mexico.

Mexican society has experienced significant changes that have modified the structure and role of the family. One major factor behind these changes is the transition from a rural to an urban population. This process has accelerated since the 1970s. At that time women started gradually to participate in the labor force. They were mostly young and educated, and worked for the public administration and in private services, contributing to the emergence of the middle class. In the 1980s, economic crises boosted the movement of women into the labor supply. They were mostly poorly educated and they held low wage jobs, but their role was crucial to augmenting low family incomes. Today, the participation of women in the labor force remains low, and economically active women suffer significant wage discrimination. This factor is a limitation for the potential consumer market, especially as an increasing percentage of families are headed by women living without their husbands or the fathers of their children (over 20 percent in 2000) (Gobierno de los Estados Unidos Mexicanos, 2001).

Role of the Mexican population in the United States

In addition to the increasing potential of the internal market, Mexico enjoys privileged access to the US market, where more than 30 million people of Mexican origin live.[6] The Mexican population in the United States interacts with Mexico's internal demand in several important ways. First, transfers from the Mexicans working in the United States are crucial assets for the economy. Total transfers recorded in the current account increased from $9 billion in 2001 to $25 billion in 2008 (the second-largest source of foreign income) (Banco de Mexico, 2009). These transfers are largely constituted of remittances by Mexicans working in the United States. This figure may underestimate the total amount of money that Mexican immigrants send to Mexico. Recently some banking institutions in the United States have agreed to allow immigrants to use identification cards received from Mexican consulates to open bank accounts. These accounts will allow them to send money transfers to Mexico at a lower cost and even to access other financial services (Hernández-Coss, 2005).

So far, most of the remittances have been spent on private consumption. The Mexican government and banks are trying to channel a portion of these transfers, offering special investment opportunities for immigrants in projects that could stimulate growth. The government has also encouraged the formation of associations of Mexicans from the same towns. These "home town associations" (HTAs) in the United States raise money to fund social projects in Mexico (e.g. road construction, electricity, and irrigation). The collective remittances are matched by the Mexican government (three dollars for each dollar sent back from the United States) (Hernández-Coss, 2005; Borjas, 2007).

Transportation and communication services between Mexico and the United States have improved significantly, largely because of the development of the Mexican export sector, including tourism. This factor facilitates the interaction between Mexican internal demand and the Mexican community in the United States, which is primarily concentrated in the western and southern United States. The short distance from Mexico allows Mexican immigrants to visit their families and to provide them with more sophisticated manufactured goods. They are also able to run small businesses in Mexico while working in the United States. Others work in Texas border cities while living in Mexico.

The great potential of the Mexican population in the United States is contingent on the latter's ability to generate labor opportunities for its Hispanic population. Immigration issues are a serious concern today in the United States. While the inflow of unauthorized immigrants has begun to diminish since mid-decade, more than seven million Mexican immigrants work illegally in the United States (Passel and Cohn, 2009; see Pew Hispanic Center, 2009). Mexico wants the latter to institute legalization programs for this group in return for policing Mexico's border with its neighbor more closely. So far, no agreement has been reached.

Companies' marketing strategies

As we have seen, the growth of the Mexican consumer market is contingent on many competitiveness factors. The fact remains, however, that there is the potential for the emergence of a strong middle-class consumer market. The prospects for this development are bolstered when one considers the high probability that Mexican immigrants in the United States will continue to be not only a source of economic stimulation but also a model for consumer culture. It is not difficult in this context to envisage an emerging consumer market that extends over at least the north of Mexico and is integrated with concentrations of Mexican immigrants in the United States. Such a market could resemble patterns of regional growth in the United States, such as the emergence of the Sunbelt.

Although the prospect of a stable and growing middle-class consumer market is far from certain, it represents a significant marketing opportunity. The question for businesses, both Mexican and international, is to decide on a strategy for approaching this market. Most firms will take a skim-and-wait strategy. Their approach will be to offer products and services to higher income consumers and to market these over time to new consumers as the income of these consumers rises. These firms will not target the very affluent consumer who is already well served and has established buying patterns. They will target consumers at the high end of the middle-income group. The strategy will be to get as much revenue from these consumers as currently possible but to count on growth coming from new consumers who reach this income level over time.

A bank with a skim-and-wait strategy might offer a prestige credit card that is coupled with personal services. With this card, the consumer can contact a personal banker to discuss a variety of needs – a personal loan for instance. Many consumers will not qualify to receive this card; their income or credit worthiness will be too low. However, the card would be marketed so that potential clients become aware of it and aspire to it. When these consumers attain the necessary income level, they will essentially be presold on the card. The bank need only wait for newly minted target consumers to emerge.

The skim-and-wait marketing strategy has obvious merits. It certainly reduces risk and avoids the problem of offering quality products at lower price levels than those to which the firm may be accustomed. In our opinion, however, it should not be the only marketing strategy considered. The Mexican consumer of tomorrow with a higher income may not be the same as today's higher income consumer. Particularly because of their proximity to US consumer culture, Mexican consumers are likely to change over time in many ways.

Consumers in an emerging market such as Mexico must be understood in terms of social change. At any given point in time, consumers are oriented by established social values. By social values, we are not referring to the monetary worth placed on products. Rather we refer to the manner in which the culture implies how people should live their lives. Social values provide direction and justification for how people behave. In Mexico there is, for instance, a strong value placed on the role of the mother. In particular, a very special sentimental value is associated with the mother-son relationship. This leads consumers to direct their lives in ways that emulate the household practices of the mother.

At any given time, traditional values anchor the culture. But in the case of a society that is changing, such as Mexico, there are also new values that emerge from or are imported into the culture. These new values often conflict with the traditional ones. People must resolve these conflicts in their daily lives. Out of this process comes social change. Conflict is resolved by adopting new behaviors that initially bridge the conflicting values until the conflict is resolved, usually with the new value becoming the traditional value.

A number of such value conflicts among Mexican consumers have been identified by Letelier, Spinosa, and Calder (2000). One important value conflict is between the traditional importance of family and an emerging value of individual independence from it. Others revolve around festive freedom (celebrating in the present with family and friends) versus planning and delaying gratification for future benefits. There is also the traditional value orientation to fate (things that happen in life are predetermined and one should not try to control them) versus trying actively to control one's life. Another current value conflict surrounds seeking patronage from a higher status person versus learning new skills for advancement.

Value conflicts such as these represent significant marketing opportunities in Mexico. Consider an example from the work of Letelier, Spinosa, and Calder (2000) on a new bank credit card product. A new card was designed that reflected the value conflict experienced by consumers around the traditional values of festive living and trusting fate versus a more planned, independent life. The new card was designed around a family money-market checking account that was shared by the husband, wife, children, and often extended family. The card was a family card, shared according to traditional values. Interest was based on all of the funds available. But the card allowed all family members to have a sub-account in their names and to have control over the money in their accounts. Thus, the wife could have a "*guardadito*" of her own. This account would be valued according to the new value of independence but would still be aligned with traditional values of family unity. Sub-accounts for extended family members have a similar appeal, especially for Mexican immigrants in the United States, in that they facilitate sharing with relatives and being independent of them at the same time.

The new card was also designed to resolve the conflicts many Mexican consumers experience over credit and loans. These can violate the traditional values associated with fate and not planning for the future. The account was designed so that consumers would feel that credit or loans would be available only after the card had been used for some time. The bank would act as a patron, giving credit as a reward for the past, not as an incentive for consumers to plan their futures in advance. The final step in this predetermined sequence would be access to investment services, again not as part of an active consumer planning process but as something determined by the consumer's status with the patron bank. In this way, the new card is appealing precisely because it speaks to the value conflicts experienced by consumers.

The skim-and-wait marketing strategy is obviously applicable to the Mexican consumer market. We believe, however, that there is potentially even greater opportunity in Mexico for what we call a penetrate-and-develop marketing strategy. With this strategy, a company does not assume that tomorrow's more affluent consumer will be the same as today's. Mexico is undergoing social change – the result of traditional values conflicting with new values. There is an opportunity to address today's consumer in terms of this change. If we can provide products designed to fit today's consumer, we can acquire consumers now rather than waiting for a future that may or may not happen.

Conclusion

Today's Mexico has one of the highest standards of living in Latin America. The liberalization of the economy initiated in the early 1980s and further spurred since 1995 by membership of NAFTA, as well as the improved democratization of the political system during the past decade, have contributed to Mexico's prosperity. However, income growth has been concentrated in a few large states. Income inequality and disintegration between the northern and the southern states continue to be a major economic and social problem.

Mexico enjoys an abundance of natural resources and an advantageous geographical location that have also enhanced prosperity. However, the country has taken neither full nor sustainable advantage of its endowments. Greater stringency and enforcement of environmental laws, as well as better infrastructure and development of the primary and energy sectors, are needed to foster sustainable long-run growth.

While the large population of Mexico is a great asset, during the next decades the country faces the huge challenge of creating millions of jobs, increasing labor productivity, and generating enough savings for the retirement contribution system. In order to do so, Mexico has to improve its competitiveness significantly. Our analysis suggest that the main competitiveness strengths of Mexico are based on the openness to trade and to foreign investments (with some exceptions) and the presence of a strong network of clusters of related and complementary industries in selected manufacturing and tourism activities. The main weaknesses are the very poor social infrastructure and political institutions. In particular, the quality of the rule of law and the political institutions is far behind other large emerging economies. The business community has raised serious concerns about the severe organized crime, corruption, and the lack of effectiveness of law-making bodies. Mexico should continue the reform of these institutions and improve the innovation infrastructure in order to be able to generate millions of jobs and sustainable long-run growth.

Mexico has been, and will continue to be in the foreseeable future, an unpredictable economy. The growth of a middle-class consumer market presents excellent marketing opportunities. But, as we have seen, the size and level of affluence of this market is contingent on many competitiveness factors. This lack of predictability favors a penetrate-and-develop marketing strategy. If a company can design products to appeal to today's Mexican consumer because of their fit to the consumer's changing social situation, the company will not have to rely on higher priced offerings that can only be afforded by most consumers at some future point. A company that pursues this strategy, furthermore, will provide the type of innovation needed by the economy and will participate in the realization of the potential of the Mexican economy.

Notes

We are grateful to Richard S. Brown and Richard Bryden for great data assistance.

1. The GDP distribution across sectors refers to the year 2007 (based on 2003 prices), and the data are sourced from INEGI (Dirección General Adjunta de Cuentas Nacionales).
2. International Cluster Competitiveness Project (ICCP), Institute for Strategy and Competitiveness, Harvard Business School; Richard Bryden, Project Director. See also Porter (2009).
3. This section draws on the information in Economist Intelligence Unit (2001).
4. See Porter *et al.* (2008) for a detailed list of the indicators used to measure each competitiveness component.
5. World Bank, WDI, Distribution of Income (based on 2004 survey).
6. Data from the Consejo Nacional de Población (CONAPO), based on the Current Population Survey of the US Census Bureau.

Bibliography

Acemoglu, D., S. Johnson, J. Robinson, and Y. Thaicharoen (2003). "Institutional Causes, Macroeconomic Symptoms: Volatility, Crises and Growth," in *Journal of Monetary Economics*, 50(1), pp. 49–123.
Acevedo, D., D. Garza Sada, J. L. Romo, B. Vogel, M. E. Porter and N. Ketelhöhn (2008). "The Baja California Sur Tourism Cluster in Mexico." Microeconomics of Competitiveness, Harvard Business School. http://www.isc.hbs.edu/econ-student_projects.htm
Alcaraz, C., D. Chiquiar, M. Ramos-Francia (2008). "Diferenciales Salariales Intersectoriales y el Cambio en la Composición del Empleo Urbano de la Economía Mexicana en 2001–2004." Banco de Mexico, Working Paper, No. 2008–06.
Arber, J., A. Chick, G. De Loyola, I. Mogollon, B. Novick, and M.E. Porter (2009). "Electronics Cluster in Guadalajara, Mexico." Microeconomics of Competitiveness, Harvard Business School. http://www.isc.hbs.edu/econ-student_projects.htm
Banco de México. http://www.banxico.org.mx
Banco de Mexico (2009). *Las Remesas Familiares en 2008*.
Bolsa Mexicana de Valores. http://www.bmv.com.mx
Borjas, G. J. (ed.) (2007). *Mexican Immigration to the United States (National Bureau of Economic Research Conference Report)*. Chicago: The University of Chicago Press.
Browne, C., R. Bryden, M. Delgado and T. Geiger (2009). "Executive Opinion Survey: Capturing the Voice of the Business Community," in *The Global Competitiveness Report 2008–2009*. World Economic Forum (ed.), 2008. Basingstoke: Palgrave Macmillan.
Conference Board and Groningen Growth and Development Centre, Total Economy Database, January 2009. http://www.conference-board.org/economics/
Consejo Nacional de Población (CONAPO). http://www.conapo.gob.mx
Cooper, J. C. and K. Madigan (2001). "Mexico: Congress Faces a Taxing Time," in *Business Week*, November 19th.
Economist Intelligence Unit (2001), EIU Country Profiles, 2001.
Economist Intelligence Unit (2002), "Country Commerce. Mexico." *The Economist*, March.
The Economist (2000). "Survey: Mexico. Revolution Ends, Change Begins." October 26th.
The Economist (2009), "After Mexico's Mid-term Election: Calderón's Hatful of Troubles." July 9th.
Fuentes, C. (1996). *A New Time for Mexico*. New York: Farrar, Straus and Giroux.
Giugale, M. M., O. Lafourcade and V.H. Nguyen (eds.) (2001). *Mexico: A Comprehensive Development Agenda for the New Era*. Washington, DC: World Bank Publications.
Gobierno de los Estados Unidos Mexicanos, Presidencia de la República (2001). Plan Nacional de Desarrollo, 2001–2006.
Gobierno de los Estados Unidos Mexicanos, Presidencia de la República (2007). Plan Nacional de Desarrollo, 2007–2012. http://pnd.presidencia.gob.mx
Hall, R. E. and C. I. Jones (1999). "Why Do Some Countries Produce So Much More Output per Worker than Others?," in *Quarterly Journal of Economics*, 114(1), pp. 83–116.

Hernández-Coss, R. (2005). "The U.S.-Mexico Remittance Corridor: Lessons on Shifting from Informal to Formal Transfer Systems." World Bank Working Paper No. 47.
Instituto Nacional de Estadística, Geografía e Informática (INEGI). http://www.inegi.gob.mx
Inter-American Development Bank (2001). *Competitiveness: The Business of Growth. Economic and Social Progress in Latin America*, London: The Johns Hopkins University Press.
International Monetary Fund (IMF), World Economic Outlook Database. http://www.imf.org/external/data.htm Last accessed in April, 2009.
Ketels, C., G. Lindqvist, and Ö. Sölvell (2006). *Cluster Initiatives in Developing and Transition Economies*. Stockholm: Ivory Tower AB.
Letelier, M. F., C. Spinosa, and B. Calder (2000). "Taking an Expanded View of Customer's Needs: Qualitative Research for Aiding Innovation," in *Marketing Research*, 12(4), pp. 4–11.
Meyer, M. C. and W. H. Beezley (2000). *The Oxford History of Mexico*. Oxford: Oxford University Press.
Passel, J. S. and D. Cohn (2009). "Mexican Immigrants: How Many Come? How Many Leave?" Washington, DC: Pew Hispanic Center. http://pewhispanic.org/files/reports/112.pdf
Pew Hispanic Center (2009). "Mexican Immigrants in the United States, 2008." http://pewhispanic.org/files/factsheets/47.pdf
Porter, M. E. (1990). *The Competitive Advantage of Nations*. New York: Free Press.
Porter, M. E. (2009). International Cluster Competitiveness Project (ICCP), Institute for Strategy and Competitiveness, Harvard Business School. Richard Bryden, Project Director. http://www.isc.hbs.edu/data.htm
Porter, M. E. and S. Stern (2001). "National Innovative Capacity," in Michael E. Porter and J. Sachs (eds.), *Global Competitiveness Report 2001–2002*. New York: Oxford University Press, pp. 102–18.
Porter, M. E., M. Delgado, C. Ketels, and S. Stern (2008). "Moving to a New Global Competitiveness Index," in *The Global Competitiveness Report 2008–2009*. World Economic Forum (ed.), 2008. Hampshire: Palgrave Macmillan.
Secretaría de Economía. http://www.se.gob.mx
Secretaría de Turismo (SECTUR). Turismo de Internación, 2001–2005. http://www.sectur.gob.mx
Sistema de Información Empresarial Mexicano (SIEM). http://www.secofi-siem.gob.mx
Schneider, F. (2002). "Size and Measurement of the Informal Economy in 110 Countries Around the World." Washington, DC: Rapid Response Unit, The World Bank.
UNCTAD (2009). World Investment Report, 2009.
Warman, A. (2003). "La Reforma Agraria Mexicana: Una Visión de Largo Plazo," in FAO (ed.), Land Reform, 2003/2. http://www.fao.org/sd/Ltdirect/landrf.htm
World Bank (2009). World Development Indicators, 2009.
World Economic Forum (ed.) (2009). *The Travel & Tourism Competitiveness Report*. http://www.weforum.org
World Trade Organization, Trade Profiles (2009). http://stat.wto.org

10
Panama

Nicolás Ardito Barletta

Panama is an S-shaped isthmus located in the middle of the Western Hemisphere, linking North and South America. It is the narrowest landmass separating the Pacific and Atlantic oceans. At the turn of the twenty-first century, Panama consolidated its territory by receiving the Panama Canal and adjacent military bases from the United States. The country is managing the canal efficiently and has begun its expansion to serve the needs of world trade in this century, developing the emerging clusters of maritime and commercial activity at both entrances to the canal, strengthening its democratic and economic institutions, and extending the benefits of development to all its population.

With a very small population base, Panama emerged in a strategic geographical location used through the centuries by world powers to enhance their international trade interests. The nation has been consolidated slowly as various technologies were applied to develop its potential as a key transit center for transportation and commercial activity. Today it looks toward a future of integration within Latin and North America serving the trade and transport needs of the world.

The land and its people

Geography and climate have determined Panama's destiny. Because of its location, it became a crossroads for flora and fauna, for peoples, cultures, goods, and services. The inhospitable tropical climate did not stimulate a large population settlement until the technologies of the twentieth century improved living conditions. Today standard health, sanitary, and comfort practices make it an attractive country in which to live, to visit, and to do business.

As part of the ecological corridor of Mesoamerica, Panama has one of the richest biodiversities in the Western Hemisphere. Panama has a coastline of more than 2000 kilometers on both the Pacific Ocean and the Caribbean Sea. It is a narrow strip of land between the two, ranging in width between 50 and 165 kilometers, with a generally low mountain range. Thus nature has defined Panama as a crossroads (see Table 10.1).

The Panamanian people are a mixture of races and cultures. The majority are mestizos, combining European and indigenous ethnic groups, with an additional significant component of whites, blacks, and Chinese. The early inhabitants – mostly Gnobe Bugles, Kuna, and Emberá indigenous and ethnic groups – were partially replaced by the Spaniards during the colonial period.

The Spaniards mixed with these groups, resulting in the mestizos. In the second half of the nineteenth century, significant groups of

Table 10.1 Country data, Panama

Location	Central America, bordering both the Caribbean Sea and the North Pacific Ocean, between Colombia and Costa Rica
Geographic note	Strategic location on eastern end of the isthmus forming the land bridge connecting North and South America; controls Panama Canal, which links North Atlantic Ocean via Caribbean Sea with North Pacific Ocean
Area	Total: 78,200 square kilometers Water: 2210 kilometers Land: 75,990 square kilometers Slightly smaller than South Carolina
Land boundaries	Total: 555 kilometers Border countries: Colombia, 225 kilometers; Costa Rica, 330 kilometers.
Population	3.4 million (UN 2008)
Capital	Panama City
Life expectancy	74 years men; 77 years women
Natural resources	Copper, mahogany forests, shrimp, hydropower
Land use	Arable land: 6.72% Permanent crops: 2.08% Other: 91.2% (1998 est.)
Main exports	Services, bananas, sea products, sugar, coffee, and fruits
Average annual per capita income	US$5800

Source: Economic Commission for Latin America (ECLA) and United Nations Organization (UNO).

Europeans and Chinese came at the time of the trans-isthmian railroad construction and during the initial work to build the Panama Canal. At the beginning of the twentieth century, Caribbean-African groups came as laborers for the canal construction. Together with the Afro-Panamanians of the colonial period, they make up over 18 percent of the population today. Small communities of Jewish, Arab, and Hindustani peoples are members of the Panamanian ethnic and cultural mosaic.

Roman Catholicism is the faith of 85 percent of the population. Most of the rest participate in Protestant Christian churches, with significant minorities belonging to the Jewish, Muslim, and Hindu religions. Panama today is made up of three regions. Metropolitan Panama is located in the transit area where the Canal, Panama City, and Colón are located. It hosts 80 percent of the nation's economic activity and 64 percent of the people. Interior Panama, on the Pacific coast to the border with Costa Rica, is typified by savanna and low hills, by agricultural and agribusiness activities in small towns, and by open country. This region has 17 percent of the country's economic activity and 27 percent of the population. Frontier Panama, on the Caribbean coast up to Darien, between the borders with Costa Rica and Colombia, has 3 percent of Panama's economic activity and 9 percent of the population, mostly indigenous ethnic groups. This region preserves the Mesoamerican biological corridor.

Geographically, Panama is part of Central America. Historically, it has been part of South America through the Andean nations. It received an influx of Caribbean culture at the time of the Canal construction. The Western, indigenous, and Caribbean cultural traditions mix in this tropical land. US traditions, present throughout the twentieth century, have likewise left an imprint.

History

The Panamanian isthmus emerged some three million years ago, linking North and South America and separating the oceans. The resulting changes in ocean currents changed the European and African climates. Flora and fauna from the north and south met at the isthmus, creating a rich biodiversity. For more than 10,000 years, people coming from the north came through the isthmus and settled, going through the stages of migratory peoples and then settling in sparse towns supported by agricultural practices. Population centers evolved with distant links to the Mayan and Incan cultures.

Rodrigo de Bastidas and Columbus (on his last trip) explored the Caribbean coastline of Panama in 1501 and 1502. Several small Spanish towns were built. In 1513, Vasco Núñez deBalboa crossed the isthmus and discovered for the Europeans the "Southern Sea" (Pacific Ocean). That event sealed the modern destiny of Panama. The Chagres River in the middle of the area going to the Caribbean was navigated in the 1520s. That led Charles V, Emperor of Spain and Austria, to order the study of a canal connecting the river to the Pacific Ocean. The project was not pursued.

Panama City on the Pacific Coast was founded in 1519 and, together with Nombre de Dios and Portobello on the Atlantic side 70 kilometers away, became the route for South American treasures and goods going to Spain. Panama City was the point of departure for Pizarro to conquer Peru and Almagro, Chile. Nicaragua, Ecuador, and other Pacific countries were colonized from Panama.

The transit of goods and treasure through Panama City, Camino de Cruces, and the Chagres River to Nombre de Dios and Portobello led to the organization of the annual trade fairs in Nombre de Dios (1544–1596) and in Portobello (1597–1739), bringing the Spaniards and the colonies together to enhance commercial activity. British pirates made their presence felt from time to time, disturbing and blocking trade and even sponsoring contraband routes near the main Spanish routes. Henry Morgan sacked Panama City in 1692. The city was then rebuilt in a nearby, safer place in 1693.

The evolution of Panama over the past 500 years has three basic stages:

1. The shock and clash between indigenous and European peoples and cultures between 1502 and 1600
2. The colonial settlement period between 1600 and the middle nineteenth century
3. The modern period when more urban and international links were developed

Transit through Panama has developed in stages according to available technologies. During the colonial period it was done with mules, barges and slaves. After 1855, the crossing was made via the first cross-continental railroad of the Americas – built by a US corporation – and steamships. After 1914, transit was simplified thanks to the Panama Canal, also built by the United States, and modern ships. In the past 50 years, complementary trade has been enhanced by airline transportation.

Colonial trade declined after the Portobello fairs were discontinued in 1739. The activity moved to Cartagena. When transit activity declined, agricultural activities increased in the rest of Panama.

Panama declared its independence from Spain in 1821, following the Bolivarian independence movement in South America, and joined Great Colombia (with Ecuador and Venezuela) under Simón Bolívar, until it broke apart in 1830. Thereafter, a country with a very small population (150,000 inhabitants in 1840), it remained attached to Colombia as a forgotten federal state and then a province. However, it was always aware of its international transit potential. Meanwhile, in the 1850s, the United States, the United Kingdom, and Colombia made agreements to guarantee safe transit through the isthmus.

The French Canal Company, under Ferdinand de Lesseps (the builder of the Suez Canal), attempted to build a canal in the 1880s but failed due to disease, poor management, and insufficient financing. The United States became interested in building the canal at the turn of the twentieth century and, after failing to reach agreement with Colombia, supported an independence movement initiated by Panamanians in 1903 and negotiated a treaty to build a canal through Panama with the new republic.

The unequal partnership ("very favorable to the US and not so favorable to Panama", said US Secretary of State Hay) defined for Panama the long-term struggle to regain its ability to benefit from the Canal and to reincorporate the Canal Zone, which had been segregated from national jurisdiction "in perpetuity". Two amendments to the treaty (in 1936 and 1955) eliminated the protectorate status of Panama and increased the economic benefits to the country.

The treaties of 1977 abrogated previous agreements, eliminated the Canal Zone, increased Panamanian economic participation and benefits, and defined procedures for the joint management of the Canal until 1999, when it was to be placed totally under Panamanian ownership and control. Since 2000, Panama has managed the Canal successfully through an autonomous public company, the Panama Canal Authority.

During most of the twentieth century, the Republic of Panama evolved with western-style democratic institutions. Democracy was interrupted by three coups that quickly returned to civilian democratic control, except during the 1968–1980 period. During that period, the National Guard controlled the government, which was managed by civilians. After the 1977 canal treaties, there was a commitment to return to fully democratic institutions with the 1984 elections.

However, the new government was overthrown in 1985 and military continued in control until 1989, when the United States intervened militarily to remove General Noriega and the defense forces from the scene. From 1990 to the present, governance has taken place through democratic institutions.

The economic tradition

Panama has always had a small population. From 320,000 inhabitants in 1904, the population grew rapidly to 3.45 million in 2008. Nevertheless, Panama remains a small market economy.

As stated, the economic history of Panama evolved for 500 years with increasing international transit and trade as world commerce grew and new technologies were applied to the narrow geographic strategic location. Tropical agrarian activity complemented that evolution. In the twentieth century the transit economy, with the Canal and US presence, gradually became the main engine of growth.

Since 1904, Panama has defined a monetary system without a central bank, using the US dollar as the medium of exchange-in effect a "dollarized" economy. Over the years, it has added legal definitions and administrative infrastructure to enhance the economic value of its transit economy. An example is the Corporation Law of 1927, based on the Delaware (US) law. In the 1930s, the tax system was defined as "territorial", meaning that economic transactions of Panamanian firms made outside of the country were not taxed in Panama. In 1924 and in the 1940s, a legal framework was established to stimulate Panamanian registration of the international merchant marine, which led to the largest ship registration in the world. In 1948, a new international airport was built and a free trade zone was created in Colón, the city at the Caribbean entrance to the Canal.

In 2008 it had an annual turnover of $19.0 billion; it is the largest in the Western Hemisphere. In 1970, a new, modern banking law was approved to set up the framework that led to the creation of an international banking center fully integrated with the international financial community. This is the largest such center in Latin America. In 1976, legislation was passed to sponsor the creation of a regional reinsurance center. In 1978, an agreement was signed with a US company to build a trans-isthmian oil pipeline that for 15 years transshipped Alaskan oil to the US East Coast.

In the 1990s, the construction of private container transshipment ports and the privatization of the public ports of Balboa and Cristobal were carried out to complement the Canal operations, leading to dynamic growth in container transshipment. The transisthmian railroad was privatized and rebuilt in 1998 and moves containers between ports. Since 1998, new submarine communication cables cross the isthmus alongside the Canal, broadening the communications potential of Panama.

All of the preceding legislation and activities have generated an international maritime and business cluster around the canal, which is now accelerating with the full integration of the former Canal Zone with Panama.

The long tradition of the Panamanian people of providing transportation and trade services was deepened and diversified in the twentieth century in the metropolitan transit region of Panama. The agrarian tradition of the country's other regions has evolved toward agribusiness. Manufacturing as a productive tradition grew after the 1940s.

From 1904 to the 1950s, the economy was heavily influenced by Canal activity. Two extensive booms (1904–1914 and 1939–1947) were led by canal construction and US military activities to protect the canal during the Second World War. The Great Depression in the 1930s also led to an extended depression in Panama.

In the 1950s, the fashion for import substitution policies in Latin America led Panama also to initiate such a strategy, which led to inward-looking industrialization. The sector had high growth through 1975, when the narrowness of the local market and rigid new labor legislation reduced the profitability of the activity. Protection of agricultural production had similar results over the same period. The heavy influence of trade did not allow tariff policies to become as protective in Panama as in other Latin American countries.

For the period 1955–1975, all the previous activity led Panama to have one of the highest economic growth rates in Latin America. The international trade sector was most active, representing 33–36 percent of gross domestic product (GDP).

The Panamanian economy is diversified, with a strong service sector that has grown to become 78 percent of total economic activity. Manufacturing reached 19 percent and then shrank to 11 percent of GDP. The primary sectors fell from 24 percent of GDP in 1959 to 9 percent by 1990.

Between 1970 and 1995 the export-oriented service sectors (the Canal, the Free Trade Zone (FTZ), offshore banking, the oil pipeline, maritime registration services, and tourism) were the most dynamic, as they were not hampered by social legislation and strong protective legislation.

The primary and secondary sectors slowed and produced mainly for the local market, and were affected by labor and social legislation. In the 1980s the Latin American external debt crisis and the Panamanian internal political crisis affected economic performance negatively. Panama accumulated high external debt between 1970 and 1984, which was mostly used for investment in infrastructure, social projects, and some state enterprises. Hydroelectric dams, a fishing port, a new airport, tourism infrastructure, highways, water and sewage systems, schools, and hospitals were expanded more than ever before. The political crisis impeded the application of a sustainable stabilization and structural adjustment policy during the 1980s.

In the 1990s, Panama returned to governance through democratic institutions. As a result, economic stabilization and structural adjustment advanced. Economic policies changed in the direction of trade opening, privatizing public utilities and other state enterprises, increasing competition in the economy, and introducing some flexibility to labor markets. Panama joined the World Trade Organization (WTO) in 1997, refinanced and reduced its external debt in 1996, and changed sector specific incentives to a generalized incentive system favoring technology, training, and exports across the board. Several regulatory agencies (banking, stock market, competition and consumer protection, insurance, and public utilities) were updated and strengthened. The thrust of policies was to increase market flexibility and efficiency through competition, trade opening, regulation of natural monopolies, and protection for consumers. Panama regained an average GDP growth rate of 4.5 percent. The FFTZ reached a gross volume of US$10 billion, the largest in the Western Hemisphere. Banking recovered to reach US$38.0 billion in assets. Maritime ship registration became the largest such sector in the world and international legal and financial services continued to grow.

Tourism grew 15 percent per year. Container port transshipments grew to 1.5 million maritime volume units (twenty-foot equivalent unit, TEU). Exports of fishery products and agribusiness, as well as industrial goods, picked up. Furthermore, the country prepared itself institutionally to receive both the Canal and the US military bases located near the Canal, whose considerable infrastructure was worth over $3 billion.

The Canal's institutional and management procedures were made part of the National Constitution. Based on that, the Canal Authority Agency was created as a public entity with an independent board and complete autonomy, separate from normal political processes. The Canal Treaties between the United Sates and Panama were fully complied with. By the time of the hand over to Panama on December 31, 1999, 97 percent of Canal employees, as well as senior management, were Panamanian. It was a seamless transition. The Canal's performance indicators have improved since then.

At the same time, the Interoceanic Region Authority was created to receive all former Canal Zone lands and properties and to incorporate them into national development.

A medium-term development strategy was prepared for the Interoceanic Region around the Canal with the clear objectives of protecting Canal operations and future expansion, consolidating an economic cluster of maritime and business activity, incorporating social development, guiding and providing for urban development in the former zone around Panama City and Colón, and protecting the Canal watershed and the surrounding rich biodiversity with a combination of National Parks and reforestation projects. The plan has entailed the development of 100,000 hectares of land and 14,000 structures and buildings (see Figure 10.1).

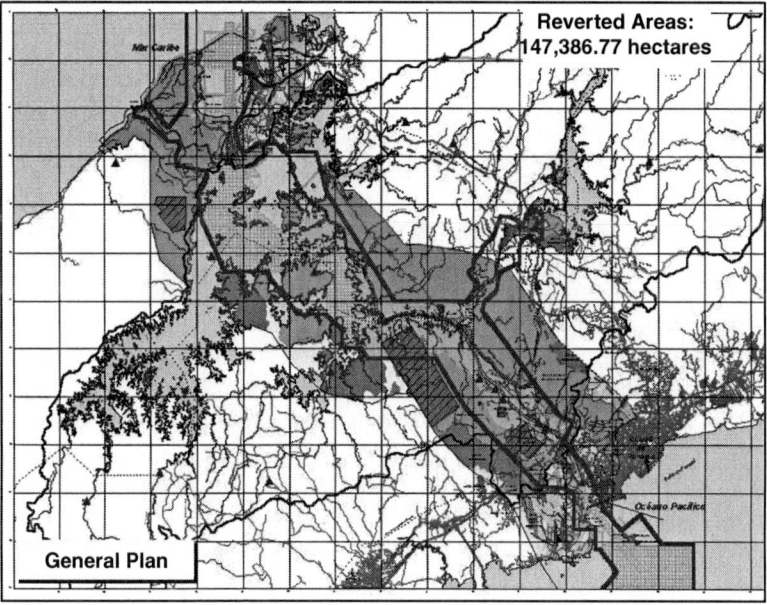

Figure 10.1 Zoning use plan prepared for the former Canal Zone, Panama
Source: General Master Plan: Interoceanic Region Authority.

Today many of the initiatives in the Interoceanic Region have been launched: the modernization of the canal and now its expansion; container transshipment ports on both sides linked by the railroad; tourism and communication infrastructure, including cruise ships; increased services to 13,000 ship transits, such as ship repair and maintenance and bunker fuel; and growing commercial and product processing activities. A "City of Knowledge", combining a research park and an academic center, is growing at a former military base; intermodal transportation logistic activities have started; and international submarine optic fiber cable communications have been built.

Tourism facilities and hotels, commercial centers, Export Processing Zones, and a Special Pacific Trade area at the Pacific entrance to the Canal at a former US air force base, have been built and organized. A locally owned international airline (COPA) has reestablished the hemispheric air traffic hub that operated in the 1960s but had disappeared as a result of the North-South overflights.

Panama is building a cluster of transportation, logistics, maritime, commercial, tourism, and manufacturing activities around the Canal. Indeed, as noted many significant steps have already been taken in that direction.

The economy in the twenty-first century

After a slow start in 2000–2003, due to the international recession, Panama averaged 8.7 percent annual growth during 2004–2008. It reached 11.5 percent in 2007 and 9.2 percent in 2008. Exports growth, a main driver of that growth, averaged 14.2 percent per year and foreign direct investment (FDI) averaged US$1594 million per year, reaching the highest per capita level in Latin America, with over $2.2 billion per year, in 2006 and 2008 (see Figure 10.2 and 10.3).

Panama now has US$23.1 billion total and US$6800 per capita GDP.

That economic boom, the longest sustained growth period since the 1960s, was due to the positioning of export activities, mainly services, over the past 30 years to take advantage of favorable world growth and policy decisions of the government to complement the policy framework advanced in the 1990s.

The main policy decisions included improvements in public finances that achieved three consecutive years of budget surpluses, tripled public investment allocations financed mostly by current savings, and reduced external debt from 70 percent of GDP in 2004 to 45 percent in 2008. Besides tax increases and expenditures changes, the Panama Canal

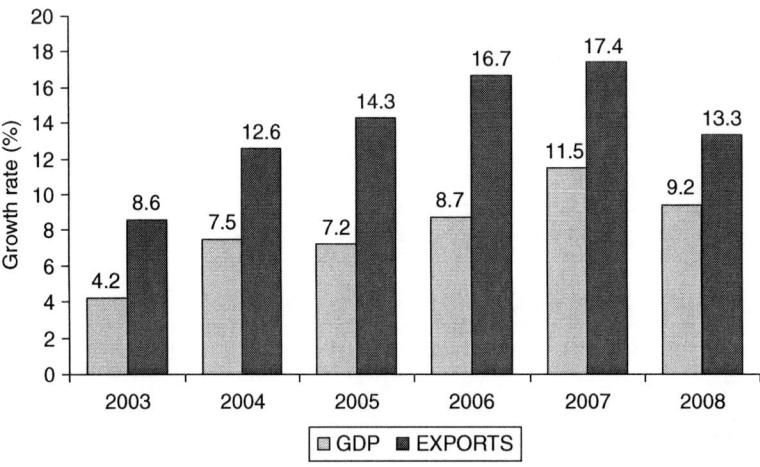

Figure 10.2 Growth of exports and GDP, Panama, 2003–2008 (%)
Source: Contraloria General de la República.

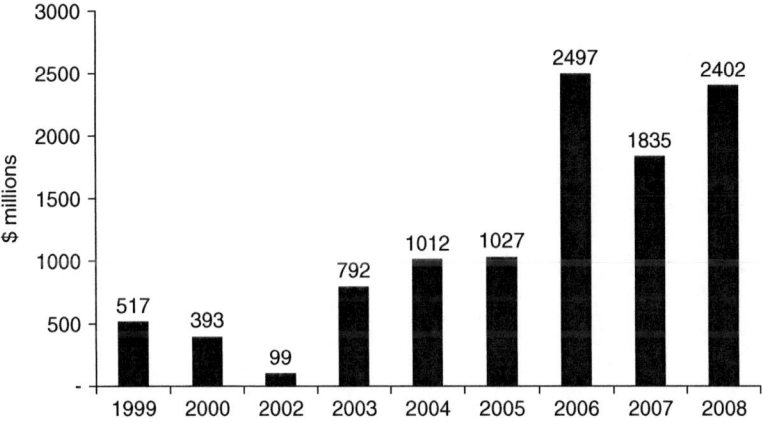

Figure 10.3 Foreign direct investment, Panama, 1999–2008 (US$ millions)
Source: Contraloria General de la República.

contributed a very significant increase to fiscal revenues. Changes were made in the Social Security revenue base to make the retirement funding solvent. These included decisions to expand the Canal and to promote trade expansion through free trade agreements (FTAs) and support to exports. Improvements in public services for economic activity in general and promotion and incentives to specific sectors such as tourism and construction were also undertaken. Table 10.2 shows macrofiscal indicators for the period 2004–2008, and Figure 10.4 charts Panama's risk rating over the years 1997–2008. The dynamics of export sectors have moved the Panamanian economy (see Table 10.3). Table 10.4 shows sectors GDP growth rates from 1990 to 2008. The most dynamic sectors are those geared to exports, (those indicated *) largely the main services sectors.

Table 10.2 Macrofiscal indicators, Panama, 2004–2008

	2004	2005	2006	2007	2008
Total current savings (US$ millions)	–217.0	33.3	576.5	1,375.3	1,387.0
Public investment (US$ millions)	501.5	466.0	530.3	973.6	1,619.4
Public sector financial balance (US$ millions)	–691.0	–500.1	87.7	683.0	97.8
Deficit/surplus (%)	–4.9	–3.2	0.5	3.5	0.4
Total debt/GDP (%)	70.2	66.1	61.1	53.0	45.2
Total public debt (US$ millions)	9,976.8	10,231.3	10,452.7	10,470.6	10,437.4

Note: The terms of payment to suppliers changed from 175 days in 2004 to 73 days in 2007.
Source: Ministry of Economy and Finance.

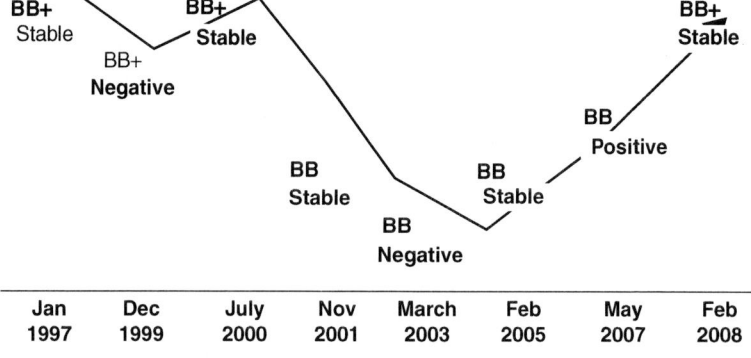

Figure 10.4 Country risk rating, Panama, 1997–2008
Note: The annual average spread (basis points) decreased by 162 points between 2004 and December 31, 2007.
Source: Ministry of Economy and Finance.

Construction has had a most dynamic growth changing the urban landscape of Panamá City, a city of 1.2 million people now full of modern skyscrapers. These are apartment and office buildings, a significant number of which are occupied by retired foreigners and by foreign companies doing regional business from Panamá.

The control by Panama of the Canal and the former Canal Zone lands has accelerated the creation of a cluster of complementary activities around the Canal and the "transit" area. (See Figure 10.5)

The Panamanian Service Economy (78 percent of GDP) is based on service exports (75 percent of total exports). A high percentage (42 percent) is directly related to the Canal and an additional 20 percent is related to the cluster of complementary service activities (i.e. banking, the FTZe, the airport, the merchant marine, and tourism) that have a symbiotic connection with the Canal and logistic services. They are of some international significance.

The canal normally transits 4.2 percent of world maritime trade. The ports transshipped 4.6 million containers (TEUs) in 2008. The FTZ had total turnover of US$19.2 billion the same year. Both are the highest in Latin America. The trans-isthmian railroad moved 360,000 containers. The sale of bunker fuel to ship traffic (4,767 transits in 2008) was 3.3 million metric tonnes, one of the highest in the region. Some 230 cruise ships with over 0.5 million tourists stopped in Panama ports. The merchant marine ship registration is by far the highest in the world (202 million gross tons). The Tocumen Airport had 4.5 million passengers of

Table 10.3 Most dynamic export sectors, Panama, 2003–2008

	Average annual export growth (%)
Canal	13
Tourism	16
Free Trade Zone	14
Container ports	15
International banking	10
Airport hub	15
Fruits	25
Real estate to foreigners	18
Telecommunications	10
Professional services	10

Source: Estimated from data of Contraloria General de la República.

Table 10.4 Growth by economic sector, Panama, 1990–2008 (%)

	1990–2000	2000	2001	2002	2003	2004	2005	2006	2007	2008
Agriculture	1.4	1.3	-2	-5.7	-1	1.8	4.5	7.4	3.5	2.2
Fisheries*	8.7	49.6	32	19.7	12.6	1.2	1.6	-5.9	-1.4	13.4
Mining*	16	-10.6	-4.1	18.3	31.9	12.7	0.1	16	20	29.8
Industry	3.2	-7.1	-6.3	-2.8	-1.5	3.5	3	5.1	5.4	3.8
Construction	12	1.3	-21.8	-7.1	32.5	14.4	1	17.4	19	30.0
Commerce	4.2	-4.4	-5.2	4.9	4.1	10.7	3.5	11.2	8.7	7.0
Free Zone*	7	16	11.1	-4.3	2.4	22.9	13.1	11.6	7	6.1
Ports*	42.1	6	12.1	8.2	21.5	18	11.5	8.2	31	12.9
Tourism*	15	7	8.7	8.5	18.6	15	18	15	21	12.0
Canal*	3	-5.5	3.2	7	16.3	13.3	6.1	10.3	11	7.1
Finance*	15.7	9.7	-2.9	-1.1	-8.1	-5.6	16	12.8	19	2.3
Telecommunications*	30.9	18	-0.9	4.6	3.6	3.6	14.2	16	14.3	21.6
GDP	4.3	2.7	0.6	2.2	4.1	7.6	7	8.1	11.2	9.2

* Sectors geared to exports.
Source: Contraloria General de la Republica.

whom 1.6 million were transits. Air cargo was 86.6 thousand tons, with a high percentage from the FTZ. The regional banking center has 91 banks with US$71 billion in assets. Ten of the largest shipping companies in the world have offices in Panama and coordinate some regional logistics activities here. Over 26 legal offices take care of maritime and other international business from Panama. More than 12 insurance and reinsurance companies complement those activities. Telecommunications with submarine fiber optic cables are among the best in Latin America and related businesses are growing fast. The Canal and trade tourism is a significant percentage of overall tourism.

Figure 10.6 illustrates the international maritime transportation connectivity with the main ports of the world that the Canal brings to Panama with more than 13,000 ship transits per year. Over 30 percent of merchandise shipments from Asia Pacific to the US east coast go through the Canal.

Combined with the container ports, railroad, the FTZ, the airport hub, and the telecommunications systems, Panama is positioned in the middle of the emerging logistics center made up of South and Central America and the east and Gulf coasts of the United States, and Canada and Mexico

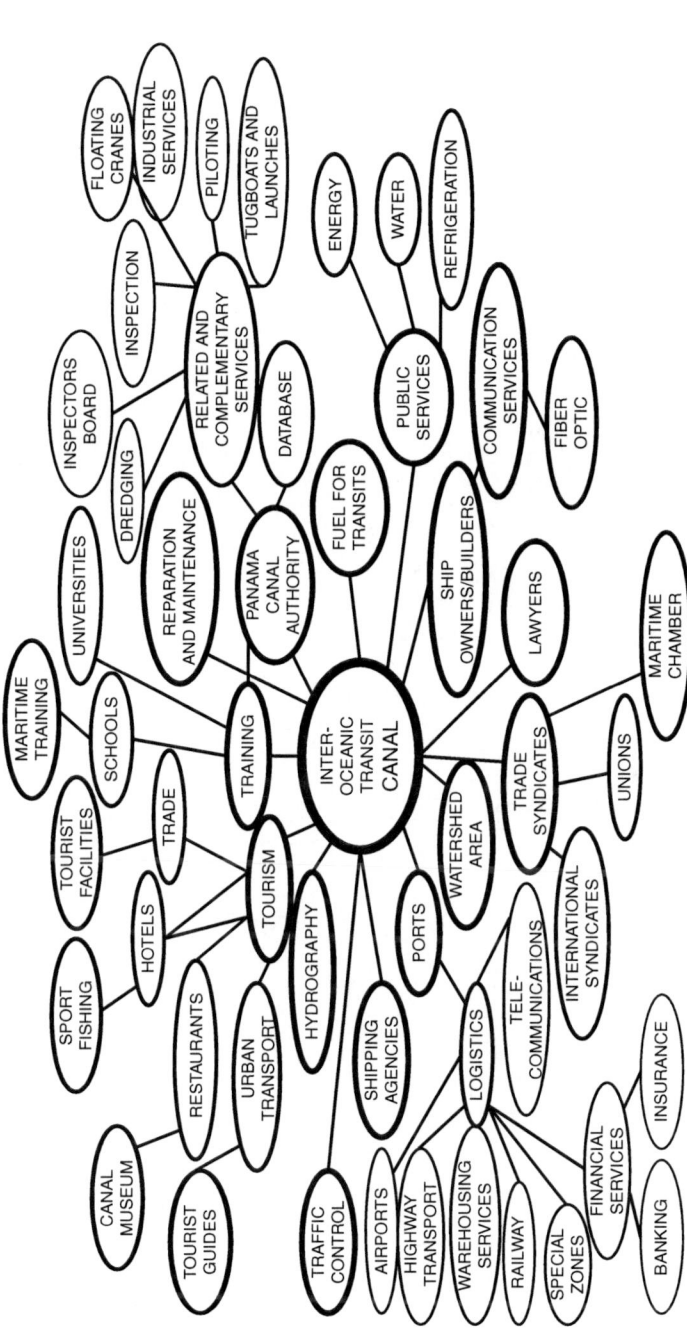

Figure 10.5 Cluster of complementary activities around the Canal and the "transit" area, Panama
Source: Panama Canal Economic Impact on the Republic of Panama. ACP, Intracorp-Asesores study.

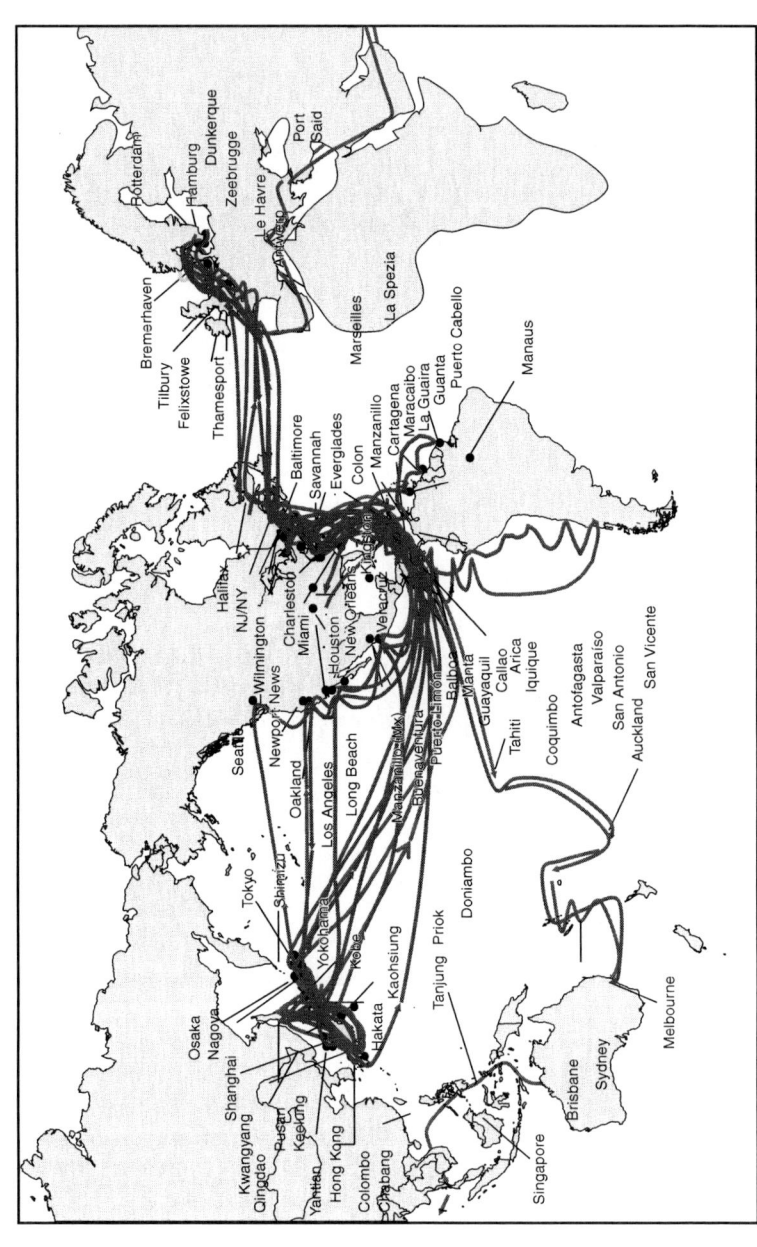

Figure 10.6 World maritime ports linked by the Panama Canal
Source: Compair data.

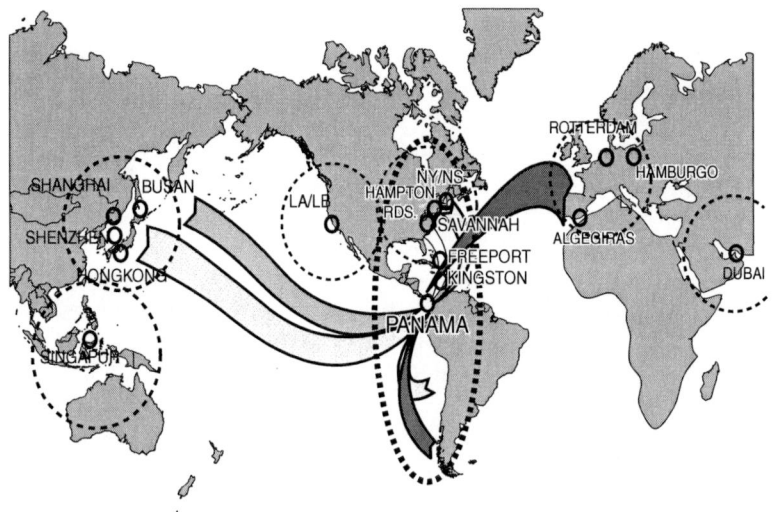

Figure 10.7 Main world logistics centers
Source: Panama Canal Authority.

(see Figure 10.7). Globalization has increased the importance of the logistics centers and Panama is becoming the main hub of the Americas.

The Canal expansion project now under way (a US$5.2 billion investment) will increase transit capacity for more Panamax ships and open the way for post-Panamax ships to transit as well. Post-Panamax ships increasingly move container traffic between Asia-Pacific and North America as well as long distances around the world. The Canal and container ports will increase the transshipment capacity of Panama and the productivity of the other maritime, transportation, logistics, commercial, banking, and tourism activity, in sum, of the cluster.

A main component of the cluster is maritime activities. These are summarized in four categories: services to ship owners, mostly legal, banking, and accounting; services to the ships include bunkering, ship repair, maintenance, registration, and certification; services to the cargo, from container ports to processing, logistics, and trade; and other services, such as banking, insurance, telecommunications, and transportation. All of the above and a normal world economic recovery in the next few years will position Panama for sustained economic growth in the forthcoming 15 years.

The 2008–2009 world recession has also affected Panama. The drop in the macro factors that led to the 2003–2008 performance (exports, local and foreign investment, and credit) caused the 2009 slowdown, although the economy is expected to grow at the rate of 2.5–3.0 percent, still among the best in the region. But the export potential and the evolving opportunities provide a good positioning for the future of Panama. In addition to the geographic location potential, growth opportunities have been evolving in tourism, agribusiness, fisheries, industry, mining, regional offices for multinationals, and communication technologies.

Tourism has rapidly become the second main service export (after the Canal) growing annually at more than 15 percent in recent years. The country packs into a relatively small space a very rich ecology, beaches on both coasts, highlands, an interesting transit cultural heritage including autochthonous communities, colonial Spanish structures, rich fishing areas, and sports attractions. It is a land of geographical, ecological, ethnic, and cultural contrast. Local and foreign investors are beginning to take advantage of this potential (see Figure 10.8).

During 2003–2008, increasing numbers of foreigners chose Panama to retire, in the city and in mountain and beach communities. Apparently factors such as nearness to North America, good transportation and communications facilities, a cosmopolitan ambience, a relatively low cost of living, a stable dollarized economy and democratic political institutions, relatively good security, and quality of life dimensions are the main attractions.

Over 55 percent of agricultural production is now exported. This includes bananas, sugar, coffee, and meat products. Nontraditional products (mostly fruits) exports have grown 25 percent per year recently. The potential for forestry and bioenergy exports as well as tropical fruits and horticultural products is significant as long as the proper production, processing, transportation, credit and marketing technologies, and linkages are developed and applied. Both foreign and local investment is entering these areas.

Fisheries in domestic and nearby international waters generate significant exports. Together with aquiculture, with the application of the proper environmental protection and technologies, it remains a strong source of growth.

The submarine optic cable communication systems, the best of the region, have opened opportunities for a telecommunications and electronic hub in Panama. Call centers, data and voice traffic, e-commerce in the FTZ, in banking, and in merchandise dispatching and other areas are examples of evolving opportunities.

Industrial and processing activities, mostly in agribusiness and those international products that can take advantage of locations next to the

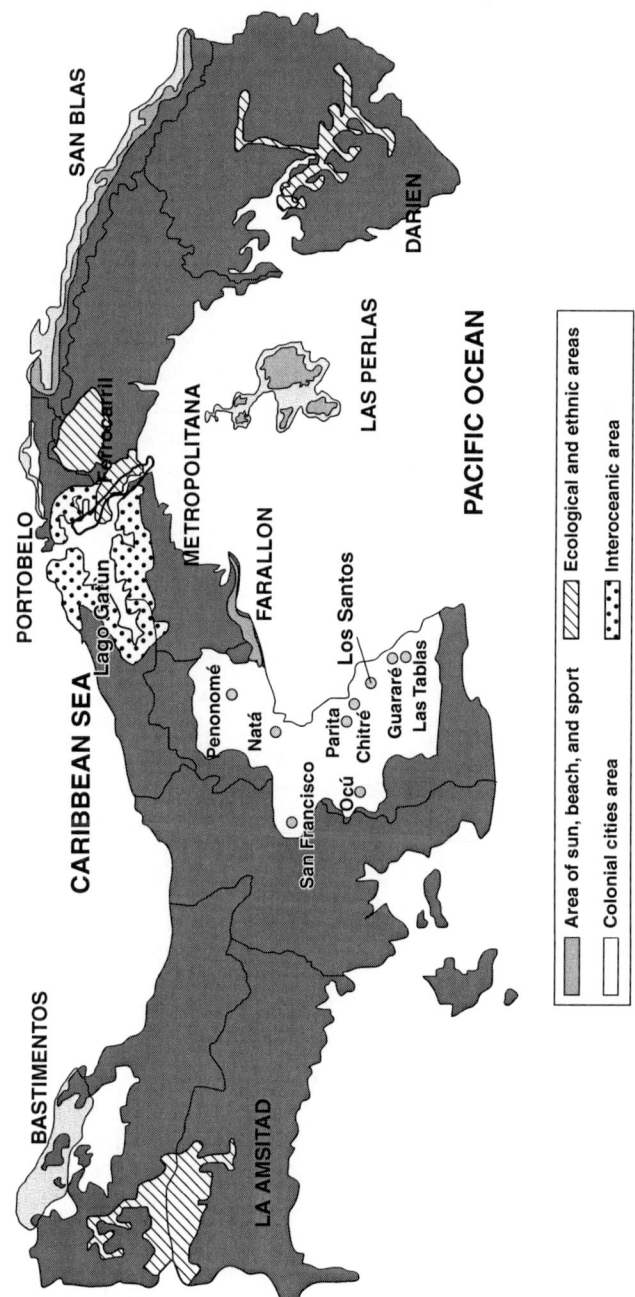

Figure 10.8 Main tourism areas, Panama
Source: Asesores Estrategicos Consulting Firm.

canal and the ports have also been proven to be good sources of growth. Technology, training, and good labor–management relations are critical to success in this area.

Mining activity, long dormant, has increased in recent years especially for gold and copper. Development of hydroelectric projects has also picked up through foreign and local investors now that private development is possible and the energy needs of the country are increasing.

In short, Panama has been positioning itself to have a diversified exports based economy, taking advantage of its strategic geographic location and its natural resource base.

In internationally measured competitive indices (World Economic Forum) Panama has been classified as fifty-eighth out of 145 countries in the world. It is rated third in Latin America. Many of the factors already outlined contribute to that rating but there are still major deficiencies in other areas such as training and education, institutional factors, and technology and innovation.

For Panama to be successful, it needs to emphasize productivity and competitiveness. These goals are necessary not only at the corporate, labor, and sector levels but also at the national level. Improvements in public administration services, institutional and legal security and transparency, infrastructure, technology, education, labor, and professional training are indispensable to achieving this goal.

The dollar-based monetary system provides a stable foundation for local and international activity. The system works for Panama because it is a small economy whose exports are primarily geared to the United States. Service exports provide a steady stream of hard currency without wide fluctuations, and the international banking center integrated with the international financial system offers a stabilizing monetary support and cushion. As a result, Panama has had the lowest inflation in the Western Hemisphere in the past 60 years and it has the greatest financial depth in Latin America.

Such an economy needs to stimulate growth in real productivity and must avoid excessive external debt. Panama needs to continue emphasizing its policies in that direction. This policy emphasis will also be effective in continuing to improve the export-led economic growth. Besides the services cluster, the potential to increase exports of maritime and agricultural products and manufactured goods was proven in the 1990s. Development in these areas has contributed to generating much-needed employment.

Panama is among the top ten Latin American middle-income countries. Although 40 percent of the people are fully geared to modern employment, another 28 percent are poor. Such social disparities are clear in the regional contrasts of the country. Seventy percent of the poor are located

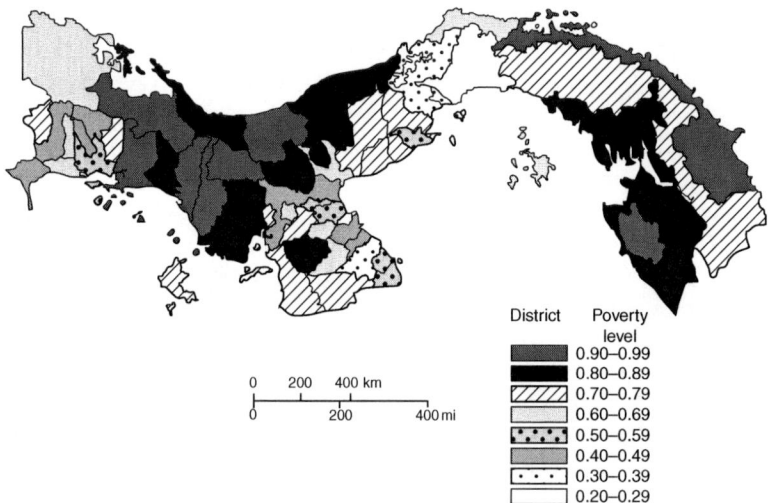

Figure 10.9 Poverty map, Panama
Source: Asesores Estrategicos Consulting Firm.

in the agrarian border regions, which offer insufficient training, infrastructure, and communications. Panama needs a sustained policy effort to maintain high export-led economic growth and human development with full participation of all members of the population.

Considerable human development advances were made in the 1970s that subsequently slowed down in the 1986–1997 period. High levels of unemployment, in the 11–14 percent range, did not help the situation. High budgetary allocations to education and health, the fifth highest in Latin America, did not significantly improve the situation mostly because of insufficient quality control, focus, and execution geared to results. Between 2000 and 2007 poverty decreased from 37 to 28 percent of the population. Unemployment decreased from 13 percent in 2003 to 6 percent in 2008, improving the situation. An expansion in projects combating poverty, mostly in rural areas – focused on nutrition, schooling, water, preventive health care, electricity, and basic housing – have contributed to that performance (see Figure 10.9)

Panama in the Western hemisphere

In the 1970s Panama turned down the opportunity to join the Central American Common Market. Membership would have led to more trade deviation than trade creation, behind a high tariff wall, protecting a relatively small market – 20 million people. Instead, Panama negotiated bilateral FTAs with each of the five Central American countries. It also began to look southward to the Andean Community; however, negotiations have not advanced.

The Caribbean Basin Initiative (CBI), a unilateral policy of the US government toward the region, opened up export opportunities to the US market in 1982. Panama has not taken full advantage of the CBI. The initiative favors US imports of manufactured goods with 35 percent value added in the Caribbean Basin economies through tariff exemptions.

In the 1990s a new open trade policy took hold in most Latin American countries with Chile leading the way. The Latin American countries organized Mercosur, the Andean Pact and the Central American Common Market. Mexico joined NAFTA. The Caribbean countries improved their internal arrangements. These new integration schemes were predicated on low tariff walls in order to enhance trade and increase exports. Within that framework, the new regional integration schemes eliminated tariffs within each group of countries. By the late 1990s, most Latin American countries had adopted uniform tariff levels for imports from the rest of the world at levels between 10 and 15 percent. As a result, trade within each integration scheme increases as Latin American exports to the rest of the world grow.

The United States proposed the creation of a Free Trade Association of the Americas (FTAA) by 2005, a proposal that was adopted by the region at a Heads of States meeting in 1994. Work advanced in that direction but is now stalled. Thereafter, the United States initiated negotiations with Chile, the Central American countries, Colombia, and Peru for them to make FTSs with the United States; most of them are now in place. The agreement with Panama has been signed and is pending approval by the US Congress.

After entering the WTO, Panama decided to improve the FTA agreements it had with the other Central American countries and to seek association with the Andean Community. The goal was to benefit from freer trade with the Andean countries and with the Mercosur countries, once those two associations finished their internal negotiations. At the same time, Panama actively participated in the FTAA negotiations. The new FTAs with all the Central American countries, with Chile, Singapore, and Taiwan are completed. The one with Canada is quite far advanced.

Panama perceives the ongoing development of the transportation, trade, and business cluster around the Canal as an important link with the Latin American integration movements. A large part of Latin

American exports and imports go through the Canal. The new container transshipment facilities are processing cargo going from and coming to the region at lower cost. The Colón Free Trade Zone reexports goods, primarily to Latin American countries. The development of an intermodal logistic transportation center in Panama will be inextricably linked to Latin American trade. The Latin American Export Bank (BLADEX), partially owned by Latin American central and commercial banks and located in Panama, has financed over United States$130 billion in Latin American trade in the past 30 years.

In this context, the increased trade links resulting from new FTA agreements with Central American countries, with the Andean Community, and with the whole of the Western Hemisphere are important priorities for Panama.

Most of Panama's international trade is with the United States, South and Central America, and the Caribbean, in that order. The full development of the country's strategic geographical location with modern transportation and communication systems, maritime and trade facilities, merchandise processing centers, warehousing and manufacturing facilities, and logistics and communications infrastructure is based on doing business with Latin America and the rest of the world.

The present Canal can only transship Panamax vessels, that is, ships of up to 75,000 tons. Already 50 percent of transits are Panamax vessels. The increasing numbers of post-Panamax vessels of up to 150,000 tons has opened the opportunity to add new and wider locks to the present Canal in order to service such ships. The maritime transportation revolution using containers, land bridges, and loading and unloading techniques from bigger to smaller ships is leading to the use of larger container ships, carrying some 7000 containers, and to building ports with deeper drafts.

Some experts consider that the expanded Panama Canal, with additional locks and deeper channels, will open the opportunity for the establishment of an "equatorial" route for post-Panamax container ships. The ships would load and unload large quantities of containers in some 12 key ports around the equatorial route in the world and smaller ships would carry them from their ports of to their final destinations. Panama would increasingly become one of such ports, servicing the Americas.

The Panama Canal Authority is advancing the expansion of the Canal, which should be finished by 2014. The project is fully financed. Most studies foresaw that the present Canal would reach its traffic limit by 2012 and that world maritime trade would require its expansion.

The ongoing project will contribute to consolidating the development of the international transport, trade, and business cluster around the canal. It should increase the trade links with all American countries. The next six years will witness the expansion of the Panama Canal to serve world maritime trade. The ongoing development of a cluster of complementary economic activities around an intermodal transportation center will continue and will certainly gather momentum as the Canal is expanded. The Panamanian people are aware that opportunities such as these are enhanced through greater integration with the Western Hemisphere.

Conclusion

Panama is not only a crossroads for world trade in a strategic geographic location. The country is also at a crossroads in its national development. Strategic national priorities include full modernization of its democratic institutions, consolidation of the economic opportunities around the Canal servicing the region and the world economy, a more dynamic integration of the different regions of the country, greater social integration based on human development and greater opportunities for the poor, the creation of a more participative society, and the strengthening of the institutional base of the country so that both political democracy and a market economy may prosper. The international services economy base needs a free and open system guided by strong institutions that stimulate healthy economic activities and keep illegal activities such as money laundering and trafficking in drugs and humans in check.

Now in full possession of its national destiny, Panama is making considerable progress in that direction. It needs to continue to develop toward joining a fully interdependent world, becoming more integrated within the Western Hemisphere, and creating closer economic ties to Central America and the Andean Community. A growing awareness of the opportunities and limitations of such realities is guiding the Panamanian people, sustained by their long tradition as a crossroads for world trade.

Bibliography

Ardito-Barletta, N. (2003). "Panamas Economic, Transportation and Service Hub: Forecasts." *Financial Panama*. Bogotá: Ediciones Gamma.
Ardito-Barletta, N. (ed.) (2003). *Financial Panama*. Bogotá: Ediciones Gamma.

Ardito-Barletta, N. (2004). "La Economía de Panamá en el Siglo XX." *Dimensiones de la Historia de Panamá*. El Club Unión de Panamá (ed.). Panamá: Imprelibros, S. A.
Castillero, A. C. (1984). *La Ruta Transístmica y las Comunicaciones Marítimas Hispanas Siglos XVI a XIX*. Panamá: Editora Renovación, S. A.
CEPAL, ONU (2003). *Panamá: Evolución Económica Durante 2002 y Perspectivas para 2003.* LC/Mex/L.563. México.
CEPAL, ONU (2004). *Balance Preliminar de las Economías de América Latina y el Caribe 2003*. México.
Club Unión de Panamá (ed.) (2004). *Dimensiones de la Historia de Panamá*. Panamá: Imprelibros, S. A.
Ediciones Balboa (1999). *The Panama Canal*. Madrid: Ediciones San Marcos.
Instituto Geográfico Tommy Guardia (1998). *Atlas Nacional de la República de Panamá*. Panamá: Instituto Geográfico.
Intracorp Estrategias Empresariales, S. A./Asesores Estratégicos, S. A. (2004). *Panama Canal Economic Impact on the Republic of Panama*. Study Prepared for the Panama Canal Authority, Panama.
Jaen, O. (1981). *Hombres y Ecología de Panamá*. Panamá: Editorial Universitaria and The Smithsonian Tropical Research Institute.
Jaen, O. (1998). *La Población del Istmo de Panamá*. Madrid: Ediciones de Cultura Hispánica.
Jorden, W. (1984). *Panama Odyssey*. Austin: University of Texas Press.
Leigh, E. G. and C. Ziegler (2002). *A Magic Web: The Forest of Barro Colorado.* Oxford: Oxford
University Press.
Linares, O. (1977). *Ecology and the Arts in Ancient Panama*. Washington, DC: Harvard University,
Dumbarton Oaks.
McCullough, D. (1977). *The Path Between the Seas*. New York: Simon and Schuster.
Ministerio de Economía y Finanzas. *La Economía Panameña: Situación y Perspectivas: Informes de Coyuntura Trimestrales.* 2000–08, Panamá. http://www.mef.gob.pa
Morales F. P. (1981). *Historia del Descubrimiento y Conquista de América*. España: Editorial Nacional.
Public Law (1997). *The Organization of the Panama Canal Authority*. Panamá: Asamblea Legislativa.
Public Law No. 61 (1997). *The General Plan for the Use, Conservation and Development of the Canal Area and the Regional Plan for the Development of the Interoceanic Region*. Panamá: Asamblea Legislativa.
Revista Lotería (1977). "Documentos de la Lucha Panameña y los Nuevos Tratados del Canal," in *Revista Lotería*. August, September, October, Panamá.
UNDP (ed.) (2002). *Informe Nacional de Desarrollo Humano: Panamá 2002*. Panamá.
World Bank (2000). *Panamá: Estudio sobre Pobreza*. Washington, DC: WB Country Study Series.

11
Uruguay

Carlos Steneri, Sebastián Sosa, and Ignacio de Posadas

One of the smallest countries in South America, wedged between the two largest, Argentina and Brazil, Uruguay has a population of slightly over three million, a temperate climate, and geography devoid of spectacular features. Low demography, calm geography, and moderate climate quite possibly account for some of the country's traits.

Origins

Unglamorous to the conquistadores due to its lack of gold and silver, Uruguay was noticed late in the colonizing process and then only because of its military potential as an outpost from which to keep an eye on the River Plate estuary and, even more importantly, on the Portuguese, ever eager to extend their domination all the way to the Atlantic coast.

These port origins also help to explain part of the country's history. Even today, the city-port of Montevideo accounts for virtually half of the total population and most of the political power. From garrison to commercial center, the region, attached to the Viceroyalty of the River Plate, slowly started to develop and to develop its rivalry with the capital city of Buenos Aires. The area – roughly bordered by the Uruguay and Plate rivers, the Atlantic and its diffuse, and changing land border with Brazil – was sparsely populated by a few Indian tribes. These tribes were very primitive, mostly nomadic, and in some cases (the Charrúas) quite indomitable. With the exception of the period during which the Jesuits established their missions, ending in the mid-1770s, roughly the northern half of present-day Uruguay was a part of the Jesuit *Estancias* (pasture lands), worked by the sedentary and civilized Guaraní Indians. The natives of this area built no cities, did not know how to write, cultivated close to nothing, and divided their time between hunting and warring.

There were vast numbers of wild cattle, descended from species introduced from Spain by Hernandarias. It is not difficult to see the spirit of the Charrúa Indians in the latter-day gauchos or in the farmhands that lived – some still live there today – in the large *estancias*. Originally, these pasture lands were huge, fenceless tracts populated by wiry longhorns, which Indians and gauchos would lasso or "bowl" using the *boleadoras*. The latter was an instrument or weapon consisting of three stones attached by long leather straps. In the early days the animals were caught and immediately slaughtered in the open fields for their hides and meat, which was cooked and eaten on the spot – including such delicacies as tongue. The rest of the carcass, being of no value, was left for predators.

Only much later did a primitive meat industry begin around Montevideo. The beef was salted to provision the ships in port and for military clients. Fencing and branding became mandatory in the 1870s.

Outside Montevideo and a few small towns scattered over the countryside, government and authority in general were generally absent, leaving ample scope for the individualism of Indians and gauchos and the greed of the Portuguese.

Facts about Uruguay

Uruguay is located in southern South America, bordering the South Atlantic Ocean, between Argentina and Brazil. It is the second-smallest South American country (after Suriname); most of the low-lying landscape (three-quarters of the country) is grassland, ideal for cattle and sheep raising. It has a total area of 176,220 square kilometers: 173,620 of land and 2600 of water, and it is slightly smaller than the state of Washington. Its land boundaries have an extent of 1564 kilometers: 579 with Argentina and 985 with Brazil. The capital is Montevideo. The population of 3.4 million (UN, 2003) has a life expectancy of 72 years for men and 79 years for women. Its chief natural resources are arable land, hydropower, minor sources of minerals, and fisheries. Arable land covers 7.21 percent of the country, permanent crops 0.27 percent and 92.52 percent is used for other purposes (1998 estimate). Its main exports are meat, rice, leather products, vehicles, dairy products, wool, and electricity. The average annual income is US$5710.

Independence

Uruguay's struggle for independence was particularly protracted and complicated. Its beginnings, however, do not differ substantially from those of other South American colonies. In Montevideo, much as in Buenos Aires or Lima, the non-Spanish population (Criollos) increasingly resented the normative and socially discriminatory measures that characterized the heavily bureaucratic, centralized, and snobbish Spanish colonial system and society. Among other things, Criollos were barred from high, and lucrative, offices. This was a very important issue for caballeros, who, as such, were not supposed to work and yet had to spend according to their rank. The same Habsburg-spawned mentality toward trade resulted in a forest of paperwork, regulations, and privileges, which not only added insult to injury with the Criollos, but also irritated even the local, pureblooded peninsulares who engaged in commercial activities. This land, thus fertilized, was also intellectually irrigated by a combination of philosophical and ideological movements.

Uruguay's independence – or rather that of the Montevideo part of the River Plate Viceroyalty – is intertwined with the evolution of its two neighbors, the Viceroyalty, then the United Provinces of the River Plate, and the Portuguese colony, then the Empire of Brazil. The better part of the struggle was against one or both of these neighbors.

In fact, loosening the Spanish yoke was the shorter and easier part. Once Buenos Aires dispensed with the viceroy, the citadel of Montevideo fell to the rebels and the Spanish practically vanished from the picture, giving rise almost immediately to a rupture between the revolutionary authority in Buenos Aires and a part of the local forces in the then-named Oriental Province, that is, the province east of the Uruguay River.

These were agitated, convulsive, and recurrently chaotic times, which spilled over into the Civil War period. At one and the same time, the so-called United Provinces of the River Plate fought the Spanish in Chile and in the north (Alto Perú), wrangled among themselves as to what sort of government they should settle on (or whether Buenos Aires should wield power), and witnessed fierce infighting among factions. The last phenomenon produced a rapid succession of triumvirates and directorships, reminiscent of revolutionary France. In this process, the Oriental Province confronted Buenos Aires's centralism, favoring and fighting for a federality or confederate whose capital could be anywhere but Buenos Aires.

The Federalist forces, led by the Oriental José Artigas, were not successful. The province, which had been the arena of confrontation with Buenos Aires, became the battleground for independence from the Portuguese. Chased from the Iberian Peninsula by Napoleon, the Portuguese court moved to Rio. From there the court watched how anarchy devastated the United Provinces and left the Oriental Province tantalizingly weakened. The old dream of the "natural" frontiers on the Uruguay-Plate rivers was impossible to repress. Portugal invaded the Oriental Province and occupied Montevideo. Buenos Aires declared war, but at the time could do little else, as it was bogged down in part by the war against the Spanish armies and in part by the differences among the provinces. These differences at the best of times meant no cooperation with the war effort, and the rest of the time signified direct military confrontation. In the Oriental Province, part of the local population, primarily Montevideanos, opted for collaboration with the lusitanos (Portuguese/Brazilians), while others migrated to Argentina.

King Dom Pedro's decision to remain in Brazil when the court decided to return to Napoleon-free Portugal did not change the situation in the Oriental Province. Only after the Spanish threat had definitely vanished and a short period of relative harmony was enjoyed in the United Provinces did a combined army of Orientals and Argentinos defeat the Imperials of Brazil.

However, defeat in the field did not equate with independence. It did mean that a negotiating process could be initiated. This, too, was hard and complicated, with many conflicting interests at play. Argentina (actually only Buenos Aires at that time), wanted its Oriental Province back, but knew it would be very difficult to hold it over time. The empire had lost its stomach for a fight, but was reluctant to give in to Argentina. Meanwhile, the Orientals, more and more distinct from both their neighbors and internally cohesive, after so many years of distrusting and battling both, had a growing nationalist party. They were strongly averse to the Montevideanos who had collaborated with the Imperials. Viewing this, the United Kingdom decided it had vital interests in the area that were not served by this never-ending succession of wars and guerrillas with constantly changing sides and issues. The United Kingdom pushed for and obtained a solution through the recognition of the Oriental Province's political reality. The province became the República Oriental del Uruguay in a treaty signed by all the belligerents, including the Oriental army, which was guaranteed by Her Majesty's government.

Such was the end of a historical period, but not of the various strands that made up history.

The period of the civil wars

In 1830, under a new written constitution that included a centralized government and a strong, indirectly elected presidency, the Senate selected as its first president one of the two most important national military personalities, one who had been for a time a collaborator with the Imperials – General Rivera. A certain degree of bad blood was inevitable. Nevertheless, General Rivera ruled through the end of his term, albeit in a very individualistic and disorderly fashion. In the second election, the presidency fell to another general, this time of totally different personal and historical extraction. Manuel Oribe was a career officer, unlike his predecessor, and also unlike General Rivera had never bowed down before the Portuguese invaders. Democracy, alternation in office, and political parties as opposed to factions – these were the aims of many in the young republic, although they were more theoretical concepts than accepted truths. Such change was resisted by the former president. Revolution ensued with the exile of General Oribe to Argentina, which at the time was going through a bloody feud between Federalists and Unitarians. Uruguay was once more plunged into war in the crosscurrent of Argentinean and local factions.

The first phase of its history saw the birth of the country's so-called traditional parties: the Blancos who followed Oribe, and the self-proclaimed Defenders of the Law who allied with the Federalists of Argentina. Both parties had strong ties with the country's interior. Both were enemies of Buenos Aires's centralism under the Unitarios and of the urban, European elitist culture that was favored by the other party, the Colorados. This party was perceived by its opponents as opposed to the true national values that were preserved in the country and were free of foreign, liberal, and frequently irreligious influences, all of which were present in the Colorado ranks.

Once again, Britain, this time aided by France, intervened in the local feuding to protect its interests. These interests were the free navigation of the rivers Plate, Uruguay, and Paraná, as well as the commercial ventures of some of its subjects, established in Buenos Aires and Montevideo. This time the powers went beyond persuasion, blockading the Argentinean ports held by the Federalists and aiding Montevideo, then in the hands of the Colorados and besieged by a Blanco army.

This first phase of the Civil Wars period ended, more out of exhaustion than for any other reason, in a peace treaty, which allowed for a relatively tranquil institutional interregnum. Unfortunately, the peace was of short duration. During the same period, Argentina continued to face fierce and frequently violent confrontations between Buenos Aires and a variable coalition of provinces, while Brazil, internally stable under the empire, never missed an opportunity to influence events beyond its ever-expanding borders. In that context, another Blanco president tripped over a tangle of internal and geopolitical interests. Paraguay, under the absolute rule of Solano López, had interests and ambitions opposed to those of both Brazil and Buenos Aires. Buenos Aires was locked in its never-resolved struggle with the other provinces. A faction of the Colorado Party, linked to Brazil, coveted power. The immediate outcome was another revolution, the ousting of the constitutional president, and a secret treaty between the Colorado revolutionary president, the imperial government, and the governor of Buenos Aires to put a stop to the expansionist dreams of Paraguay's dictator, General Solano López. The next step was one of the most infamous episodes of the history of South America, the so-called War of the Triple Alliance, which devastated Paraguay to such an extent that the country is said to suffer still from its consequences.

By this time, the 1870s, some of Uruguay's distinct political and cultural traits were in place. The small country was wedged between two giants that were a constant source of problems, forever trying to meddle in its internal affairs. The country was divided into two distinct realities. On the one hand, Montevideo was a port – cosmopolitan, modern, and already bearing a strong presence of non-Peninsular Europeans. The city was the seat of government and of effective power in most of the country. The other Uruguay was the interior – sparsely populated, agrarian, more Spanish in its culture, and more primitive. Here, authority was a personal condition dependent on courage and charisma. In Montevideo, the Colorado Party was predominant, whereas the Blancos held sway in most of the rest of Uruguay. Economically, the country was also a juxtaposition of two realities: trade in Montevideo and extensive cattle raising in huge estancias in the interior. As mentioned above, there was an incipient industry of salting and packing meat in and around Montevideo.

This turbulent period of the Civil Wars had a hiatus in the form of three military regimes. These regimes were a result of reactions against the constant turbulence and disorder of partisan warring. During this calmer period, the country managed to advance in important areas such as the enclosing of lands, civil and commercial codes, the establishment of a system of public education, etc.

By this time, Montevideo was already on its way to becoming a cosmopolitan society, with the presence of citizens from many West and East European nations. In the interior, the Indian population had been almost entirely exterminated. The few tribes that had populated the vast countryside never adapted to the pace of progress, however slow it might be. Once their usefulness as warriors in the various wars of independence and civil strife was over, their indomitable ways moved them toward banditry. The last tribe was lured to a banquet by a senior officer and then, once duly plied with food and liquor, every single Indian was exterminated.

Enter modernity

Toward the end of the nineteenth century Uruguay started to move into a new phase under the presidency of one of its more outstanding and polemical leaders, José Batlle y Ordóñez. He was very much the man of his age: modern, enlightened, and a believer in progress. He identified with rationalism, invention, industry, and education. Later, he was also an opponent of the Catholic Church, which had denied him the permission to marry a divorcée. Batlle y Ordóñez relied heavily on his party, the Colorados, and its grassroots militants, mostly located in Montevideo. The party had a heavy presence of immigrants, mostly of Italian and French origins.

Batlle pushed forward a full agenda of progressive reforms, which included labor legislation, favoring unions, protecting infant industries, and unburdening the Church of some of its traditional vital activities, namely education and social activities in the area of health, old age, and the like. Not to be outdone, leaders of the other party, by then named Partido Nacional, pushed in Congress for the first pieces of legislation in the area of social security which were to convert Uruguay to one of the earliest welfare states in the world. This modernism was completed with legislation on the family, rights of women, divorce, etc.

Even though there were some further attempts after 1904, the era of the Civil Wars was over, but not before having marked very strongly and for many years the different paths of the two traditional parties. The Colorados were confirmed as a mostly urban party, with their power base in Montevideo and adjacent cities. With a bent toward the interests and ideas of the city and of industry and its unions, the Colorados were the party of government and power, having won the elections steadily for many years. They were the party of modernism and positivism, of anticlericalism, and freemasonry. On the other hand, the Blancos, generally out of government, with their power base in the interior, were the party of tradition, closer to the old Spanish roots and to the interests of the ranchers – which were frequently at odds with those of Montevideo.

Despite such well-defined differences and an ill-disguised antagonism, this was an era of political deal making between them, or, more precisely, between factions of each party, as frequently internal feuds were stronger and bitterer than party differences.

This was also the time of progress in electoral legislation and of dabbling with constitutional engineering. The Partido Nacional had made the former its main banner in the later uprisings. They campaigned for electoral honesty and against fraud and gerrymandering. The divisions within the parties finally led to legislation that guaranteed free, clean elections. In fact, the legal structure was so well designed that not only has it been substantially the same since, but it has also served as an inspiration for other countries in South America and beyond. As for the constitution, a combination of realpolitik by the leading groups within the parties and the optimistic rationalism of the times produced a number of constitutional changes, some more felicitous than others, many short-lived. This is a national weakness the political classes have not entirely shed to this day.

On to the welfare state

By the second decade of the twentieth century, Uruguay was a vigorous country, sought after by young, hard-working immigrants, with a flourishing agricultural sector. It was progressive in certain areas like genetics and possessed a budding industry, thriving trade, and a battery of modern legislation. All of this legislation concerned the state: public health, public education, public works, state companies (monopolies in most cases), preferential financing by state banks (including a housing mortgage bank), labor legislation, a widespread social security system covering retirement (at 55 and 60), and a constellation of pension causes. Everything added up to an almost ideal country, by then politically stable. And so it was, while it lasted, or, rather, while agricultural income sufficed to pay for both industrial protection and distribution policies.

At the end of the Second World War, Uruguay adopted the import substitution model as its growth strategy. This model implied the protection of industrial activities through high tariffs (sometimes prohibitive) and the taxation of primary sector exports (mainly agriculture) as a way to subsidize the domestic production of agricultural raw materials. By definition, the domestic market became the main driver of growth, but its limited size set unsurpassable constraints on its growth. In addition, an array of labor market regulations, price controls, and distorted exchange rates surrounded a bloated public sector. This distorting framework imposed additional burdens on an already weakened economic growth path. As a result, the model began to show symptoms of exhaustion just as the favorable external conditions stemming from the Korean War elapsed. In fact, the Uruguayan economy stagnated between 1955 and 1973.

The stagnation process fostered a chain of events characterized by the onset of inflationary pressures, banking and balance of payment crises, and political tensions stemming from a middle class now exiled from a lost paradise. As a reaction, the main political outcome was the rise of an urban guerrilla movement (the "Tupamaros") in the mid 1960s that ultimately led to a military coup in 1972. Hence, the traditional stability of Uruguay's social foundations broke, and the import substitution model collapsed.

The 1970s were characterized by a changing international environment. In 1971, the dollar's convertibility with a fixed parity to gold was abandoned, and the liberalization of the balance of payments capital account began. These events signaled the end of the Bretton Woods paradigm, born at the end of Second World War, which had promoted a stable international macroeconomic environment. Since then, higher exchange rate volatility and the emergence of autonomous capital flows have constituted the new working patterns of the global economic system. In consequence, domestic economic policy management faced unknown challenges, especially in emerging economies such as Uruguay.

Uruguay's stance during that period was characterized by severe external sector problems. While the current account recorded surpluses from 1965 to 1973, the capital account showed continuous deficits, due to persistent private capital flight. Following two large negative external shocks – the oil price shock in 1973–1974, and the closure of the European market (the main export destination) to Uruguayan beef in 1972 – the trade balance also shifted to a deficit, exacerbating the balance of payments problems.

After two decades of inward-looking economic policies and financial repression, Uruguay launched a series of liberalization reforms in the mid-1970s. These reforms included trade and financial liberalization, and the deregulation and elimination of distortions in domestic markets. This reform process led to substantially higher GDP growth rates, but also to an increased influence of external factors (i.e., international financial conditions, global growth, terms of trade, and regional influences) and a higher incidence of financial crises. Hence, the post-liberalization period has been characterized by higher trend GDP growth rates than in the past, but also by pronounced boom-bust cycles – in part because financial liberalization was associated with risky capital inflows, lending booms, financial fragility (due to dollarization), real exchange rate appreciation, current account deficits, and occasional crises. Uruguay's 1982 and 2002 crises are perfect examples of the collapse of the economic cycle fostered by the joint action of negative external shocks, macroeconomic inconsistencies, and fragilities in the financial sector.

After the 2002 crisis, Uruguay recovered rapidly and – maintaining the market-oriented policies of economic openness – has shown stellar growth since then. The 2008 global crisis put a drag on that trend, but the economy did not enter recession. In fact, a moderate but positive rate of economic growth is projected in 2009. In sum, the export-led growth model coupled with economic liberalization and structural reforms delivered unsurpassed positive results in terms of long run growth.

Liberalization, growth, and crisis, 1974–1983

As mentioned before, two decades of endemic stagflation, coupled with recurrent balance of payments crises, led to social tensions that disrupted the country's political stability. Uruguayan society gradually began to accept that major economic policy changes were needed to overcome the situation.

The answer was the introduction of a new growth model based on promotion and diversification of exports, implementation of market-based economic reforms aimed at fostering total productivity, and liberalization of the financial system – including the foreign exchange market – as a way to address the external imbalances. In this endeavor, Uruguay opted first to liberalize the capital account of the balance of payments and then to open up the current account through a gradual process of protection reduction.

As a result, between 1974 and 1979 all restrictions on capital flows and foreign exchange controls were eliminated, and the dual exchange market was unified. Moreover, interest rates were freed, guidelines for credit allocation by sector and Central Bank rediscounts to commercial banks were discontinued, and barriers to entry into banking were lifted.

Moreover, price controls and subsidies, which were widespread in Uruguay, were progressively removed.[1] Trade policy, in turn, started to shift gradually toward liberalization and openness. Export taxes were lowered, and some trade barriers – import quotas for instance, in 1975 – were abolished. Later, by end-1978, a timetable was introduced for the unification and reduction of existing import taxes into a global tariff.[2]

In addition, a tax reform was implemented in 1974 aimed at simplifying the tax system and making it more efficient and neutral. Personal income tax was eliminated, and the tax structure increased the emphasis on indirect taxes – especially VAT.

The reforms took place in an environment of high international liquidity arising from current account surpluses in oil exporting countries, which enjoyed the extraordinary bonanza (the so-called "petrodollars") associated with the first oil shock. The international banking system recycled this upsurge in global liquidity thorough huge lending to emerging economies. These events were a blessing for Uruguay, which was starving for growth financing, but also disguised the seeds of a bubble that would burst years later in banking and in a debt crisis that fostered high social costs.

The impact of the liberalization and reform process coupled with abundant external financing was reflected in strong macroeconomic performance (see Figure 11.1). Real GDP – which had remained stagnant since the mid-1950s – grew at an average annual rate of 4.5 percent in 1974–1980, exports and imports increased dramatically, investment levels rose significantly, and the balance of payments recorded surpluses. Furthermore, the public sector deficit declined from more than 5 percent of GDP in 1974, to about 0.5 percent of GDP in 1977–1978, shifting into surplus in 1979–1980.

Inflation, however, remained high, becoming the authorities' main policy concern. Although it fell from the 1972–1974 levels (more than 90 percent on average), it remained high and volatile during 1975–1978, at 52 percent on average. The inability to bring down inflation persuaded the authorities to change the stabilization strategy in October 1978. A new stabilization plan, known as "the tablita", was launched with the objective of reducing inflation to world levels. The key feature of the plan was the use of the exchange rate as the nominal anchor of the system. The idea was that the devaluation rate would be set below the inflation rate and would be gradually lowered converging to a fixed exchange rate. It is worth noting that this type of stabilization program was a common feature of the experiences of the Southern Cone (Argentina, Chile, and Uruguay) in the 1970s.

The initial stages of the stabilization plan constituted a period of prosperity, characterized by consumption and investment booms, an increase in output, a deterioration of the trade balance and current accounts, and a steady appreciation of the real exchange rate. The

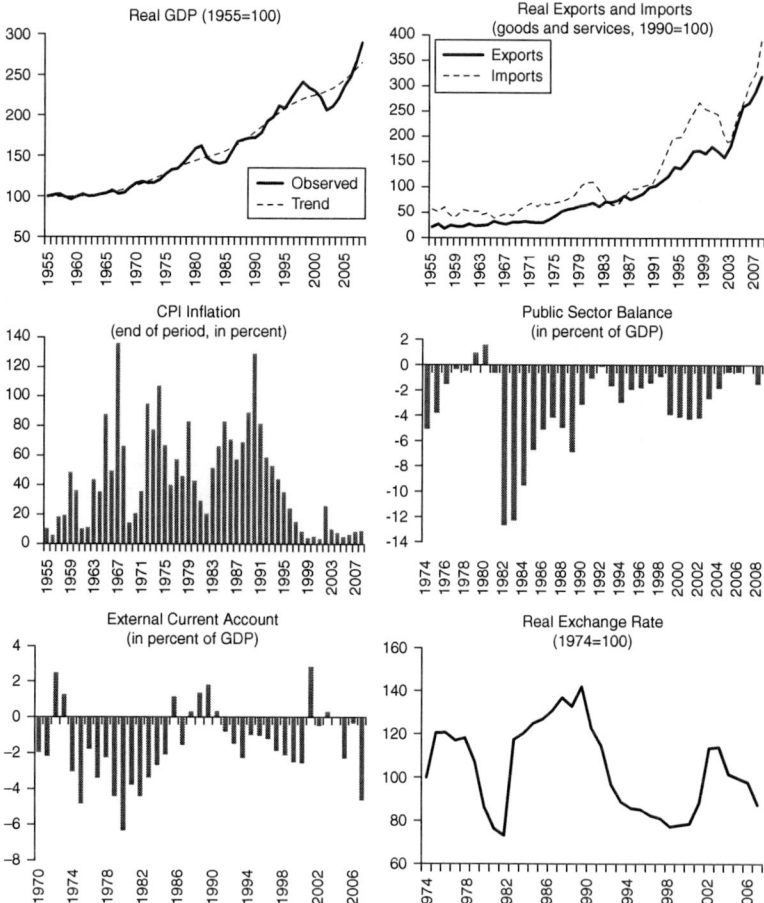

Figure 11.1 Selected macroeconomic indicators, Uruguay
Sources: IFS, WEO, BCU, MEF.

Uruguayan economy was strongly influenced by positive regional and global shocks during those years. The Argentine economy was booming, in part because a similar stabilization plan had been launched there. This, coupled with a stronger real exchange rate appreciation in Argentina – which improved Uruguay's competitiveness vis-à-vis its big neighbor, resulted in a sharp increase in Argentina's demand for Uruguayan goods and services. The effects of this positive regional influence were augmented by two additional shocks stemming from the global economy. First, international prices of Uruguay's main export goods rose significantly. Second, international financial conditions for Uruguay were extremely benign during that period. The associated large capital inflows fostered the expansion of domestic demand through the increased current account deficit.

The Uruguayan macroeconomic picture between 1978 and 1981 resembled developments in the region, where large foreign capital inflows, increasing domestic spending, widening trade and current account deficits, high real GDP growth rates, increasing stocks of foreign exchange reserves, and real exchange rate appreciation were the common standard.

In Uruguay, the large capital inflows, coupled with the liberalization of the domestic financial sector, triggered a boom in credit to the private sector. No specific action was taken to control credit by the private banking system. On the contrary, credit expansion was promoted through the relaxation of regulation and supervision of the banking system, thus facilitating also asset price bubbles.

The "tablita" crisis

Despite the apparent success in the early stages of the stabilization program, there were important shortcomings that would become evident in the second half of 1981, when the benign external conditions suddenly deteriorated. First, the adjustment of public wages, pensions, and public tariffs was linked to past inflation and not to the evolution of the exchange rate. This implied a large increase in these sums and tariffs measured in dollars, which affected the competitiveness of the economy. Second, fiscal policy was inconsistent with exchange rate policy. Third, the liberalization of cross-border capital flows and the deregulation of the domestic banking system contributed to the buildup of asset price bubbles, excessive corporate debt levels, and currency mismatches in the balance sheets of firms and households.

Furthermore, the external environment started to change dramatically. In the US, the FED tightened monetary policy to fight inflation, leading to a large increase in real interest rates that triggered a reversal in capital flows and increased the external debt burden. Furthermore, commodity prices collapsed, deteriorating Uruguay's terms of trade. In addition, after Argentina's real exchange rate devaluation, Uruguay's external competitiveness was eroded further.

In consequence, capital started to flow out of Uruguay rapidly and on November 12, 1981, the Central Bank let the exchange rate float. After an initial overshooting, the exchange rate stabilized at a level 50 percent higher than the pre-float level. This increased the burden of corporate and households' dollar-denominated debt, and as a result, bank nonperforming loans soared. Moreover, the loss of confidence in the banking system triggered a bank run by both residents and nonresidents (mainly Argentineans). This situation brought most banks to the verge of insolvency, including BROU – the large state-owned commercial bank. The bank resolution strategy consisted of a recapitalization program under which Central Bank promissory notes were exchanged for banks' nonperforming loans.[3] These measures implied heavy losses, aggravating the deterioration of the overall public sector's fiscal accounts and augmenting government indebtedness. In fact, the combined public sector deficit reached more than 18 percent of GDP in 1982, with the Central Bank accounting for 8 percent of GDP.

Real GDP declined by about 9.5 percent in 1982 and 6 percent in 1983. Unemployment, in turn, jumped from 6.5 percent in 1981 to 12 percent in 1982, and to more than 14 percent in 1983–1984. Moreover, real wages plummeted, falling by more than 30 percent in 1983–1984. Uruguay's external debt rose from 45 percent of GDP in 1982 to more than 100 percent in 1985. However, Uruguay tried to protect its longstanding tradition of prompt debt service by seeking international bank refinancing to avoid a default. This led to negotiations with creditors to reschedule maturing debt obligations.

The reconstruction period, 1985–1990

Democracy returned in 1985. In addition to the main challenges of regaining political stability and achieving social healing, addressing macroeconomic imbalances and fostering growth were imperative goals of the constitutional government. The difficulties faced by the elected authorities at that moment should not be underestimated. The fiscal deficit was still very large, at about 10 percent of GDP. Also, external public debt required prompt restructuring, with multilaterals such as the IMF being the only source of net financing. Meanwhile, the health of the banking system remained fragile, with some banks still facing liquidity and/or solvency problems.

This number of difficulties made more evident certain policy implementation constraints inherited from the military period. For instance, an extraordinary upsurge in expenditure was expected mostly to cover wage claims, indemnities, and the reinstatement of public servants laid off arbitrarily during the dictatorship.

Notwithstanding these difficulties, a modest economic recovery began in 1985, followed by two years of rapid growth in 1986–1987 (9 percent and 8 percent respectively). This was in part driven by positive regional shocks – an expansion of demand in Argentina and Brazil associated with the early stages of new stabilization plans in these countries (the "Plan Austral" and the "Plan Cruzado", respectively). Moreover, a decline in international real interest rates and a sharp fall in oil prices constituted positive external developments. The expansion of output proved to be short lived, though. In fact, real GDP growth slowed to an annual average of only 0.5 percent in 1988–1989, in part due to limits in the operating capacity of the manufacturing sector and a severe drought.

Although some fiscal consolidation was achieved, persistent fiscal deficits remained large (at 5.5 percent of GDP on average during 1985–1989). The objective of reducing inflation – which was secondary to regaining growth – also proved to be elusive during this period, as inflation rates remain high at about 75 percent on average.

Debt was wisely managed, with the aim of improving the maturity profile of public debt. The extension of the average debt maturity was achieved through mechanisms such as the Baker Plan and a MYRA (Multi-Year Rescheduling Agreement), which was also supported by financing – at favorable terms – from the IMF and the World Bank.

The health of the banking system continued to be extremely fragile. A new episode of financial turmoil ended with the purchase of two private banks (Pan de Azúcar, and de Italia) by BROU. Two other domestic banks (Comercial and Banco Caja Obrera) were nationalized with the idea of being reprivatized later. Meanwhile, BROU and BHU (the public mortgage bank) were undercapitalized, and had to obtain forbearance from their supervisors to continue operations. In addition, a domestic debt refinancing law was passed to address the severe solvency issues of a large fraction of the economy.

In sum, the first constitutional government attempted to achieve macroeconomic consolidation, with mixed results. Real wages and social indicators improved in this period, and social reconciliation was achieved after several years of dictatorship. However, a number of structural problems remained, including: a high degree of indexation of wages, pensions, and housing rents; a large fiscal burden to finance social security; the fragile financial position of the public sector; large inefficiencies in public services; a high level of labor conflict; broad exposure to regional developments (aggravated by the high macroeconomic volatility of Uruguay's big neighbors); and low investment levels.

The roaring 1990s, 1991–1998

A new government took office in March 1990. The main challenges of the new administration, headed by the Blanco Party, included consolidating the fiscal position (the fiscal deficit amounted to 7 percent of GDP in 1989), reducing inflation (which had remained high – reaching 90 percent in late 1989 – due to the monetization of the large public sector deficits), addressing the external debt sustainability problems, and promoting higher economic growth. In addition, the new government aimed to implement an ambitious structural reform agenda, which included the privatization of some public sector enterprises, a number of market-oriented reforms, and the deregulation of some sectors of the economy.

Fighting high inflation and reducing the large fiscal imbalances that were at its root were urgent objectives. The situation was worsened by a constitutional reform approved during the presidential election in November 1989. This reform indexed social security benefits to past inflation, shifting from yearly to quarterly adjustments. The higher frequency of adjustments implied a substantial increase in real social security spending,[4] equivalent to 2 percent of GDP per year on average. This higher expenditure (as well as the transition costs of the social security reform implemented later, in 1996) had to be financed by higher public debt, and social security became an obstacle to reaching fiscal consolidation. Moreover, the reform created a perverse inverse relationship between real social security benefits and inflation, which would in the future become an additional constraint to bringing down inflation.

The new government promptly approved a tough fiscal package, with an adjustment of approximately 4 percent of GDP, mainly consisting of tax increases. Meanwhile, Uruguay accelerated external debt negotiations in the context of the Brady Plan, initiated by the previous administration, to obtain a debt reduction agreement and refinancing of the remaining debt.[5] These negotiations ended with the conclusion of the Brady Agreement in February 1991, and resulted in a debt reduction of about 20 percentage points of GDP. In 1992, Uruguay regained access to international capital markets through the issuance of a dollar-denominated bond.

In December 1990 a new stabilization plan was launched, with the objective of bringing inflation down to 30 percent over a period of three years. The plan used the exchange rate as the nominal anchor of the system but allowed it to fluctuate within a band. Although not as quickly as was envisaged under the program inflation declined steadily, from 130 percent in 1990 to 45 percent in 1994.

The Blanco Party's administration was also characterized by an ambitious structural reform agenda. A key element of this was the reduction of the size of the state, including the privatization of public sector enterprises. With this aim, a law was passed in September 1991 authorizing the government to partially privatize ANTEL, the state telecommunications company. However, a referendum against the law was promoted by the left and later backed by a faction of the Colorado Party, with strong support from the unions. In December 1992 the population overwhelmingly voted against the privatization law, with 72 percent of the voters rejecting it. The strong opposition to the law sent a clear message to the political parties, constituting a landmark against any future plans to privatize or even reform public enterprises. Notwithstanding the failure regarding ANTEL, the government was able to privatize some port services and the state airline company. Furthermore, in November 1993 a law was approved to deregulate the insurance industry, which implied the elimination of the state monopoly.[6]

The government also attempted to undertake a comprehensive social security reform, which was perceived as a necessary condition to achieving long-run fiscal sustainability.[7] The efforts to pass the law through Parliament failed. Various factors contributed to a gradual shortage of funds in the social security system, including demographic factors, certain inadequate parameters and regulatory aspects of the system,[8] and – especially – the effects of the constitutional reform approved in 1989, which implied a huge increase in social security expenditure in real terms. Efforts to reform the social security system continued in the next administration headed by the Colorado Party, and – finally – a law was passed approving the reform in April 1996. The reform introduced a new "mixed" system, with contributions and benefits determined through a combination of a "pay-as-you-go" pillar (or "intergenerational transfer") and an "individual saving/investment" pillar.[9]

Trade policy was also modified. Uruguay joined Argentina, Brazil, and Paraguay to sign a free trade agreement in 1991, formally launching the Southern Common Market (Mercosur). The main objective was to remove trade barriers within the region and improve bargaining power vis-à-vis other trade blocks in order to facilitate integration with the global economy. Uruguay's external trade had been largely dependent on the region. The trade openness process initiated in the 1970s was accompanied by a high concentration of trade with both Argentina and Brazil, due not only to geographic reasons ("regional determinism") but also to institutional considerations.[10] The formation of Mercosur resulted in an important decrease in tariff and nontariff barriers to trade within the region, thus strengthening the concentration of Uruguay's exports in the region. In fact, the share of Brazil and Argentina in Uruguayan trade increased from 30 percent in 1986–90 to 45 percent in 1996–2000.

As a result, Uruguay became more region-dependent, given in particular that a large fraction of exports to these countries consisted of goods and services tradable only within the region. Therefore, in the absence of a regional demand for them, they would be mainly nontradables. The risks entailed would become evident later on, when Brazil devalued its currency in 1999 and then Argentina fell into recession. Other risks associated with Mercosur included potential trade diversion due to still relatively high external tariffs, and the lack of macroeconomic policy coordination – in particular exchange rate policy. Finally, Mercosur de facto lowered Uruguay's flexibility to engage in bilateral trade agreements with other trade blocks or individual countries, curtailing its transition toward integration with the global economy.

Despite all the problems and risks involved, it was very difficult for Uruguay not to participate in the regional integration process promoted by Argentina and Brazil. But in any case, the regional trade agreement reinforced the high correlation between Uruguay's economic cycle and those of its neighbors, adding more challenges to economic policy implementation.

The period between 1991 through 1998 was characterized by high real GDP growth rates (4.5 percent on average). During 1991–1994, growth was facilitated both by Argentina's high growth rates and by benign international financial conditions for emerging markets. Strong capital inflows led to high levels of aggregate expenditure, large trade and current account deficits, and substantial real exchange rate appreciation. In consequence, the Central Bank's international reserves increased and public debt ratios declined substantially. Social indicators improved dramatically, with the incidence of poverty declining by one half in 1991–1994. It is worth noting that most of these phenomena were not specific to Uruguay, but mainly constituted a regional syndrome.

After the negative impact of the Mexican crisis in 1995, the economic boom resumed in 1996 and continued through 1998. From 1995 on, the second Colorado administration continued to implement sound macroeconomic policies, internalizing the high regional and global growth rates coupled with high liquidity in global financial markets to fight inflation. Thus, inflation continued to decline, finally reaching single-digit figures by 1998. Moreover, the fiscal deficit steadily declined from 3 percent of GDP in 1994 to 1 percent of GDP in 1998. As a result of these positive outcomes, Uruguay reached investment grade in 1997, joining Chile as the only country in the region enjoying this credit rating.

The 1990s also witnessed a recomposition of the Uruguayan economy's structure, with the increasing importance of tourism and financial services. The banking system expanded significantly, with both domestic credit and deposits growing rapidly. Deposits from nonresidents – mainly Argentine – also increased sharply, accounting for approximately 40 percent of total bank deposits and roughly 60 percent of dollar deposits in private banks. Tourism services receipts reached values comparable to those from the main traditional exports – such as beef and wool.

However, significant vulnerabilities remained, including:

- High liability dollarization levels, which implied currency mismatches in the balance sheets of the private and public sectors, including banks (especially BROU and BHU)[11]
- Strong exposure to the region – especially to Argentina, not only through trade concentration but also through financial channels, including the large stock of Argentinean deposits in Uruguayan banks
- Highly dollarized public debt
- Potential banking system fragilities stemming from the existence of "zombie" banks (Banco la Caja Obrera and Banco Pan de Azúcar y Banco de Crédito)
- High rigidities in public spending, given the large share of nondiscretionary expenditures (wages, pensions, and debt interest)
- The stock of Central Bank international reserves not being large enough to finance a reversal of external capital inflows and to perform its role as a lender of last resort in the event of a run on public banks' dollar deposits

External shocks, recession, and crisis, 1999–2002

The generally favorable external environment deteriorated dramatically in the late 1990s. First, the Russian crisis in August 1998 caused severe disruptions, bringing a reversal in capital inflows to Latin America. Second, the sharp devaluation of the Brazilian real in January 1999 affected Uruguay's competitiveness vis-à-vis Brazil, the main destination of its exports of goods.

Moreover, Argentina was also strongly affected, entering a stage of declining growth and inconsistent macroeconomic polices. This led to a political crisis that promoted subsequent rounds of distorting policies. The multiple linkages with that country caused additional negative effects in Uruguay's economic system. This combination of negative shocks from the region brought the economy into recession. Moreover, in 2001 an outbreak of foot-and-mouth disease stopped beef exports, throwing the whole agricultural sector into disarray. Thus, real GDP recorded a cumulative decline of about 10 percent between end-1998 and end-2001.

Lower economic activity meant a decline in tax revenues, a deterioration of the fiscal position, and an increase in public debt. The declining public sector deficit, which had been less than 1 percent of GDP in 1998, increased sharply, reaching about 4 percent of GDP in 1999–2001. This development implied an increase in public debt-to-GDP ratios, from around 35 percent in 1998 to more than 50 percent by 2001. Moreover, the debt was highly dollarized and thus serving it was extremely vulnerable to an exchange rate depreciation.

In addition, significant vulnerabilities remained in the financial sector, in part due to inadequate banking supervision. The main risks included currency mismatches in the balance sheet of corporations and households – which also implied credit risks for banks – due to high levels of financial dollarization, the large share of deposits by Argentineans, and endemic vulnerabilities in public banks. In particular, BHU had extensively lent long in pesos indexed to wages and borrowed short in dollars.

The continued deterioration of Argentinean macroeconomic fundamentals eroded Uruguay's situation even more, reversing its traditional role as a safe haven for financial outflows from that country. The turning point was Argentina's decision to declare a freeze on bank deposits (the "Corralito") in December 2001. Argentinean firms and households – facing strong liquidity constraints – began to withdraw their deposits from Uruguayan banks. The withdrawals particularly affected two private banks with strong links to Argentina: Banco Galicia Uruguay and Banco Comercial.[12,13]

The withdrawals became a full-fledged run on deposits amid fears that the Uruguayan Central Bank could either run out of reserves or (like Argentina) confiscate the deposits. Argentina's decision to abandon the peg, to force by decree the financial pesofication of all contracts (including deposits), and to default on public debt sent an array of negative signals that further deteriorated Uruguay's domestic market sentiment.

Problems in another large commercial bank (Banco de Montevideo) helped fuel deposit outflows, and by June 2002 it was intervened in by the Central Bank.[14] BROU and BHU, representing more than 50 percent of the banking system, also faced strong withdrawals. Hence, Central Bank reserves declined steadily, as the monetary authority played its role as a lender of last resort. Finally, the Central Bank let the peso float freely – causing an immediate overshooting of the exchange rate. On impact, this event fostered the melting down of banks' solvency due to the currency mismatch on their balance sheets.

The banking crisis exacerbated the real sector problems, triggering a collapse of output with severe social consequences. GDP fell by an additional 8 percent in 2002, with unemployment reaching record high levels (about 20 percent) and real wages declining sharply. Poverty levels also rose dramatically, from about 15 percent in 1998 to more than 30 percent after the crisis.

Crisis resolution, recovery, and growth, 2003–2009

The reaction of the government to the financial crisis constituted a comprehensive crisis management strategy. This strategy consisted of several stages including the provision of liquidity assistance to support the banking system, measures to stop the bank run, the resolution of insolvent banks and a restructuring of the public banking system, and strengthening the financial sector's regulatory and supervisory framework. Furthermore, the government implemented a very successful and market-friendly sovereign debt restructuring, which was key to regaining debt sustainability, strengthening market confidence, and sharply lowering the country's risk premiums.

The policy responses to deal with the bank run evolved starting in early 2002 as the crisis intensified. From the beginning, the Central Bank supplied liquidity support to the affected banks using its own reserves. The IMF and other multilaterals helped to replenish part of the reserves through current programs in place. The liquidity assistance discriminated between a group of core banks (mostly domestic) with critical participation in the payment system and a nationwide branch network and client base, and other noncore banks (mostly foreign branches and subsidiaries).[15] The liquidity support by the Central Bank focused on the former, with the latter relying on their own liquidity support. That represented an explicit policy decision taken by authorities. As the deposit run intensified, a United States$2.5 billion facility – the Fondo para la Fortificación del Sistema Bancario (FFSB) – was created in June 2002 to supplement the debilitated lender-of-last-resort facilities, and to provide additional liquidity and equity support to troubled core banks.[16] Deposit withdrawals, however, continued through July, contributing to further draining Central Bank reserves and curtailing its ability to continue to provide further liquidity to the system. The FFSB ultimately proved to be insufficient and, as stated before, a bank holiday was declared on July 30.

In late July, 2002, Uruguay's authorities decided to negotiate an emergency loan with the US Treasury aimed at financing a new program, which entailed a bank restructuring backed by an extraordinary amount of reserves readily available to stop the deposit run. Thus, an emergency credit line of US$1.5 billion was instantly wired to the Central Bank with the explicit purpose of providing liquidity to the banks involved, BROU and BHU. Meanwhile, further negotiations with the IMF began at top speed, which resulted in a new program that included the refinancing of the emergency line of credit provided by the US Treasury as well as measures to consolidate the banking system.

The new program created the Fondo de Estabilización del Sistema Bancario ("FESB"), a US$1.4 billion stabilization fund financed by multilateral institutions, which fully backed all dollar sight and savings deposits at core banks. Dollar time deposits of the public banks (BROU and BHU), in turn, were rescheduled to extend their maturities.[17] As regards foreign banks, no restrictions were imposed on their operations. No restrictions were placed on peso deposits in the system either. Finally, the operations of the four banks intervened in were permanently suspended – except for paying out sight and savings deposits with FESB – and actions were initiated toward their resolution.

The implementation of these measures backed with the extraordinary amount of liquidity, ultimately halted the bank run in August 2002. By then, the banking system had lost about 50 percent of total deposits and 65 percent of nonresident deposits. Moreover, a total of US$2.4 billion (roughly 20 percent of GDP) had been injected by the government through different liquidity support facilities. An important lesson could be derived from this crisis: a large sum of up-front liquidity is crucial to fighting a bank run. Other policy responses are typically ineffective and foster higher exit costs.

Once the deposit withdrawals stopped, the government implemented additional measures aimed at liquidating the insolvent banks, including BHU. Moreover, the government strengthened prudential regulation and the supervisory framework, including the creation of a more formal deposit insurance scheme, and introduced a new legal framework to improve banking resolution.

Another key element of the crisis management approach was a sovereign debt restructuring, completed by mid-2003. In fact, after the large devaluation of the peso and the sharp GDP contraction in 2002, the debt-to-GDP ratio had grown to about 100 percent. This development raised concerns about debt sustainability. In the Uruguayan authorities' view the problem was temporary illiquidity stemming from extraordinary circumstances rather than insolvency. Therefore they believed that getting an extension of the debt maturity profile was the optimal policy. The result was a market-friendly voluntary debt exchange implemented in May 2003. This exchange implied a formal process of consultation and negotiation with affected domestic and international creditors, which ended in a very high participation rate (of about 95 percent of investors).[18] The debt exchange drastically reduced short-term financial needs, enhancing the government's ability to service its debt obligations. The successful exchange also reduced financial risks sharply and improved market confidence, with country risk premiums falling from 2,300 basis points in April 2003, to near 600 basis points at end-2003. In October 2003 Uruguay regained access to external financing, issuing a bond in pesos indexed to inflation in global markets. This was actually the first time a Latin American country tapped international markets in a local currency.

Furthermore, the government attempted a fiscal consolidation. As a result, the public sector primary balance shifted into surplus, reaching 3.5 percent of GDP in 2003 and 4 percent of GDP in 2004.

The results of the crisis management strategy were quite impressive. Macroeconomic stability was regained, the banking system started to recover, debt sustainability issues were resolved, and some vulnerabilities of the past began to be addressed. The economy initiated a mild recovery in 2003 and GDP growth reached 5 percent in 2004. Inflation was kept under control in the aftermath of the exchange rate float, reaching single-digit figures in 2004. Exports recovered significantly and capital inflows (including foreign direct investment – FDI) resumed, facilitating a rapid recovery of Central Bank international reserves. In fact, reserves reached about US$2.5 billion in 2004, roughly 75 percent of the pre-crisis level. Bank deposits were also recouped, reaching about 80 percent of the pre-crisis level – although dollarization remained high.

A new administration took office in March 2005. A center-left coalition (Frente Amplio) was in office for the first time in Uruguay's history. The coalition's economic program was based on two basic pillars: prudent macroeconomic policies coupled with social expenditures (health, education, and subsidies targeted to the poor, who were severely affected by the 2002 crisis).

Supported by favorable external conditions, Uruguay's economy boomed in 2005–2008. Relatively prudent macroeconomic policies benefited from an exceptionally benign global and regional environment, including strong global and regional growth, a boom in Uruguay's main export prices, and favorable global financial conditions. These factors supported an expansion of economic activity, with real GDP annual growth rates averaging 7 percent during this period, and peaking at close to 9 percent in 2008. Private investment rose to record levels benefiting from large flows of FDI, especially to the pulp mill industry and to the agricultural and agribusiness sectors. Meanwhile, unemployment fell to historic lows, real wages increased, and poverty levels declined substantially, with inflation maintained at single-digit level.

The 2008–2009 global crisis

The global crisis temporarily interrupted the expansionary cycle in Uruguay. However, due to the reduction of some vulnerabilities and the improvement of macroeconomic fundamentals after the 2003 crisis, the Uruguayan economy was better prepared to face the global shock than in the past. This enhanced macroeconomic stance included single-digit inflation; a healthier and well-regulated banking system;[19] substantial international reserves; a more flexible exchange rate regime; moderate current account deficits financed mostly by FDI; adequate public debt management that greatly reduced financing vulnerabilities, in particular by lengthening the debt maturity structure; a lower exposure of Uruguayan banks to Argentina;[20] and a more diversified structure of export destinations.

All these factors – combined with low leverage levels of private sector credit by companies and households,[21] and low exposure of banks to foreign toxic assets – contributed to dampening the impact of the current global crisis, which was transmitted mainly through real channels. In fact, while activity slowed down with the global recession, the impact appears to have been short lived, and the financial sector has held up considerably well.

Conclusion

The past three decades of economic history in Uruguay are rich in providing important lessons:

- First, the inward-looking growth model based on import substitution, in place since the mid-century, was incompetent to foster sustainable economic growth. Expansionary fiscal policies were not

the solution, as they led to high inflation and therefore substantial economic and social costs.
- Second, the liberalization process and structural reforms initiated in the 1970s as a result of the failure of the previous economic model triggered some fundamental transformations in the Uruguayan economy which led to higher growth rates. The new economic policy stance relied mainly on an export-led growth model for which trade openness, financial liberalization, and price setting deregulation were the basic fundamentals.
- Third, the external environment began to play an enhanced role in explaining domestic events. The end of the Bretton Woods system in the early-1970s facilitated the resurgence of autonomous cross-border capital flows. This fact, coupled with capital account and financial liberalization, resulted in a greater exposure of the domestic economy to external factors, posing new challenges to the design of domestic economic policy. Moreover, higher economic cycle volatility stemming from international and regional events added to these challenges. In this regard, the Mercosur agreement reinforced the impact of regional influences through the trade channel.
- Fourth, the 2002 crisis made the importance of a well-regulated and supervised financial system very clear. This episode showed once again that weaknesses in those areas are the key transmission channels for negative external impacts.
- Finally, the export-led growth model coupled with adequate macroeconomic policy management, in particular aimed at fiscal consistency, was capable of successfully passing the acid test of the 2002 crisis. In fact, since then, the country has been able to regain robust growth rates, to consolidate its fiscal stance, to improve public debt indicators, and to reduce poverty.

As a result, Uruguay was only mildly affected by the 2008 global crisis, and is now well positioned to benefit from a recovery in the world economy. However, Uruguay still has a number of challenges remaining to foster stronger long-term growth. In this regard, enhancing total factor productivity remains a key, but elusive, economic policy goal. These challenges include the achievement of a more diversified trade structure; an increase in investment in the infrastructure, technology, and energy sectors; the modernization of the public sector, including public enterprises; the revamping of the education system; a reduction in the levels of poverty and social inclusion.

Notes

1. In early 1974, 94 percent of the items included in the consumption basket were administered by COPRIN, a governmental office.
2. This timetable, however, was not completed; it was discontinued due to fiscal needs following the 1982 crisis.
3. The pricing of the exchanged assets was done according to the likely residual asset value. As in any crisis resolution process, the metrics used were in most cases arbitrary.
4. Social security expenditure accounted for about half of public sector spending.
5. By the end of the 1980s, several years after the 1982 debt crisis, most Latin American countries were still facing severe debt sustainability issues. Against this background, in March 1989, the new Secretary of the US Treasury, Nicholas Brady, launched a plan to restructure sovereign debt with the objective of reducing the heavy burden imposed by overindebtedness in the region.
6. Two specific segments of the market remained under state company monopoly: the risk coverage of public enterprises and insurance for labor accidents.
7. Uruguay pioneered in Latin America the creation of a very generous social security system. However, the financial health of the system deteriorated over time, and by the early 1990s was it heading toward bankruptcy.
8. For instance, a low minimum retirement age, a short period used to calculate the base salary to determine pension entitlements, and great flexibility in meeting the years-of-service requirement.
9. The state maintained an active role in the system, administrating the pay-as-you-go pillar and regulating and competing with the private pension funds (the AFAPs).
10. Uruguay signed two preferential trade agreements with its regional neighbors. The first one was signed with Argentina (CAUCE) in 1974; the second one was signed with Brazil (PEC) in 1975.
11. Reducing dollarization through market-friendly measures has proved to be extremely difficult not only in Uruguay, but also around the world. Dollarization constitutes a structural problem derived from economic agents' reluctance to save in domestic currency, in part as a result of the trauma of past episodes of high inflation and devaluation.
12. Banco Galicia operated almost fully as an offshore bank, receiving deposits from and lending to Argentina. It began losing deposits in December 2001, and by February 2002 – as the parent bank was unable to support it – the Central Bank intervened.
13. The problems of Banco Comercial, which was strongly linked to an Argentinean bank, originated in a fraudulent activity that depleted the bank's capital. The news about the fraud triggered withdrawals in January and February 2002, with the bank losing 20 percent of deposits.
14. Two other domestic private banks were subsequently intervened in: Banco La Caja Obrera and Banco de Crédito.
15. The group of core banks included BROU, BHU, the three banks intervened in, and some small domestic cooperatives.

16. The initial resources of the FFSB came from the IMF, with additional resources to be provided by other multilateral institutions and the government in the form of dollar-denominated bonds.
17. BROU absorbed all foreign currency and timed deposits of the BHU, which was no longer allowed to receive deposits.
18. Domestic participation was especially high, with 100 percent participation by domestic financial institutions and 98 percent by domestic retail investors.
19. Banks showed high liquidity and capital ratios, and very low levels of nonperforming loans. Moreover, credit and deposit dollarization had declined somewhat.
20. Nonresident deposits (mainly Argentinean), which accounted for more than 40 percent of total deposits by end-2001, represented less than 20 percent by late 2008. Moreover, while some Uruguayan banks used to be heavily exposed to Argentine assets in the past, this type of exposure has recently been quite small. This change in part reflects the improvement of regulation and supervision of the financial system and the measures taken to internalize credit risks from dollarization and cross-border activities.
21. Private sector credit levels, which reached almost 60 percent of GDP in December 2001, are now substantially lower, at 25 percent of GDP.

Bibliography

Abdala, W. and S. Maciel. *Manual de Ciencia Política*. Editorial Fondo de Cultura Economica.
Aguilera de Prat, C. R. and P. Vilanova (1987). *Temas de Ciencia Política*. Barcelona: PPU.
Almond, Abraham Gabriel and Albert Battle (1997). *Diez Textos Básicos de Ciencia Política*. Barcelona: Editorial Ariel.
Arendt, H. (1999). *Crisis de La República*. Taurus.
Aristóteles. *Obras*. Aguilar.
Aron, R. (1997). *Introduction a la Philosophie Politique: Démocratie et Révolution*. Livre de Poche.
Aron, R. *Une Histoire du XXe. Siecle*. Plon.
Arthur, J. (1992). *Democracy*. Belmont, CA: Wadsworth Publishing.
Baran, P. A. *The Political Economy of Growth*. Modern Reader.
Barber, B. (1988). *The Conquest of Politics*. Princeton, NJ: Princeton University Press.
Berlin, I. (1996). *The Sense of Reality: Studies in Ideas and Their History*. Pimlico.
Bobbio, N. (1987). *The Future of Democracy*. Minneapolis, MN: University of Minnesota Press.
Bobbio, N. (2004). *El Filósofo y la Política (Antología)*. Editorial Fondo de Cultura Economica (FCE).
Braud, P. *Science Politique, L'Etat*. Paris: Du Seuil.
Braud, P. *Science Politique, La democracie*. Paris: Du Seuil.
Brittan, S. (1983). *The Roles and Limits of Government*. Minneapolis, MN: University of Minnesota Press.
Broadie, A. (1997). *The Scottish Enlightenment*. Edinburgh: Canongate Books.

Bronner, S. E. (ed.) (2006). *Twentieth Century Political Theory*. New York: Routledge.
Brown, B. E. and R. Macridis. *Comparative Politics*. Harcourt Brace.
Buchanan, J. M. (1975). *The Limits of Liberty*. Chicago: University of Chicago Press.
Buchanan, J. M. (1977). *Freedom in Constitutional Contract*. College Station, Texas: Texas A & M University Press.
Burke, E. and T. Payne (1973). *Reflections on the Revolution in France*. New York: Anchor.
Burke, E. and T. Payne. *The Rights of Man*. New York: Anchor.
Burns, J. M. (1982). *The Vineyard of Liberty*. New York: A. Knopf.
Burns, J. M. (1986). *The Workshop of Democracy*. New York: Vintage Books.
Burns, J. M. (1987). *The Crosswinds of Freedom*. New York: Vintage Books.
Caminal, Badia, M. *Manual de Ciencia Política*. Madrid: Tecnos.
Cappella, J. N. (1997). *Spiral of Cynicism*. New York: Oxford University Press.
Chilcote, R. H. (1981). *Theories of Comparatives Politics: The Search for a Paradigm*. Boulder, CO: Westview Press.
Cohen, J. L. and A. Arato (1994). *Civil Society and Political Theory*. Cambridge, MA. MIT Press.
Cohen, M. and N. Fermon. (1996). *Princeton Readings in Political Thought*. Princeton, NJ: Princeton University Press.
Collin, D. *Les Grands Notions Philosophiques La Justice et Le Droit*. Seuil.
Collin, D. *La Societe, Le Pouvoir, L'Etat*.
Crick, B. *In Defense of Politics*. Penguin.
Crozier, M. (1987). *Etat Modeste, Etat Moderne*. Fayard.
Dahl, R. A. (1989). *Democracy and Its Critics*. New Haven: Yale University Press.
Dahl, R. A. and C. A. Lindblom (1953). *Politics, Economics and Welfare*. New York: Harper and Row.
de Brun, Julio and Gerardo Licandro (2006). "To Hell and Back: Crisis Management in a Dollarized Economy. The Case of Uruguay," in *Financial Dollarization: The Policy Agenda*. Adrián Armas, Alain Ize, Eduardo Levy Yeyati and International Monetary Fund (eds.), pp. 147–76. New York: Palgrave MacMillan.
de Posadas, Ignacio and Carlos Steneri (2004). "Mercosur" in *Latin American Business Cultures*. Robert Crane and Carlos Rizowy (eds.). Prentice Hall.
Denquin, J. M. (1992). *Science Politique*. Paris: Presse Universitaire.
Denquin, J. M. (1994). *Introduction a la Science Politique*. Paris: Hachette.
Desai, M. (2002). *Marx's Revenge*. London: Verso.
Diamond, Larry. *Politics in Developing Countries: Comparing Experiences with Democracies*. Lynne Pienner.
Diaz, Ramón (2003). *Historia Económica del Uruguay*. Montevideo: Editorial Taurus.
Doyenart, J. C. (2003). *El Problema está en Nosotros*. Montevideo: Editorial Fin de Siglo.
Durkheim, E. (1988). *Les Regles de la Metode Sociolique*. Paris: Flammarion.
Duverger, M. (1962). *Métodos de las Ciencias Sociales*. Barcelona: Ariel.
Duverger, M. (1975). *Sociología de la Política*. Barcelona: Ariel.
Easton, D. (1969). *Enfoques Sobre Teoría Política*. Beunos Aires: Amorrortu Editores.
Etzioni, A. *The Communitarian Thinking*. University Press of Virginia.

Etzioni, A.(1995). *New Communitarian Thinking: Persons, Virtues, Institutions and Communitites.* Charlottesville, London: The University Press of Virginia.
Franco, R. (1985). *Democracia'A la Uruguaya.* Montevideo: El Libro Libre.
Friedman, M. *Capitalism and Freedom.* Chicago: University of Chicago Press.
Gaus, G. F. (1996). *Justificatory Liberalism: An Essay in Epistemology and Political Theory.* Oxford: Oxford University Press.
George, R. P. (1996). *Natural Law, Liberalism and Morality.* Oxford: Clarendon Press.
González, L. B. *Political Structures and Democracy in Uruguay.* South Bend, Indiana: University of Notre Dame Press.
Gordon, S. (1995). *Historia y Filosofía de las Ciencias Sociales.* Barcelona: Ariel.
Gorosito, R. *El Nacimiento de la Política.*
Gray, J. *Liberalism.* Minneapolis, MN: University of Minnesota Press.
Gray, J. (1997). *Endgames: Questions in Late Modern Political Thought.* Polity.
Gray, J. (2001). *Las Dos Caras del Liberalismo.* Barcelona: Paidós.
Grompone, A. M. (1962). *La Ideología de Batlle.* Montevideo: Arca.
Hall, J. A. *Powers and Liberties: The Causes and Consequences of the Rise of the West.* Penguin Press.
Hamilton, A., J. Madison and J. Jay (1961). *The Federalist Papers.* New York: Mentor Press.
Hamilton, Garcia J. I. *El Autoritarismo y la Improductividad.* Sudamericana.
Hayeck, F. A. *Camino de Servidumbre.* Alianza.
Hayeck, F. A. (1960). *The Constitution of Liberty.* Chicago: The University of Chicago Press.
Hayeck, F. A. (1973, 1976, and 1979). *Law, Legislation, and Liberty.* 3 Vols. Chicago: The University of Chicago Press.
Heilbroner, R. L. *The Worldly Philosophers: The Lives, Times and Ideas of the Great Economic Thinkers.* Clarion.
Hofstadter, R. (1961). *The American Political Tradition and the Men Who Made It.* 15th Printing/Edition. New York: Vintage.
Horowitz I. L. and S. M. Lipset (1978). *Dialogues on American Politics.* New York: Oxford University Press.
Jacobs, L. A. (1997). *An Introduction to Modern Political Philosophy.* Upper Saddle River, NJ: Prentice Hall.
Joyce, P. *Politics.* Teach Yourself.
Keynes, J. M. *Teoría General de la Ocupación, el Interés y el Dinero.* Editorial Fondo de Cultura Económica.
Khon, J. *Le Contral Social Liberal.* Ed. Presse U.
King Gamble, J. *Introduction to Political Science.* Englewood Cliffs, NJ: Prentice Hall.
Kung, H. (1998). *A Global Ethic for Global Politics and Economics.* Oxford: Oxford University Press.
Kymlicka, W. (1991). *Contemporary Political Philosophy.* Oxford: Clarendon Press.
Larraín, Felipe (1986). "Liberalización Financiera en Uruguay: Éxito o Fracaso?" I Jornadas de Economía. Banco Central del Uruguay.
Lijphart, A. (1992). *Parliamentary Versus Presidential Government.* New York: Oxford University Press.
Lijphart, A. and C. Waisman. (1996). *Institutional Design in New Democracy.* Boulder, CO: Westview Press.
Locke, J. (1965). *Two Treatises of Government.* New York: Mentor Books.

López Murphy, Ricardo, Elbio Nattino and Michele Santo (1988). "Un Ensayo Sobre la Economía Uruguaya en la Década de los 80." III Jornadas de Economía. Banco Central del Uruguay.
Marquand, D. (1988). *The Unprincipled Society*. London: Jonathan Cape.
Marquand, D. (1997). *The New Reckoning: Capitalism, States and Citizens*. Cambridge: Polity.
Marx, K. *El Capital*. EDAF.
McClelland, J. S. (1996). *A History of Western Political Thought*. London: Routledge.
Meynaud, J. *Introducción la Ciencia Política*. Madrid: Tecnos.
Mill, J. S. *Politics and Society*. Glasgow: Fontana.
Montesquieu, C. *Persian Letters*. Penguin.
Montesquieu, C. *The Spirit of the Laws*. Berkeley, CA: University of California.
Mulhall, S. (1992). *Liberals and Communitarians*. Oxford: Blackwell.
North, D. C. (1990). *Institutions, Institutional Change and Economic Performance*. Cambridge: Cambridge University Press.
Oliveria, A. C. (1997). *Marco Regulador de las Organizaciones de la Sociedad Civil en Sudamérica*. Washington, DC: PNUD.
Ophulus, W. (1997). *Requiem for Modern Politics*. Boulder, CO: Westview Press.
Panizza, F. E. *Uruguay: Batllismo y Después*. Montevideo: De la Banda Oriental.
Pilar del Castillo and Ismael Crespo (1997). *Cultura Política*. Valencia: Tixrant Blanch.
Platon. *La República*. Tesoro Literario.
Porter, R. *Enlightenment*. London: Penguin Press.
Prieto, F. (1989). *Lecturas de Historia de las Ideas Políticas*. Madrid: Unión Editorial.
Putnam, R.O. (1993). *Making Democracy Work*. Princeton, NJ: Princeton University Press.
Rama, G. (1987). *La Democracia en Uruguay*. Beunos Aires: Latinoamericano.
Rauch, J. (1994). *Demosclerosis*. New York: Times Books.
Rauch, J. (1999). *Government's End*. New York: Public Affairs.
Real de Azúa, C. (1969). *La Clase Dirigente*. Montevideo: Nuestra Tierra.
Real de Azúa, C. *Partidos, Política y Poder en el Uruguay*. Montevideo: Universidad de la República.
Rosanvallon, P. (1981). *Le Crise de L'Etat Providence*. Paris: Du Seuil.
Rosanvallon, P. (2000). *La Démocratie Inachevée. Histoire de la souveraineté du peuple en France*. Paris: Gallimard.
Rothschhild, E. (2001). *Economic Sentiments*. Cambridge, MA: Harvard University Press.
Runciman, W. S. *Weber Selection*. Cambridge University Press.
Sabine, G. *Historia de la Teoría Política*. Madrid: Fondo de Cultura Económica.
Sahakian, W. and M. L. Sahakian. *The Ideas of the Great Philosophers*. New York: Barnes and Noble.
Sartori, G. *Comparative Constitutional Engineering*. New York: New York University Press.
Sartori, G. *Teoría de la Democracia*. Alianza.
Sartori, G. *Elementos de Teoría Política*. Madrid: Alianza.
Schmitt, K. *El Concepto de lo Político*. Madrid: Alianza.
Schumpeter, J. *Capitalism, Socialism and Democracy*. Allen and Unwin.
Serrano, N. P. *Tratado de Derecho Político*. Madrid: Civitas.

Shunway, N. (1993). *The Invention of Argentina*. Berkeley, CA: University of California Press.

Smith, A. *The Wealth of Nations*. Chicago: University of Chicago Press.

Sosa, Sebastián (2009), "The Influence of 'Big Brothers': Does Uruguay Face Two Rests of the World?" IMF Working Paper. Forthcoming.

Steneri, Carlos (1995). "El Endeudamiento Externo del Uruguay Desde la Crisis de los 80 al Plan Brady." *Revista de Economía*, 1(1). Segunda Época. Banco Central del Uruguay.

Steneri, Carlos. *Theory of Wordly Sentiments*. Oxford: Clarendon Press.

Tawney, R. H. *Religion and the Rise of Capitalism*. Penguin.

Taylor, P. B. (1960). *Government and Politics of Uruguay*. New Orleans: Tulane University.

Touchard, J. *Historia de las Ideas Políticas*. Madrid: Tecnos.

Touraine, A. *Qué es la Democracia*. Fondo de Cultura Universitaria.

Valadier, P. (1997). *L'Anarchie des Valeurs*. Paris: Albin Michel.

Van Parijs, P. (1995). *Real Freedom for All: What (If Anything) Can Justify Capitalism?*. Oxford: Clarendon Press.

Van Parijs, P. (2004). "Uruguay Debt Exchange: Lessons From Experience." *Georgetown Journal of International Law*, 35(4). Summer.

Van Parijs, P. (2009). "Uruguay 2002–03: Recovery from Economic Contagion." Comment in "Successes of the International Monetary Fund: Untold Stories of Cooperation at Work." Eduard Brau and Ian McDonald (eds.). New York: Palgrave Macmillan.

World Bank and Ministry of Finance, Uruguay (2007). "Uruguay: ¿Qué Aprendimos de la Crisis Financiera de 2002?" Presentations from the Conference, "Uruguay: ¿Qué Aprendimos de la Crisis Financiera de 2002?". Montevideo, May 29.

Zakaria, F. (2003). *The Future of Freedom: Illiberal Democracy at Home and Abroad*. New York: W.W. Norton & Company.

12

Spain: Influence, Inspiration, and the Roots of Latin America's Development Process

Alvaro Eguiron Vidarte

The country and its people

Spain is located in southwestern Europe, on the Iberian Peninsula. It occupies, together with Portugal and Andorra, the westernmost of all three southern peninsular zones of Mediterranean Europe. Thanks to its privileged geographical position, the Iberian Peninsula has, all through its history, been a vital gateway between the European Continent, Northern Africa, and America. As a result, there have been many migrations of various people into Spain: in addition to its original people, the Celts, the Phoenicians, the Greeks, the Carthaginians, the Romans, the Visigoths, and the Arabs and other Muslims, as well as people from other parts of Europe and from all over the world, who, in the contemporary period, have helped make up a diverse society.

Spain's mainland is bordered to the north by the Cantabrian Sea, France, and Andorra; to the east and south by the Mediterranean Sea; to the south by Morocco; and to the northwest and west by the Atlantic Ocean and Portugal. With an area of 504,000 square kilometers, Spain has a total population of 45 million inhabitants, which accounts for a population density of 89 people per square kilometer (a population denser than that of Latin American nations, but within an average range in continental Europe). However, the distribution of the population across the country is very unequal. The most populated areas lie in the conurbation around the capital city, Madrid, as well as along the coast; the hinterland is more depopulated.

Due to Spain's historical vicissitudes, various languages co-exist within different cultural spaces. This situation has helped increase the country's cultural and linguistic resources: Castilian, Galician, Basque, and Catalan-Valencian. In 1978 Spain established a parliamentary monarchy, to conform to its historical tradition. From an administrative point of view, in 1833, Spain was divided into 50 provinces and two cities in the North of Africa (Ceuta and Melilla). Ever since the Constitution of 1978, the country has been divided into 17 autonomous communities (equivalent to the different regions) and two autonomous cities, a status which conforms to the cultural and historical affinities of the different provinces, regions, towns, and villages that make them up.

The Spanish Constitution of 1978 establishes the division of the executive, legislative, and judiciary powers of government into separate, independent bodies. The legislative body is elected every four years through universal suffrage to appoint the executive body. This executive body is made up of the President of the Government (Prime Minister) and the Ministers of State, who are nominated by the former. The legislative body is made up of two chambers: the Congress of Deputies and the Senate. The Congress is made up of 350 deputies, elected by proportional representation on popular votes in closed lists; the Senate is made up of 225 senators, with territorial representation. The judiciary, on the other hand, has independent governmental bodies: the General Council of the Judiciary Power of Spain, whose main institutions are the Constitutional Court, the Supreme Court, the High Courts of Justice (i.e., the highest judiciary body of each autonomous community), and the Provincial Courts. The National Court has its seat in Madrid, with jurisdiction over the whole of Spain. Through its criminal chamber, for instance, it tries cases involving organized crime, terrorism, and drug trafficking in order to achieve maximum efficiency in the fight against such crimes.

The services sector in Spain is the country's main economic activity, followed by the industrial, building, and agricultural sectors respectively. Within the services sector, tourism, along with financial services and distribution are the country's major economic activities.

Historical outline

The history of the Iberian Peninsula began with the settlement of Greek and Phoenician colonies and with the outbreak of the Punic Wars between Carthage and Rome, prior to the conquest of the peninsula by the Roman Empire (beginning in 217 BC). This conquest experienced periods of strong resistance, because of the bellicose nature of its inhabitants, and its climate and geography. Thus, the conquest occurred through different invasions. The Roman Empire brought with it the adoption of a cultural, legal, and administrative body that would serve as the basis for Spain's reorganization for centuries. However, the adoption of Roman culture (*Romanization*), which was followed by Christianity, was really unequal on the Peninsula, since it extended south to the Mediterranean rather than to the north and west, where its impact was weaker. For example, the Basque language survived despite a long period of colonization. On the whole, the Roman period can be considered as a positive era for economic and social development, despite the negative factors derived from it.

During the period of decadence of the Roman Empire, Germanic peoples such as the Suebi, Vandals, and the Sarmatian Alans invaded the Peninsula, among whom only the Suebi settled in present-day Galicia and northern Portugal. Thereafter, the Visigoths ruled the peninsula (AD 476–711), except for the territories under the command of the Suebi and the Bascons. The Visigothic period was characterized by economic recession which impeded growth, as a result of years of continuous wars; slowing trade; and the conscious destruction of part of the road links from the Roman Empire in order to avoid another European invasion. The Visigothic monarchy was traditionally elected, and therefore not hereditary, which resulted in chronic institutional instability. The last of the hereditary disputes culminated in the invasion of the peninsula by the Arabs in AD 711, in the first of a series of campaigns that lasted until they were defeated near Poitiers in France by the Franks in AD 732.

In the early period, the Arabs were a civilization of conquerors who would ultimately leave an indelible mark of their culture all over Europe, to remain for centuries. In this respect, it is worth mentioning the University of Cordoba and the School of Interpreters of Toledo, for such languages as Latin, Hebrew, and Arabic. In an earlier phase, the territories that did not fall under Arab dominion were circumscribed in the Cantabrian Strip and the valleys in the High Pyrenees.

Shortly after the Battle of Covadonga (AD 789) the *Reconquista* or Christian reconquest of Spain began, with the recovery of the Hispanic territories, now ruled by the Christian Kingdoms. This process gave rise to a defragmented panoramic map of different kingdoms and territorial units: Portugal, León, Castilla, Navarra (sometimes with, and sometimes without, the Basque territories of Biscay, Guipúzcoa and Álava), Aragón, and Catalonia. The vast majority of these territories converged under the Reign of the Catholic Monarchs and the Surrender of Granada (AD 1492), thus putting an end to the Reconquista. As a result, the date was adopted as the foundation of Spain. The politics of the Catholic Monarchs revolved around the unification of the peninsula. Their politics of marriage to try to form an alliance with Portugal, however, were in vain. The only achievement was the annexation of the Kingdom of Navarra (AD 1520).

But in the year Spain was founded, another notable event occurred that would remain as an important landmark in its history: the discovery of America on October 12, 1492. This fact, along with subsequent Portuguese and Spanish expeditions, was to disseminate the idea of a New World in Renaissance Europe. This New World with fertile land and unknown products offered a unique opportunity for territorial expansion.

The organization of the American territory

After the conquest of the American territories, the Kingdoms of Spain and Portugal extended their geographical limits. This development would define their overseas empires and disseminate their religion and cultures. Hence, they obtained high returns in the form of gold and silver reserves, as well as through other unknown products at the time like maize (corn), potatoes, tomatoes, and tobacco – grown in extremely fertile lands. Among the goods that were introduced by the Spanish into the New World were animals like horses, cattle, and sheep for the production of milk and meat.

Once the conquest was over, the Hispanic monarchy faced a new challenge: organizing and administering a vast territory, which extended far beyond Spain itself and was sparsely populated. Politically, the American Territory depended upon the Council of the Indies, and was divided into viceroyalties, where each viceroy resided. He was the Minister Plenipotentiary to His Majesty the King with legal authority over militia, laws, taxes, etc. In the beginning, there were two viceroyalties, the Viceroyalty of New Spain and the Viceroyalty of Peru. The former was made up of the *Audiencias* (Courts and administrative boards) of Mexico, Guadalajara, Guatemala, Santo Domingo (with jurisdiction over The Antilles, Florida, and Venezuela), and Manila. The latter was made up of the Audiencias of Lima and Charcas, governing all South American territories and Panama with the exception of Venezuela. From 1580 to 1640, Portugal was annexed to the Crown of Spain. Thus, the Portuguese territories were integrated into the Spanish administered territories.

Shortly thereafter, new viceroyalties in New Granada and Río de la Plata were created under the rule of the Bourbon Dynasty in Spain.

The former, whose headquarters was in Bogotá, was to govern the territories of Colombia, Ecuador, Panama, and Venezuela; the latter was to have jurisdiction over the areas of "Upper Peru" (now called Bolivia), el Chaco, la Pampa, and the surrounding territories of Río de la Plata (which now constitute the nations Paraguay, Uruguay, Rio Grande do Sul in Brazil, and centre-northern Argentina). The latter viceroyalty had its headquarters in Buenos Aires, so as to boost trade and facilitate the defense of these territories.

As mentioned earlier, the viceroyalties were subdivided into *Audiencias*, which held administrative, judiciary, and fiscal powers. If the governor of a viceroyalty were a military man, he was given the name *captain general* and governed a division of a viceroyalty, a *"Captaincy-general"*[1] (i.e., an established district that was under serious pressure from foreign invasion or Indian attack).

The *cabildo* constituted another basic institution in colonial Spanish America. It was the competent body to rule the life of towns and cities, and was elected by the proprietors and major merchants. Thus, the cabildo was the fundamental unit of local government or a council. As Spanish colonization spread around towns and cities, Spanish–American trade developed, transporting European products to the New World and colonial products from Spanish America to Spain.

Trade with the New World was the main source of wealth in Europe from the time of the discovery of the American continent to the Industrial Revolution. As a direct result of the wealth generated by this trade the slave trade, smuggling, and piracy became common – especially in the Caribbean. European countries adopted different measures to combat this phenomenon. In some cases, they allowed free trade, whereas in others they restricted it to vessels with their own national flag. What is more, in some territories a private company monopolized trade through governmental concession. The Hispanic monarchy established a monopoly of trade through *La Casa de Contratación*, (*The House of the Indies*), an instrument of the Spanish crown's policy of centralization and imperial control. The company's headquarters was in Seville, the only port authorized to trade with America until the nineteenth century.

Seeking to suppress piracy and kidnapping, the Hispanic monarchy organized shipping on a regular basis to defend trade. There were three *galeones* annually; that is, military galleons accompanied the merchant ships. The Galleon of the Pacific cruised from Manila to the coast of New Spain, where the goods were directed toward the Port of Vera Cruz. Products coming from Upper Peru – such as gold, silver, and minerals – were sent by land to Lima and to the Port of El Callao and then transferred to Panama (first to the port of Nombre de Dios and then to the port of *Portobello*), to be finally sent to the port of Cartagena of the Indies. From Vera Cruz and Cartagena the goods were taken to La Habana (Havana), which served as a logistics base before the Atlantic crossing. In reverse order, the trade departing from Seville stopped over in the Canary Islands before crossing the Atlantic toward La Habana. Once there, the ships were repaired. The goods were again initially transferred to *Vera Cruz* and Cartagena of the Indies. Other ports were also important, such as Buenos Aires, Maracaibo, and Caracas. Their full development, however, took place only with the deregulation of trade in the eighteenth century.

This way of organizing trade not only sparked off the development of these ports as the key military logistics bases but also the development of the surrounding areas as their supply chain for primary commodities. Consequently, following the conquest there was immigration by the Indian population from their original territories toward the towns and cities that were closest to the trade routes, or toward those with mining of mineral deposits.

Among the main commercialized products were gold and silver. The mines were manned by indigenous workers, whether silver, mercury, or any other minerals. Large communities grew up around the mining centers and created an internal market for primary commodities, supplying themselves.

In the Viceroyalty of New Spain extensive livestock rearing played a key part. Such was the case in hinterland areas of today's Mexico, the coast along the Gulf of Mexico, and the early settlements of the Great Plains and Upper California. In Central America, the development of the lands of the Pacific Basin was remarkable. These lands were of volcanic origin, very fertile for farming, unlike the Caribbean coast, where there were lush tropical forests.

In the Viceroyalty of New Granada, the Panamanian economy and that of the areas close to Cartagena of the Indies developed around trade and its inherent needs. There were important craft guilds, centers for the transport of cattle, and arsenals with weapons, minerals, and precious metals that were a powerful lure for the populations from other areas. At the same time, cocoa and coffee were produced in large quantities, and cattle centers were concentrated in the Venezuelan Llanos (*Plains*). In the South American region, colonies of indigenous peoples settled down, in settlements called *reducciones*. The manpower shortage in the mining and farming industries was chronic throughout the entire subcontinent.

The mining centers were to be found in the Viceroyalty of Peru. Their economy spread around the commercial axis, which ran from Potosi,

Lima, and El Callao through La Paz and Cuzco. Depending on their climate, the lands lying between the coast and the mountains grew wheat, grapevines, and even sugar cane. In the Andean region, however, there were cocoa and coffee fields.

Large populations settled in the Rio de la Plata (River Plate) basin, concentrating in haciendas (plantations), which had all the facilities necessary for their supply. In hinterland areas, extensive livestock raising was the main activity.

Shipbuilding played an essential part in the development and expansion of trade. The main shipbuilding areas were Vera Cruz, Honduras, the Caribbean coasts, the Antilles, Cartagena of the Indies, the Venezuelan coasts, and also those areas with maritime ports like Guayaquil, El Callao, Buenos Aires, Valparaiso, and – southernmost – Valdivia.

Another major economic institution of the Spanish colonial period was the *encomiendas* or *encomienda* system (a feudal system of trusteeship). The *encomiendas* were the system by which the King awarded Spanish conquistadors landholdings and the profit thereof in exchange for spreading Christianity to the Indians who lived and worked there. The Indians were forced to pay a tribute to the trustees in exchange for protection and religious instruction. However, The problem is that it depended on the will of the employer, in many cases offered protection in exchange for labor, but many others became a human exploitation.

The Laws of the Indies made several failed attempts to end the *encomienda* system and apply the rules of the Crown, hoping to prevent them from becoming hereditary. By contrast, the settlers prevented landowners to keep their abolition social status. Finally, the benefits of the institution of the *encomienda* can be mentioned that large farms were established which allowed to reach before profitability and boost trade and economic activity. At the same time, *encomienda* had an adverse effect: the concentration of indigenous peoples from different latitudes helped spread illness, which decimated these populations. At the same time, the Quechua and Aymara languages gradually dominated the other indigenous languages, which eventually disappeared.

In short, during the Spanish colonization period economic activity was concentrated in urban areas situated near ports, trade routes, or mining centers. In rural areas, outside the Amazon region, the population and economic activity were based on haciendas.

As far as the factors of production are concerned, the economic activity of this period was intense in terms of manpower. This fact encouraged the immigration of both Europeans and natives as well as the development of slavery, especially in the areas where sugar cane was grown and also in the mining centers.

In the urban and mining centers, various craft guilds sprang up to meet the needs derived from trade, such as armaments, shipbuilding, and auxiliary tools for farming and livestock raising. Craftsmen endeavored to concentrate in the craft guilds and merchant guilds with a view to ensuring the protection of their interests and wealth creation.

Peninsular or European Spain

During this period, the Protestant Reformation began in Spain, which set off a series of domestic wars from 1521 to 1648. These wars ultimately desolated and impoverished economic and social growth. They were followed by the War of the Spanish Succession (1700–1714), resulting in the establishment of the French Bourbon dynasty in Spain, which carried out various administrative reforms such as the creation of the Viceroyalty of the Río de la Plata, in 1776, and opened several forts in Spanish America for commerce. Generally speaking, the eighteenth century can be considered a period of economic growth, despite the wars and the disturbance of the Spanish colonies by British troops.

Immediately afterward, came the French Revolution, along with Napoleon's invasion of the Iberian Peninsula. After the downfall of Napoleon, the spread of liberal ideas from the French Revolution contributed greatly to the uprising in the American colonies, as they fought for their independence.

All through the nineteenth century, Spain was immersed in an institutional and social crisis. There was a great divide between those in favor of the Old Regime, who defended its traditions, and a more liberal group, who advocated the adoption of new governmental forms. In the meantime, the Industrial Revolution occurred, with the development of new social classes, such as the extension of bourgeois society and the emergence of the working class. The country's traditional society faced new challenges, for which it was not ready.

The restoration of the Bourbons to the throne of Spain in 1875, after their forced exile in 1868, opened a period of institutional stabilization that boosted the country's economic development. This regime remained in place, through the reigns of Alfonso XII and XIII, until 1930. All through this period, positive developments took place, such as industrial development in the textile, metallurgy, and mining sectors and the development of trade, etc. There were also deep institutional crises such as the loss of Cuba, Puerto Rico, and the Philippines to the United States (1898); the wars in the North of Africa (1921–1927); and anarchist and Marxist outbreaks of violence that had a strong anticlerical character.

From 1917 onward, Spain was affected by a deep crisis (the Crisis of Liberalism). Monarch Alfonso XIII allowed the pronouncement of General Primo de Rivera, which put an end to the democratic regime in Spain. Although political agents and trade unions initially supported the new system, it would ultimately collapse, with the impact of the 1929 financial crisis. In 1930, the general's government resigned and in 1931, the republic was proclaimed. The King lost his popular support and the royal family went into exile.

The Second Republic was set in a convulsive period, within a Europe between wars, characterized by the struggle between democracy and fascist and communist totalitarianism. In this period, Spain was beset with unstable institutions. There was no clear parliamentary majority, and there was both a social confrontation between anticlerical and Catholic traditionalist sectors and an economic confrontation between owners and employers, day laborers and farmers, and the working class. Immersed in a climate of violence, the revolutionary insurgency of 1933 in Asturias would ultimately lead to a military uprising, which culminated in civil war (1936–1939).

Franco's regime (1939–1975) was established immediately before the Second World War (1939–1945) broke out. After the defeat of Germany, General Franco was internationally isolated due to the support he had received from the Axis Powers. The support Franco received from Latin American nations, especially Argentina, and the outbreak of the Cold War, along with his eventual alignment in favor of the United States, ultimately ensured the permanence of the regime. Thereafter, Spain was ruled like a kingdom without a king, through a centralized administration supported by a single party, and with vertical trade unions. Even though Spain registered unprecedented economic growth, the absence of fundamental liberties and the isolation of the regional languages and democratic ideas became blemishes on Spain's economic achievement.

Francisco Franco died in November 1975, and King Juan Carlos I of Bourbon and Bourbon of the Two Sicilies began his reign. A new period of transition was initiated with the first elections in 1977 and the approval of the Spanish Constitution in 1979. Ever since that day, Spain's form of government has been a constitutional monarchy, with a division of the powers of the state. The country's territories are divided into autonomous communities, each possessing a parliament and governmental body.

In 50 years Spain has changed considerably. From being internationally isolated with an agricultural economy, it has transformed itself to become a player in the international arena, participating in major economic and political decision-taking centers. The incorporation of Spain into NATO in 1982, its entry into the European Economic Community in 1986 and into the constitution of the Ibero-American Community of Nations, its membership on the United Nations Security Council for a three-year-period, its adoption of the Euro and its participation in the G-20 summit are examples of the transformation Spanish society has undergone over time.

Cultural diversity in Spain

Thanks to its history, the Iberian Peninsula is inhabited by peoples of unparalleled cultural wealth. The following languages are spoken in Spain: Portuguese, Galician, Castilian (with dialects in Asturias, the Pyrenees of Aragon and in Murcia and Andalusia), Basque, Catalan, and Catalan-Valencian.

All through its history, there have been successive periods of tolerance and periods of persecution of minorities. Such tolerance and intolerance ranges from political freedom to freedom of worship and religion, and freedom of education and culture. On the other hand, there have been periods in which political power was concentrated in a single kingdom or a single political structure, and other periods when the territory was divided. Additionally in the nineteenth century, each political tendency was succeeded by an ad hoc constitution that granted privileges to those in power. These privileges were replaced by those granted with the establishment of yet another constitution and status quo whenever a new political government was installed, until the restoration of the Bourbons. In the twentieth century, only a dictatorship was able to reestablish institutional stability. However, this reality entailed the persecution and cultural isolation of all minority languages, which ultimately led to cultural impoverishment. The creation of a unique system of regional autonomy has sought to provide a more appropriate, freer path. However, a common or well-defined framework is necessary so that diversity will not lead to separatism. All in all, Spain has struggled between order and disorder, unity and separatism.

Spain's extensive tradition has created a way of thinking and of doing business in which a good relationship between the parties concerned is essential. The importance of relationships is common to Latin countries or coastal states of the *mare nostrum*, the Mediterranean. Additionally, the country's regional and linguistic diversity are reflected in dissimilar, well-defined behavior patterns. For example, doing business in Madrid is completely different from doing business in Barcelona. Primarily, larger towns and cities are different from those of medium size. Second, differences not only exist among the various regions, but also within them. It is in large urban areas where the new remote management systems offered by new technologies are more widely accepted, thus reaching larger numbers of people. However, a good business deal is one from which all parties profit. Therefore, business transactions are based upon fair service and a trusting relationship. For instance, Catalan culture attaches great value to work. The Catalans have a reputation for well organized business, though costs are high. Overall, in the northern regions, trade relations have a more direct style. It is more difficult to attract customers but such trade is sustainable. By contrast, in Andalusia and southern regions, it seems that it is easier to attract customers but polls indicate that stop being too soon. Undoubtedly, the key factor to conduct business in Spain is to have a good network of contacts who can present to potential customers. Such people, however, are less essential the larger the population of the town or city. As a result of the decentralization process, Spain has 17 autonomous regions. In them, the regional public sector has gradually replaced public sector central and regional public sector has become the first operator within its sphere of influence. In order to promote economic growth and employment in their region, and prevent the relocation of companies, regional governments have made some favoritism to companies based in their respective territories. This process partially breaks free competition and the Spanish economy is a major challenge: to reduce the weight of public sector and strengthening the private sector.

The economic transformation of Spain, 1959–2001

In this section we will recall the major changes experienced by the Spanish economy in the second half of the twentieth century.

Francoism: from isolation to development, 1939–1975

When Franco's regime began, the Spanish economy was undergoing a period of famine and poverty that would take the country nearly 20 years to overcome. For the years following the civil war, the livestock population was reduced. There was virtually no agricultural production and industry was either destroyed or barely operative. Up until 1955, there were rationing cards. The state issued currency as a function of monetary policy, which produced high inflation rates.

At the outbreak of the Cold War, Franco's regime was composed of appointed technocrats – a new breed of economists – who replaced the old military solicitors. The government of Spain drafted a stabilization plan in 1959, which served as a springboard to Spain's long-term economic growth, until the oil crisis in the 1970s. The social order imposed by the regime, including the absence of serious protests all through the 1960s, would facilitate Spain's economic stability and foreign and private investment. Thus began the golden years for the Spanish economy, with low unemployment rates, an inflation rate now under control, and an industrial development similar to that of the neighboring counties.

Economically speaking, Spain was characterized by strict control of the economy by the state, with an excessively bureaucratized managerial structure, especially for obtaining licenses for the import and export of goods, setting up businesses in other cities, or expanding businesses to other sectors. Moreover, prices were controlled, especially those of primary commodities. Despite this situation, the impact of public expenditure on GDP (Gross Domestic Product) was very low. Consequently, the tax load was low, even though the health, educational, and communications infrastructures were inadequate.

In the business world, there were major monopolies by public companies in the most important economic sectors: energy, telephones, mining, industry, transportation, shipping, the automotive industry, the mass media, and the industrial and financial sectors.

The structure of the labor market was based on paternalistic laws, which overprotected the employee and produced an inflexible working system. The model fostered low labor costs, characterized by the absence of trade union freedom and long-term employment. People developed their careers within the company they worked for, without venturing outside.

As far as concerns international relations, the Spanish economy functioned under governmental autarchy, and was thus internationally isolated in the 1940s and 1950s ultimately to be sheltered by complete protectionism. High tariffs, import duties on some products and the need to obtain a license for foreign trade diminished the economic flow. Financially, there was strict control of capital flows and of exchange rates. Once Spain had attained a certain level of economic development, it also concluded various trade agreements with the European Economic Community (EEC), which rejected, on several occasions, Spain's application for membership.

The transition period: from the oil crisis to the entry into the European Economic Community, 1975–1986

After Franco's death, Prince Juan Carlos took the oath as King of Spain, *Juan Carlos I de Borbón y Borbón-Dos Sicilias*. Thereafter, the country underwent a dramatic transformation through the renovation of its former institutions and political system to achieve democracy.

Immediately prior to the end of the Franco regime, the first oil crisis took place in 1973, after the aid granted by Western countries to Israel in the Yom Kippur War. Arab oil producing countries raised the price of crude oil. This fact alone put an end to the economic growth Spain had experienced since the end of the Second World War. Thus, a new economic era began in a completely unknown context which soon provoked an offer shock in the economy,[2] resulting in a fall in production, a fall in employment and a high inflation rate (i.e., stagflation). This crisis reappeared in 1977 and again in 1979, thus covering the period leading to Reagan and Thatcher's policies of economic liberalization, when the West returned to a sustainable growth path.

In Spain the first crisis occurred during the period known as the *tardofrancoism*, characterized by the eagerness of institutions to maintain the social order and the status quo until a new government model could be found and implemented. This fact, along with the paternalistic attitude of the state led the government to decide to accept the oil price increase initially by issuing currency, and this ultimately led to higher levels of inflation. However, the subsequent oil crises hit Spain in a period of political, social, and institutional instability, with high unemployment and inflation rates and the violent political repression of terrorism.

During the transition period, Spain carried out the most important institutional reform of the contemporary period: a parliamentary monarchical constitution was passed as the form of government. The monarchy renounced some powers and privileges. The state was transformed from a centralist structure to an autonomous, quasi-federal model. A brand new system of taxation was introduced. Industrial restructuring had just begun, with a high cost in terms of employment. The reform signaled the end of direct control of prices by the state (maximum and minimum), and of administrative licenses for business activity, which led to the modernization of the educational system. At the beginning of the democratic period, the educational system was updated and research activities were encouraged.

Both the establishment of a new state and the alteration of the country's regional configuration met strong opposition – not only from those who distrusted the new model, but also from strong terrorist pressure. Simultaneously, the division of the powers of the state, new emerging political divisions, and a change in the social and economic activities of the pubic sector at all levels (state, autonomous regions and local) took place. The whole constituted a challenge which society had to face.

In the social sphere, this transformation led to the disappearance of a single vertical trade union system for the trade unions and the emergence of class trade unions, linked to socialist and communist parties that were banned during the dictatorship. With the arrival of the three oil crises in the '70s, there was an outburst of inflation, which led to automatic wage indexation. Additionally, the high inflation set off a sharp increase in interest rates by the (Central) Bank of Spain. First, companies were affected by high financial and employment costs, within the context of a severe financial crisis. Second, the high inflation produced a consumption and sales slump and drove the country into an economic crash. This phenomenon of low growth, high unemployment, and high inflation is known to economists as stagflation. All through this period, job destruction losses accelerated a dramatic rise in the unemployment rate. As an explanation, it should be noted that since the dictatorship time until now, the Spanish labor market has been characterized by economic rigidity and the adjustment to economic cycles through employment, not through reduced wages or reduced working hours. Therefore, the Spanish economy creates more jobs than other European countries during periods of economic expansion and on the contrary, it destroys more jobs than other countries during the economic crisis. During this current year the Government has introduced a new labor law reform to reduce the cost of dismissal to encourage recruitment of new employees. Returning to the historical facts, to face the severe crisis afflicting Spain, the Pact of La Moncloa (1979), between the political parties and the social agent unions, was central to avoiding an explosion of violence.

In the field of foreign trade, during the Spanish transition period there was a simultaneous opening of the Spanish economy through agreements with the former European Community (EEC or EC) and the World Trade Organization. However, due to the crisis, most countries adopted protectionist measures, leading to a fall in international trade due to lower demand. Thus, Spain opened to foreign trade just as it integrated into Europe.

Spain's integration into the European Union, 1986–1993

The integration of Spain into the European Economic Community meant the realization of a dream held during the entire contemporary era: to regain the country's privileged position worldwide with a sphere of influence. Membership in this *European club* encouraged the consolidation of Spain's unstable democratic institutions, and generated a climate of legal security and both labor and social stability, all of which are essential to any stimulus, investment growth, and – consequently – growth in employment.

Within this context, there were two different stages: the economic boom after Spain's integration into the EEC (1986–1991) and the monetary crisis and devaluation of the peseta (1992–1993).

These developments resulted in a great increase in the public sector to adopt the guarantees of the welfare state to the economic situation. Moreover, European social and territorial cohesion policies, laid down by President Felipe Gonzalez, served to introduce capital flows into Spain that facilitated the renovation of infrastructure and boosted investment and cost reduction. On the part of the private sector, the expectations of attaining economic convergence with the more developed countries boosted investment and consumption, thus activating the country's economy. Nonetheless, high public debt originated in this period and entailed a major increase in interest rates and financial costs for both companies and households. This factor reduced liquidity for the future of both these economic agents.

To become a member of the Economic Community, Spain had to introduce into its legislation a series of community directives – which regulate the economic sector – and ultimately to transform its economic model. In this way, the country had to face a profound reconversion of all its sectors: farming, fishing, mining, and industry. Similarly, it had to dismantle all the remaining monopolistic structures in energy, telephony, and transportation. A process of privatization of publicly owned companies began and this provided the state with a source of income to finance its public debt and facilitated the development of previously public economic sectors.

During this period, women were fully integrated into the labor market and given access to higher learning. This development bolstered the economically active population and activated the economy's growth potential. The labor market had been encumbered by a rigid economic model, as mentioned above, which had to be adjusted thorough employment. The 1993 crisis brought about the introduction of temporary and part-time employment contract formulas, which reduced the costs of redundancy payments to render the labor market more flexible. However, a duality was produced in the labor market between the generation of workers over 40 years old, who enjoy a high level of protection, and younger generations of men and women workers who enjoy less advantageous contractual conditions. This dichotomy occurred despite the fact the young are often better qualified, since they belong to a period with the highest index for higher-level education in the history of Spain. The younger, temporary labor sector must bear cyclical adjustments and this holds back the growth of investment, as concerns housing and consumption, until they are employed under longer-term employment contracts.

On the financial markets, restrictions to capital flows were gradually eliminated, which helped dynamize investments. At the same time, the restructuring of the financial markets was achieved through a book entry system. It became easier to issue corporate shares, and other markets in financial instruments were encouraged, such as futures contracts, and options. Finally, with the 1992 monetary crisis, Spain had to face three peseta devaluations to finance the high public debt, while also confronting higher risk premiums.

With regard to the foreign sector, Spanish economic openness and internationalization began in earnest. At an early stage, European companies entered the country through acquisitions of Spanish companies in a wide range of sectors, especially within the auxiliary automotive and food industries. Likewise, tariffs were gradually reduced to a lower level for other countries, and to a zero level for other European member nations, thanks to the adoption of the Common Customs Tariff (CCT) of the EEC. The Spanish economy lost the protection through which it had previously been sheltered. Through pricing the peseta devaluations of 1992 facilitated the country's recovery of market share for exports. This development served as a springboard for the country's internationalization.

To sum up, even though the country's economic policy focused mainly on domestic demand-led growth, its competitiveness increased thanks to Spain's incorporation into the single European market, and to the subsequent entrance of European companies into the country. All these factors stimulated foreign trade.

Toward adopting the Euro: reconstruction of the public finances and the internationalization of the country, 1993–2000

The European single currency proposed by the European Community makes it easier to move people, goods, and capital, while encouraging international economic competitiveness. To access this single currency area, the EC set forth a series of requirements aimed at controlling inflation, public finances (debt and deficit), and exchange rates. At the same time, the European institutions were modified and the EC became the European Union.

Thereupon, Spain faced an economic crisis in 1992–1993, which seemingly made it impossible for it to join the single currency area. In 1994 and 1995, there was an economic recovery, but indicators showed underlying weakness in domestic demand. It was not until 1996, when a new government assumed control, that Spain's economic policy shifted.

Within the fiscal policy context, the new government strove to lessen the burden on the public sector through a series of privatizations and by freezing public spending. Later on, it reduced taxes, which provided the private sector with more liquidity (both households and business) and in turn stimulated consumption, investment, and consequently employment.

With regard to monetary policy, a new law of independence of the (Central) Bank of Spain was approved, to comply with the requirements of the new single currency, the euro. Interest rates were gradually reduced to converge with those of the rest of Europe. Thanks to low interest rates, the debt service became lower, which made it easier to reduce public expenditure. The private sector faced lower financing costs, thereby encouraging investment and employment. Additionally, the new policies for the reorganization of public finance lowered the market risk premium of the Spanish government and reduced its financing costs.

To sum up, joint fiscal and monetary policies in this period boosted the Spanish economy to a high economic growth rate. This fact ultimately enabled Spain's real and nominal economic convergence with the most advanced European countries. Spain also achieved its ambition to join the single currency.

Internationalization of Spanish companies in Latin America since Spain's integration into the single European market, 1992–2009

The global economic system is undergoing a process of self-integration and interdependence, which is referred to as "globalization". The free movement of capital flows, the increase in both domestic and international competition, the unification of financial systems, and the removal of the various protective economic barriers characterize this process. Likewise, those countries that decide to protect their economies will likely be marginalized within the worldwide economic context. As a result, they may well be doomed to become autarchic regimes. Spain, Portugal, and Latin American are not alien to this worldwide process. The creation of the Ibero-American Community of Nations constitutes a form of self-protection and solidarity aimed at facilitating the commercial interchange of goods and the development of our peoples and nations.

Over the past three decades, since the enforcement of the single European market in 1993, given that it was necessary to increase European competitiveness, Spanish companies have accelerated their internationalization. In this way, Spanish companies ensure their own survival, through the diversification of both their customer base and their business in the countries where they operate. They also strengthen their competitiveness, which helps them face new challenges in larger markets where barriers to competition remain low, such as the European Union and the United States.

In fact, foreign investment by Spanish companies has largely been directed to the Latin American market, where total investment flows have been increasing since the early 1990s. Major Spanish investment began with the privatization of Latin American public companies, led simultaneously by Telefónica, Iberia, and Repsol, all of which were formerly Spanish monopolistic corporations. Among the main acquisitions at the time were the purchase of Telebras by Telefónica in Brazil in 1998, the acquisition of Enersis in Chile in 1999 by Endesa, and finally the acquisition of Yacimientos Petrolíferos y Fiscales in Argentina in 1999 by Repsol.

Immediately afterward, large banking institutions followed their example. Thus, BBVA and Santander took the lead in 1995, expanding rapidly all over South America in an attempt to increase their size and scope ultimately to be able to compete with larger corporations on international markets. Being stronger and larger, these companies can defend themselves against hostile acquisitions by larger financial institutions. Thereafter, other corporations in various economic sectors – including energy, public works, and the service sector – have also made major investments in Latin America.

According to the Spanish Department of Trade and Industry, foreign direct investment, by gross domestic product, of Spanish companies in Latin America in the 1993–2006 period, amounted to €126,730 – the largest flow of foreign investment worldwide until 2001. The year 2001 is considered to be a milestone in the Argentinean economy as it underlined the impact of the crisis that hit that country. The Argentinean crisis brought about losses of millions to Spanish companies with subsidiaries in that country. This development entailed a halt in Spanish investments throughout the continent. From then onward, the way investments were made in Latin America underwent significant modifications: fewer purchases and less dispersion of these, focusing on larger companies that ensured a greater return on investment, and located in countries with larger economies and greater legal security: Mexico and Brazil. This phenomenon gave rise to yet another major Spanish investment development: by that time, major Spanish corporations had already set up in Argentina, but investment by pioneer companies would thereafter focus on the development of specific business projects. At a later stage in the internationalization process, companies in the industry and service sectors would also make investments in Latin America.

The importance of the new Spanish investment in Latin America does not only lie in the volume invested, but especially in the sectors in which the investments were made. These sectors are key for the improvement of competitiveness in Latin American countries. The determination of Spanish companies to continue to operate in such countries conferred stability to their business development. Moreover, their investment encouraged investment in other countries.

Among the key features of Spanish investment in Latin America, we must point out the pertinence of a common language and culture, even though there are different linguistic and cultural specificities, depending on the countries and regions. Such cultural resemblance is central to human communication and to efficient business management. Thanks to these similarities, business measures can more easily be implemented between the purchaser and the subsidiary company. The Spanish buyer will meet the demands and needs specific to each market. As a result, the cultural divide will not impede the economic activity of the company acquired. The fact that Spain and Latin America share a common language does not mean there is no cultural barrier when it comes to managing a business. This barrier, however, will cause less trouble when interacting with companies and people from countries with no cultural affinity. On the other hand, transaction and business costs for the purchase of shares, stocks, the creation of joint ventures, conglomerates, etc. are definitely much lower.

All things considered, according to the Spanish Department of Trade and Industry, Spanish investment in Latin America accounts for 33 percent of total Spanish foreign investment. This figure underlines the importance of the Latin American market for Spanish companies. Moreover, Spain has become the second largest investor in the region, just after the United States. In order to extend investment by Spain, by member states of the EU, or by the United States, fiscal safety mechanisms for investors need to be reinforced. Thus, a more stable social and policy environment will be established, ensuring the continuation of coherent, continuous macroeconomic policies to ease economic and social development within the Latin American Community of Nations.

Spain after the adoption of the Euro, 2000–2009

After Spain's adoption of the single European currency, its economic growth experienced a spectacular rise until 2007. However, the economy was later hit by a severe crisis that has extended up to the present.

Prior to this crisis, Spanish economic expansion resided mainly in the building, real estate, and service sectors, and in tourism. Within a framework with low interest rates that facilitated investment and indebtedness of all economic agents, a real estate bubble was generated similar to that in other countries with sound economic growth. Meanwhile, the immigration rate was very high, with immigrants coming from less developed countries – mainly from Latin America, Africa, and the Magreb (as well as from other countries in Western Europe). These countries' labor was cheaper. This fact posed a challenge to the public administration and to enterprises, since their arrival entailed greater health, educational, and housing needs. A new work force had just been created and the country's active population had increased

During this period, Spain's economic policy has experienced different stages: during the dominance of the center-right party, a public sector reduction policy continued to operate. This situation did not change until the Socialist Party took power. The first government of the Socialist Party (2004–2008) continued clearing the public finances, but later began to increase the public sector, putting future public expenditure at risk through parliamentary agreements. Generally speaking, this government did not take advantage of the economic prosperity of the time in order to undertake necessary economic reforms. Soon after the second legislature began, Spain was hit by the financial crisis originating in the United States. Ever since, economic recession has progressed at a faster rate than ever experienced previously. This turn of events eventually led the country into severe economic crisis that has raised unemployment rates to 18 percent.

The quest for investment in research, the endeavor to shift internationalization to other sectors to prompt the service sector to create employment to fill the gap left by the unemployed manpower from the building sector, and to find a solution to problems arising from delocalization are some of the major challenges that Spain is facing today.

Notes

This chapter was translated into English by Susana González Méndez.

1. The term *Capitanía*, meaning the subdivision of an area ruled by a viceroy, is translated into English as a *Captaincy*. The man who commands the *Captaincy*

is the *Captain-General*. Because of their special military responsibilities and the considerable distance of their territories from the viceregal capital, they became virtual viceroys, having a direct relationship with the king and the Council of the Indies in Madrid.
2. When developed economies are very vulnerable to price increases.

Bibliography

Béjar, Ramón Casilda (2008). *La Gran Apuesta: Globalización y Multinacionales Españolas en América Latina.* Barcelona: Ediciones Granica.

Sallier, Jean (2005). *Atlas de los Pueblos de Europa Occidental.* Barcelona: Ediciones Paidós.

de Cortazar, Fernando García y José Manuel González Vesga (2009). *Breve Historia de España.* Madrid: Alianza Editorial.

Tamames, Ramón (2008). *Introducción a la Economía Española.* Madrid: Alianza Editorial.

Index

aggression, 13
agrarian reform, 138–9
agriculture, 5, 36–7, 54, 62, 63, 67, 81, 168, 208, 223
Alessandri, Arturo, 85
Alessandri, Jorge, 85–6
Alfaro, Eloy, 142
Alfonsín, Raúl, 38–9
Allende, Salvador, 86
American Treaty on Peaceful Solutions, 11
Amplio, Frente, 3
Andean Charter for Peace and Security, 15
Andean Community, 1, 2, 6, 155–7
Andean Trade Preference Act (ATPA), 152
Andean Trade Promotion and Drug Eradication Act (ATPDEA), 152
anti-Americanism, 6
anticorruption measures, 97–8
anti-inflationary policies, 4–5
Argentina, 14
    cooperation between Brazil and, 16–21
    coups d'etat, 38
    cultural and economic history, 35–41
    culture versus globalization in, 48–9
    economy of, 39–41, 44
    foreign policy of, 16, 18–21
    independence for, 36–8
    land and people of, 34
    Latin American identity of, 19
    map of, 35
    Mercosur and, 42–8
    populism in, 38
    stability in, 38–41
    territorial disputes of, 15
    trade and growth, 41–8, 48–50
Arias, Oscar, 108–9
Aylwin, Patricio, 88

Bachelet, Michelle, 78, 89
bananas, 158–60
Betancourt Doctrine, 28
bilateral investment treaties, 100–1, 113–14
binomial system, 88
biodiversity, 109, 135–6
Bogotá Agreement, 11
Bolivarian Alternative for Latin America (ALBA), 155
Bolivia, 2, 4, 9, 84, 87, 150, 157
Bolsa Mexicana de Valores (BMV), 174
border disputes, 2, 8–10, 12–14, 25–7, 148–9
Borja, Rodrigo, 143
Brazil
    agriculture, fisheries, and forestry, 62, 64
    cities, 54–5
    colonial period, 66–7
    cooperation between Argentina and, 16–21
    culture and social profile, 58–60
    economy of, 17, 62–74
    education, 56–7
    foreign policy of, 16–20
    geography of, 52–4
    government of, 60–1
    high-tech industries, 64
    history, 61–2, 66–71
    industrial growth, 69–71
    language, 56
    leadership of, 6
    living standards, 57–8
    manufacturing, 62
    map of, 53
    Mercosur and, 43
    natural resources, 62
    political and legal system, 60–1, 72–4
    political development, 65
    population and demographics, 54–60

Brazil – *continued*
  populism in, 3
  recent trends in, 71–4
  religion, 56
  service industries, 64
  trade balance, 73
  transport and communications, 64–5
Brazilian-Argentinean Agency of Accounting and Control of Nuclear Materials (BAAAC), 20
Bucaram, Abdala, 143
business climate
  in Costa Rica, 116–20
  in Mexico, 178

Calderón, Felipe, 176
Canada, free trade agreements with, 114
Canal Zone, 195, 199–200, 203
capital movements, 100
Cardoso, Fernando Henrique, 17
Caribbean, 23–4
Caribbean Community (CARICOM), 1, 114
Caribbean Regional Security System, 15
Carter administration, 17
Central America, 23–4
Central American Common Market (CACM), 1, 111–12
Chaco War, 9
Chavez, Hugo, 3, 20, 21–3, 156, 158
Chile, 14, 19
  1891 civil war, 84–5
  1925 reform, 85
  anarchy in, 83–4
  anticorruption measures in, 97–8
  bilateral investment treaties, 100–1
  binomial system, 88
  business climate, 77–8
  colonial period, 82–3
  Concertación administrations, 88–9
  economic policies, 89–101
  economy of, 77–8
  environmental regulations, 98–9
  ethnicity and immigration, 81–2
  foreign investment, capital movements, and exchange rates, 100
  free trade agreements, 91–7, 114
  GDP growth, 80
  geography of, 75, 79–81
  health indicators, 79
  imports and exports, 93
  import substitution in, 90
  independence for, 83
  map of, 76
  natural resources, 79
  Pinochet government in, 86–7
  political development, 82–9
  political system, 78
  population and demographics, 75, 77
  privatization in, 100
  property rights, 98
  pseudo-parliamentary system, 84
  regional integration and, 90–1
  republican government in, 84
  socialism in, 85–6
  tax rates, 77–8
  trade liberalization in, 91, 101–2
  transition period in, 87–8
China, free trade agreements with, 95
Cisplatine Wars, 9
civil wars, 27, 28, 84–5, 107–8, 219–22
Cobos, Julio Cleto, 40
Cold War, 8, 11–12, 20, 24
collective defense, 27
Colombia
  conflict between Venezuela and, 21–3, 26
  drug trade in, 25–6
  foreign policy of, 22
  relations with Ecuador, 149–50
  revolutionary groups in, 3
colonial period, 4, 66–7, 82–3, 105–6, 141, 194–5, 250–4
Common External Tariff (CET), 156
communications, 64–5, 208
Concertación administrations, 88–9
Convertibility Plan, 39
Cooperation Agreement for the Development and Pacific Use of Nuclear Energy, 17

Index 271

Coronado, Juan Vásquez, 106
Corporation Law, 196
Correa, Rafael, 144, 149
corruption, 146–7
Costa, Guedes da, 27
Costa Rica
  characteristics of enterprises in, 116–20
  colonial period, 105–6
  contemporary, 108–10
  culture and values, 116–17
  democracy in, 107
  economic crisis, 108
  exports, 109
  finance, technology, and infrastructure, 120
  free trade agreements, 114–15
  future plans, 120–1
  geography of, 104
  historical background, 105–10
  independence for, 106–7
  living standards, 104
  population and demographics, 104
  pre-Columbian era, 105
  reform and civil war in, 107–8
  tourism in, 109
  trade partners, 109–10
  trade policy, 110–16
coups d'etat, in Argentina, 38
Cuba, 12, 14–15
Cuban Revolution, 12–14, 22
cultural affinity, 2
culture
  of Argentina, 35–6
  of Brazil, 58–60
  clashes, 2
  of Costa Rica, 116–17
  economic, 4–7, 36–7
  versus globalization, 48–9
  indigenous, 4, 141
  pre-Columbian era, 105
Cycle of Brazil-Wood, 66
Cycle of Sugar, 67

democracy, 2, 3, 8, 14–15, 18
  armed conflict and, 27–8
  civil war and, 28
  in Costa Rica, 107
  democratic thesis, 27–8

dependency, 8
Díaz, Porfirio, 163, 170
Difference Solution Organization (OSD), 159–60
diplomacy, militarization of, 26
Dominican Republic, 9, 12
  conflict resolution in, 129–31
  economy of, 124–8
  foreign policy of, 131–2
  geography of, 124
  government of, 124
  history of, 123–4
  intervention in, 13
  investment climate, 128–9
  population of, 124
  tourism, 129, 130
  trade balance, 127
Dominican Republic-Central American Free Trade Agreement (DR-CAFTA), 115, 126
Drago Doctrine, 11
drug trade, 2, 25–7, 151–2
Duhalde, Eduardo, 39
Duran-Ballen, Sixto, 143

Economic Commission for Latin America and the Caribbean (ECLAC), 90
economic culture, 4–7
economic integration, 27
economy
  of Argentina, 39–41, 44
  of Brazil, 62–5, 65–74
  of Chile, 77–8, 89–101
  of Costa Rica, 108–16
  of Dominican Republic, 124–8
  of Ecuador, 139–41, 152–60
  of Mexico, 166–9
  of Panama, 196–210
  of Spain, 257–66
  of Uruguay, 223–9, 232–9
Ecuador, 14
  biodiversity, 135–6
  border disputes, 148–9
  corruption in, 146–7
  drug trade, 151–2
  economy of, 139–41, 152–60
  foreign relations, 147–52
  geography of, 134–5

Ecuador – *continued*
　government of, 144–7
　history of, 141–4
　map of, 135
　migration process, 139–41
　political conditions, 145–6
　population and demographics, 136–7
　society and environment, 137–9
　terrorism and, 147
　trade agreements, 155–60
　trade balance, 153–4, 157
education, 56–7, 176, 179, 180, 182, 210, 211, 221, 222, 223, 240, 256, 259
elite, 29
environmental regulations, 98–9, 174
Estrada Doctrine, 11
ethnic conflicts, 2, 3–4
EU-Chile Association Agreement, 92–3
euro, 262–3, 266
European Economic Community, 259–60
European Union, 47, 158–60, 260–2
exchange rates, 100
Extremo Occidente, 16

FARC (Revolutionary Armed Forces of Colombia), 21, 26, 149
Febres-Cordero, Leon, 142
Fernandez, Cristina, 40
Figueiredo, João Batista, 17
finance, 120
financial services, 174
fisheries, 62, 208
Football War, 9
foreign direct investment (FDI), 100, 154, 172–4, 201, 264–5
Foreign Investment Law, 128–9, 172
foreign policy
　of Argentina, 16, 18–21
　of Brazil, 16–20
　of Dominican Republic, 131–2
　of Ecuador, 147–52
forestry, 62
Fox, Vincente, 176
Framework Treaty for Democratic Security, 15

Franco, Francisco, 255, 257–8
Franco, Itamar, 17
free trade agreements, 5–7, 91–7, 110, 114–15, 155–60, 170, 201, 211–13
Free Trade Area of the Americas (FTAA), 155, 157–8, 212
Frei Ruiz-Tagle, Eduardo, 88–9
frontiers, 25–6

Galtieri, Leopoldo, 19
Geisel, Ernesto, 17
globalization, 1–2, 5, 25, 48–9
government bureaucracy, 117, 119
government legitimacy, 3
Guadalajara Agreement, 20
Guatemala, 12, 14
　border disputes, 25
　Spanish settlers in, 105
　US intervention in, 10
guerilla warfare, 14, 26–7, 224
Gutierrez, Lucio, 143–4
Guyana, 14

Haiti, 30n1
health care, 180–1
high-tech industries, 64
historical background, 1
Human Development Index (HDI), 104
hyperinflation, 38–9

ideology, 2, 26–9
immigration, 81–2
imperialism, 8
import substitution policy, 42, 62, 65, 90, 197, 223–4, 239
indigenous movements, 3–4
indigenous population
　in Argentina, 36, 48–9
　in Chile, 81–2
　in Ecuador, 141, 146
industrial sector, 167–8, 208
inflation, 38–9, 44, 70–1, 86, 90, 101, 108, 119, 125–8, 175, 224, 226, 231, 239–40, 257–60, 262
infrastructure, 120, 178–9
institutions, 176, 181
Inter-American Committee of Peace (IACP), 13

Inter-American System, 10–12, 15, 28
Inter-American Treaty of Reciprocal Assistance, 11
International Centre for Settlement of Investment Disputes (ICSID), 100
International Cluster Competitiveness Project, 171–2
International Monetary Fund (IMF), 154, 175
inter-state conflicts, 8–10, 25–9
investment agreements, 113–14
investment climate, 128–9

Juarez, Benito, 163

Kirchner, Nestor, 40–1

labor productivity, 169
Lafer, Celso, 18
Lagos, Ricardo, 89
land reform, in Mexico, 168
language, 56
Latin America
 Spanish investment in, 264–5
 U.S. and, 1–2, 6, 10–12
 US and, 20–1
Latin American Association for Free Trade (ALALC), 155
Latin American Export Bank (BLADEX), 213
Latin American Free Commerce Association (ALALC), 30n12
Latin American Free Trade Area (LAFTA), 1, 2, 2–3, 6
Latin American Integration Association (ALADI), 30n12
Latin Americanism, 15–16
legal system, 60–1
liberalism, 107
living standards
 in Brazil, 57–8
 in Costa Rica, 104
 in Mexico, 182
Lula Da Silva, Luiz Inácio, 3, 71–2

macroeconomic competitiveness, 180–2
Madrid, Miguel de, 174
Malvinas, 15

Malvinas (Falklands) War, 9, 16, 18–19, 38
manufacturing industries, 62, 167–8
Mar del Plata summit, 158
market economies, 2, 4–5
marketing strategies, 184–7
Martinez de Irala, Domingo, 36
Mello, Collor de, 17
Menem, Carlos S., 39, 40
Mercosur, 1, 2, 5–6, 17, 18, 91–2, 112–13
 birth of, 42–3
 current status of, 46–7
 factors behind, 43–4
 future of, 47–8
 trade development and, 44
Mercosur Declaration, 15
mestizo population, 4, 106
Mexican Stock Exchange, 174
Mexico
 competitiveness of, 176–82
 consumer market in, 182–7
 culture and values, 185–6
 economic crises and policies, 174–6
 economy of, 166–9
 endowments of, 164–5
 exports, 171–2
 external sector, 169–74
 foreign investment, 172–4
 free trade agreements with, 114
 GDP distribution by region, 168–9
 geography of, 174
 history of, 163
 imports, 172
 migration to US from, 175, 183–4
 NAFTA and, 5, 20, 170, 174
 population of, 174–5
 shadow economy in, 181–2
 standard of living in, 182
 trade balance, 172
 trade policies, 170–1
 unemployment and labor productivity, 169
 United States and, 169–70
microeconomic competitiveness, 178–80
migration, 139–41
military regimes, 13, 30n4, 142
military technology, 26–7

mining, 210
Monroe Doctrine, 10–11, 19
Moreno, Mariano, 37
Muhuad, Jamil, 143
Mujica, José, 3
multiethnicity, 3–4, 81–2

NAFTA, *see* North American Free Trade Agreement (NAFTA)
national business environment (NBE), 178
natural resources, 14
  Argentina, 37
  Brazil, 62
  Chile, 79
  Mexico, 167, 174
  New Spain, 250–4
  Nicaragua, 13, 14, 15
Niemeyer, Oscar, 59
Noboa, Gustavo, 143
Nonaligned Movement, 148
nonintervention, 10–11, 13
North American Free Trade Agreement (NAFTA), 1, 5, 20, 48, 170, 174
Nuclear Non-Proliferation Treaty, 20
nuclear weapons, 19–20

oil crisis, 259
oil diplomacy, 22
oil exports, 152, 154, 175
open regionalism, 18
Organization of American States (OAS), 9–15, 29, 148
organized crime, 25–6

Panama
  colonial period, 194–5
  economy of, 196–211
  exports and GDP, 201, 203
  foreign investment in, 201
  free trade agreements, 115
  geography of, 191–2
  history of, 193–6
  independence for, 195
  macrofinancial indicators, 202
  population and demographics, 192–3
  poverty in, 210–11
  retirement in, 208, 210
  trade policies, 211–14
Panama Canal, 195–200, 203–6, 213
Paraguay, 5, 9, 17, 28, 30n11, 43, 47, 91, 221, 232, 251
Pax Americana, 10–12
Perón, Eva, 38
Perón, Juan Domingo, 38, 41
Peru, 2, 4, 6, 9, 14, 36, 43, 84, 87, 148–9, 151
pesofication, 39
Pinochet, Augusto, 86–7
Plan Colombia, 22
political institutions, 181
political parties, 3
political system
  Brazil, 60–1
  Chile, 78
  in Chile, 82–9
  Ecuador, 145–6
  Mexico, 180–2
politics, 2
populism, 2–4, 38
Portugal, 66–7
poverty, 27, 79, 82, 104, 107, 121, 132, 137, 139, 165, 210–11
pragmatism, 2
pre-Columbian era, 105
privatization, 5, 100
property rights, 98, 100
protectionism, 89–90
Protestant Reformation, 254
Puebla-to-Panama Plan, 170–1

railroads, 64–5
regional integration, 90–1
regionalism, 1–2, 5, 14–15, 18
religion, 56, 193
remittances, 154, 184
revolutionary groups, 3
Reyes, Raul, 21
Rio Group, 3
Rio Protocol, 15, 148
Rio Treaty, 13, 27, 30n2
Roman Catholicism, 193
rule of law, 181

Salinas de Gortari, Carlos, 174
San Martín, José de, 36

Sarney, José, 17
September 11, 2001, 147
service industries, 64
short-termism, 116
skim-and-wait marketing strategy, 185, 187
social infrastructure, 180–2
social institutions, 176
socialism, 85–6
social values, 185–6
SOFOFA, 90
South-American Union, 18
South-American Nations Community, 18
Southern Common Market, *see* Mercosur
Soviet Union, 1
Spain, 2
    American colonies of, 250–4
    cultural diversity in, 256–7
    economic transformation of, 257–66
    geography of, 247
    history of, 248–50, 250–6
    internationalization in, 263–5
    population and demographics, 247–8
Spanish explorers, 105, 194
Spanish settlers, 82–3
structural reforms, 5
Summit for the Unity of Latin America and the Caribbean, 1, 29
Suriname, 14

tariffs, 5, 6, 89–90, 156, 170, 197, 211–12, 223, 226, 228, 233, 262
technological modernization, 26–7
technology, 120
territorial disputes, 15, 25–6, 27
terrorism, 147
Tlatelolco Treaty, 20
Tobar Doctrine, 11
tourism, 109, 129, 130, 167, 184, 198, 208, 209
trade agreements, 1–7, 110–16, 155–60
    see also free trade agreements
trade liberalization, 5, 42–8, 91–7, 101–2, 115–16

trade policies
    Argentina, 41–50
    Chile, 91–7, 101–2
    Costa Rica, 110–16
    Ecuador, 155–60
    Mexico, 170–1
    Panama, 211–14
    Uruguay, 225–6, 232–3
trade protectionism, 89–90
traditional values, 186
transportation, 64–5
Treaty of Montevideo, 155
Tripartite Agreement, 17
Triple Alliance, 9
Turbay, Julio César, 22

unemployment, 77, 108, 139, 155, 166, 169, 179, 211, 229, 236, 258
Union of South American Nations (UNASUR), 150–1
United Kingdom, 18–19
United Nations, 147
United States
    Colombia and, 21–2
    Cuban Revolution and, 12–14
    foreign policy of, toward Latin America, 23, 29
    free trade agreements with, 94–5
    hegemony of, 9, 12, 30n5
    Mexican immigrants in, 175, 183–4
    Mexico and, 169–70
    role of, in Latin America, 1–2, 6, 10–12, 20–1
    trade with, 47–8, 153
Uribe, Alvaro, 149
Uruguay
    in 1990s, 231–4
    civil wars in, 219–22
    economy of, 223–9, 232–9
    external shocks and crises, 234–9
    facts about, 217
    geography of, 217
    growth model, 225
    independence for, 217–19
    liberalization reforms in, 224–8
    Mercosur and, 43
    modern period, 222–3
    origins of, 216–17
    populism in, 3

Uruguay – *continued*
  reconstruction period, 229–30
  stabilization plan, 226–9, 231–2
  trade policy, 225–6, 232–3
  welfare state in, 223–5

value conflicts, 186–7
Venezuela, 16
  under Chavez, 21–3
  conflict between Colombia and, 21–3, 26
  foreign policy of, 22–3
  leadership role of, 20–3
  populism in, 3

War of the Confederation, 9
War of the Pacific, 9, 30n18
war on terrorism, 27
Washington Convention, 100
World Trade Organization (WTO), 111, 170, 198, 212
World War II, 11

Zedillo Ponce de León, Ernesto, 175